Smart Thinking

www.palgravestudyskills.com – the leading study skills website

Palgrave Study Skills

Business Degree Success
Career Skills
Cite Them Right (10th edn)
Critical Thinking Skills (2nd edn)
Dissertations and Project Reports
e-Learning Skills (2nd edn)
The Exam Skills Handbook (2nd edn)
Get Sorted
The Graduate Career Guidebook
Great Ways to Learn Anatomy and Physiology
  (2nd edn)
How to Begin Studying English Literature
  (4th edn)
How to Study Foreign Languages
How to Study Linguistics (2nd edn)
How to Use Your Reading in Your Essays
  (2nd edn)
How to Write Better Essays (3rd edn)
How to Write Your Undergraduate Dissertation
  (2nd edn)
Improve Your Grammar (2nd edn)
Information Skills
The International Student Handbook
The Mature Student's Guide to Writing (3rd edn)
The Mature Student's Handbook
The Palgrave Student Planner
The Personal Tutor's Handbook
Practical Criticism
Presentation Skills for Students (3rd edn)
The Principles of Writing in Psychology
Professional Writing (3rd edn)
Researching Online
Skills for Success (3rd edn)
The Student's Guide to Writing (3rd edn)
The Student Phrase Book
Study Skills Connected
Study Skills for International Postgraduates
Study Skills for Speakers of English as a Second
  Language
The Study Skills Handbook (4th edn)
Studying History (3rd edn)
Studying Law (4th edn)
Studying Modern Drama (2nd edn)
Studying Psychology (2nd edn)
Success in Academic Writing
Teaching Study Skills and Supporting Learning
The Undergraduate Research Handbook
The Work-Based Learning Student Handbook
  (2nd edn)
Work Placements – A Survival Guide for
  Students
Write it Right (2nd edn)

Writing for Engineers (3rd edn)
Writing for Law
Writing for Nursing and Midwifery Students
  (2nd edn)
You2Uni: Decide. Prepare. Apply

Pocket Study Skills

14 Days to Exam Success
Analyzing a Case Study
Brilliant Writing Tips for Students
Completing Your PhD
Doing Research
Getting Critical (2nd edn)
Planning Your Dissertation
Planning Your Essay (2nd edn)
Planning Your PhD
Posters and Presentations
Reading and Making Notes (2nd edn)
Referencing and Understanding Plagiarism
Reflective Writing
Report Writing
Science Study Skills
Studying with Dyslexia
Success in Groupwork
Time Management
Where's Your Argument?
Writing for University

Palgrave Research Skills

Authoring a PhD
Getting to Grips with Doctoral Research
The Foundations of Research (2nd edn)
The Good Supervisor (2nd edn)
The Postgraduate Research Handbook (2nd edn)
The Professional Doctorate
Structuring Your Research Thesis

Palgrave Teaching and Learning

Coaching and Mentoring in Higher Education
Facilitating Work-Based Learning
Facilitating Workshops
Fostering Self-Efficacy in Higher Education
  Students
Live Online Learning
For the Love of Learning
Leading Dynamic Seminars
Learning, Teaching and Assessment in Higher
  Education
Learning with the Labyrinth
Masters Level Teaching, Learning and Assessment

For a complete listing of all our titles in this area
  please visit **www.palgrave.com/studyskills**

Smart Thinking

How to Think Conceptually, Design Solutions and Make Decisions

By Bryan Greetham

 palgrave

First published 2016 by
PALGRAVE

Palgrave in the UK is an imprint of Macmillan Publishers Limited, registered in England, company number 785998, of 4 Crinan Street, London, N1 9XW.

Palgrave Macmillan in the US is a division of St Martin's Press LLC, 175 Fifth Avenue, New York, NY 10010.

Palgrave is a global imprint of the above companies and is represented throughout the world.

Palgrave® and Macmillan® are registered trademarks in the United States, the United Kingdom, Europe and other countries.

ISBN 978–1–137–50208–7 paperback

This book is printed on paper suitable for recycling and made from fully managed and sustained forest sources. Logging, pulping and manufacturing processes are expected to conform to the environmental regulations of the country of origin.

A catalogue record for this book is available from the British Library.

A catalog record for this book is available from the Library of Congress.

Printed in China

*To Dax, Rogier and Zoltan, all of whom were quick to learn that education means
the passion for ideas and the joy of discovery. And to Pat,
for whom life has always meant an unending series of adventures.*

It is a lesson which all history teaches wise men, to put trust in ideas,
and not in circumstances.

Ralph Waldo Emerson

Capital isn't that important in business. Experience isn't that important.
You can get both of these things. What is important is ideas.

Harvey Firestone

Contents

Contents

Acknowledgements

There are few things more difficult than teaching someone to think; far easier just to teach them what you know and understand. That so few of us are willing to take up the challenge only increases the debt we all owe to those brave and gifted few who do. As for my own colleagues, I am grateful to them for giving me their support as I extolled the importance of teaching students how to think, especially when the institutional momentum moved irresistibly towards teaching students what to think at the expense of their skills.

Similarly, I am grateful to those of my friends who have helped me just by letting me talk through these ideas. In particular, I must thank Marek Jezewski and Philip Hall, who willingly gave me their advice, support and the benefits of their professional experience. Likewise, I owe a debt to my students. I am grateful to all those in Britain, Europe, Australia and the US, who have been generous enough to work with me as I got them to think about their thinking, rather than just teach them facts, explanations and theories.

I am similarly indebted to all those who have devoted their professional lives to unravelling the intricate mechanisms of the mind that turn us away from novel and original thoughts to the comfortable predictability of conventional ideas. The most remarkable of these are Daniel Kahneman and Amos Tversky, whose work together resulted in insights that have fundamentally reshaped our understanding. Reading Kahneman's best-selling book, *Thinking, Fast and Slow*, is a truly transformative experience.

Similarly, I must acknowledge my debt to Nassim Taleb, whose book, *The Black Swan*, is full of the most provocative insights about the way we mishandle and fool ourselves about uncertainty. In the same area, I am deeply indebted to Gerd Gigerenzer, whose book, *Reckoning with Risk: Learning to Live with Uncertainty*, makes clear a very difficult subject.

To Helen Caunce, my editor at Palgrave, I owe a special debt for investing such confidence in me, and for her quiet patience, professionalism and unfailingly sound judgement. My thanks also go to Clarissa Sutherland, who has coped with the problems I have raised with tactful patience and understanding. I am grateful also to my reviewers for their kind, encouraging words. Their sound judgement and insightful comments have opened up ways of improving the book that would never have occurred to me.

Finally, I would like to thank my partner, Patricia Rowe, for being there when silence descended and I walked around with the weight of problems on my mind. As always, when I needed someone to bring sanity and a sense of proportion to my work, she was there.

About this book

Going beyond critical thinking

We all have some idea of what is meant by 'critical thinking'. Indeed many of us have probably taken a course in it. So how does it differ from smart thinking? Critical thinking is essentially the auditor of our thinking. It teaches us the value of critically evaluating our arguments and those we read and hear to see if they are consistent: that their conclusions are validly drawn from the assumptions that support them and there are no undisclosed assumptions manipulating our thinking. We learn to identify hidden values and recognise the logical fallacies in arguments.

We also learn to evaluate the evidence on which an argument is based: is it reliable, is it relevant, is it enough to support the conclusions of the argument? Likewise, we learn to evaluate the language used to develop the argument to see if it conveys the ideas accurately, clearly and consistently. Are the implications of the argument obscured by vague language? Do words change their meaning halfway through the argument, persuading us to accept false conclusions? We learn to read between the lines to identify when a writer is using devices that manipulate our thinking by appealing to our emotions rather than our reason.

Although critical thinking is seldom defined clearly and comprehensively, ranging over various activities from courses in formal logic to social theory and current affairs, the emphasis is on the word 'critical'. The aim is to provide us with the tools and habits we need to evaluate arguments, and not just accept them on blind trust. Once we have done this we can then decide whether they can be repaired, whether there is any part worth retaining, or whether we should just abandon them entirely.

In some of this there are overlaps with smart thinking. They both encourage us to become thinkers who are self-reflective, who learn to monitor their thinking. They both draw upon our ability to analyse problems and arguments, so that we know what we are dealing with. And they both advocate the importance of imaginatively empathising with others to play devil's advocate so that we are aware of beliefs and assumptions that we would not otherwise take into account.

Creating new ideas

But the crucial difference is that on its own critical thinking will not create one new idea. When we think critically we work with what we are given to identify its weaknesses, assess its reliability and decide whether it can be repaired or needs to be discarded altogether. In contrast, smart thinking is all about generating new ideas, creating new concepts, designing solutions to problems, producing new insights, assessing risk and coming to your own decision.

If you want to be the next Mark Zuckerberg, Steve Jobs or Bill Gates, if you have ever wondered how it is that such people can come up with such stunning insights, produce new, revolutionary concepts and ideas that so change our world, then learn to be a smart thinker. In retrospect most of these ideas seem so simple. What could be simpler than a website where people communicate with their friends, auction off their property or post their videos? They are so simple that you wonder why you didn't think of it yourself. You ask yourself why you can't do it too. But, of course, you can, if you learn to become a smart thinker.

In this book you will learn the three stages of smart thinking: conceptual thinking, creative thinking and decision-making. It is a progressive method of thinking: each stage builds on the previous stage. In chapter 1 we learn the problems we all have to overcome to become smart thinkers. In chapter 2 we learn what smart thinking is and how it develops the employability skills that all employers are looking for, along with the skills we need to tackle the psychometric questions organisations set in their selection process.

Conceptual thinking

Then, in the next five chapters, we learn how to think conceptually:

- In chapter 3 we will unwrap the mysteries of conceptual thinking. You will see the creative power it brings to our thinking and how you can use this in your own thinking.
- If you have ever wanted to know how to create new concepts, which will transform our thinking, new products and services or new ways of promoting a product, read chapter 4.
- If you want to reveal the ideas that control your thinking without your knowing it, so you can recombine them in new and interesting ways, read chapter 5 and learn how to analyse concepts to see the ideas at the heart of them.
- If you want to learn how the most important breakthroughs in our thinking have occurred, so you too can generate your own insights that will surprise even yourself in their originality, read chapter 6.
- In chapter 7 you will learn how conceptual thinking can help you achieve the highest grades in your essays and dissertations and its significance as an employability skill. You will also learn how much easier it is to cope with psychometric problems once you have learned the methods and skills of conceptual thinking.

Creative thinking

In the next six chapters you will learn the skills that will release your own creative potential:

- In chapter 8 you will learn the most important characteristics that all creative thinkers share and the extent to which you have them too.
- If you've always wanted to be able to generate a wealth of original ideas on almost any problem, read chapter 9.

- In chapter 10 you will learn how to release yourself from the shackles of conventional ideas. You will learn how to structure your ideas, to represent them in different ways, so that you reveal new insights and unexpected meaning.
- In chapter 11 you will learn how creative people can always find surprising, unexpected solutions to problems; how they can interpret structures in new ways using analogies that transform the way we think.
- Have you always wanted to be able to solve the most difficult problems that others find impossible to solve? Then read chapter 12. Here you will learn four methods of designing the most incisive and surprising solutions to the most intractable problem.
- In chapter 13 you will learn how all of these methods will help you inject your own original ideas into your essays and dissertations, how employers worldwide are eager to employ graduates with these skills and how important these are to tackling the three most common psychometric problems.

Decision-making

Finally, in the last five chapters you will learn how to assess your original ideas and solutions and come to a decision that is genuinely your own:

- In chapter 14 you will learn what makes a good decision-maker and a good decision. You will also learn how to tackle the most common psychometric problems that test these skills.
- If you find it difficult to choose between competing solutions and making your own decisions, read chapter 15. This teaches us how to escape our intuitive biases that frequently result in poor decisions.
- Understanding how to make decisions under conditions of uncertainty is one of the most urgent challenges we face, yet most of us are never taught how to calculate risk so that we can make the best decision. In chapter 16 you will learn how to make the best decisions based on an accurate assessment of the risk involved.
- We all struggle to choose between those things that are so different from one another that all we can do is resort to intuitive, impressionistic judgements. In chapter 17 you will learn how to avoid this and instead make rational, objective decisions.
- Finally, in chapter 18, you will learn about the importance of decision-making in making ideas your own. You will see how it results in a depth of conviction that will radiate from your presentations and essays making them far more persuasive. You will learn how important the skills of decision-making are to organisations and professions in the twenty-first century.

Learning to be a smart thinker

As you read this book you will no doubt wonder just how many ground-breaking ideas there are out there just waiting to be revealed, if only you had the skills of a smart thinker. With the skills this book will teach you will be able to open up new insights and ways of seeing things nobody else has seen. You will learn how to solve problems you never thought possible and how to make the right decisions, when others are overawed by uncertainty.

Introduction

Trained musicians can pick up a piece of sheet music that they have not seen before and play it. They can put together different melodies and musical phrases to form an original piece of music. This doesn't require musical genius, just someone who has developed the skills to use their musical abilities. Indeed, there are many of us who have these abilities, but who haven't had our skills developed to use them, so our potential lies untapped.

The same is true of our abilities to think. It doesn't take a genius to develop original ideas; we can all do it; we all have the abilities. We have just not been taught the skills we need to use these abilities. Just as a pianist can learn to read music and translate the notes into movements of fingers across the keyboard, so we as thinkers can learn to analyse concepts, generate our own original ideas, bring them together to reveal new insights and make decisions of our own. This is what we will do in this book. The starting point is to realise that you have enormous potential. Like all teachers, my job is to release it.

The problem

The cruel fact is that, despite all we know about how to educate people, despite the quality of our education systems and the crippling sums that many have to pay for their education, most students leave universities with their enormous potential largely untapped. The reason for this is that universities have as their central mission the responsibility to attract experts in their field, to provide them with the best facilities and then to ensure that they have the time to conduct research.

Their other responsibility, of course, is to teach students. But as university teachers are the experts in their field, the gold standard in knowledge, both students and staff tend to interpret this teaching role as passing on their knowledge, which students must show they can understand and then recall in exams in exchange for the marks they need to pass. In effect, we teach students *what* to think, rather than *how* to think.

We teach students *what* to think, rather than *how* to think.

As you can see, this leads to the development of just the lower cognitive skills: the abilities to understand and recall. It doesn't develop the higher cognitive skills we need to analyse concepts and ideas, to generate new ideas and synthesise them into new ways of looking at a problem, to solve difficult problems, to critically evaluate arguments and to come to our own judgements and decisions: in other words, to think for ourselves.

The General Medical Council in the UK recognised this problem in 1996, when it criticised medical education for promoting passivity in learning and for being overloaded with factual material, which discouraged the development of higher cognitive abilities, like synthesis, evaluation and problem-solving.

> **We are busy producing a generation of the most sophisticated recyclers of received opinion.**

This authority-based approach to education perpetuates the idea that teachers know all the answers and their duty is simply to pass them on to students; that there is a single best answer to every problem and this can be found by applying set techniques and conventional logic, which can be simply learned and applied over and over again. Worst of all, it means students merely develop the skills to reproduce orthodoxy, rather than develop ideas of their own, think for themselves and create new insights and new solutions to problems. In effect, as teachers we are busy producing a generation of the most sophisticated recyclers of received opinion.

The revolt against orthodoxy

Encouragingly, students around the world are now beginning to revolt against this narrow vision of education. In November 2011 over 70 economics students at Harvard walked out of a lecture given by their departmental head. They were objecting to the unerring faith of their teachers in the economic orthodoxy they were being taught, which had brought about the financial crash and left not one of their teachers able to predict the economic meltdown.

In a manifesto signed by 42 university economics associations from 19 countries, students have condemned not just the narrowing of the curriculum to exclude the broader social and moral implications of economic decisions, but also the quality of the teaching they receive.

> **For instance. . .**
>
> At the University of Manchester students complained that they were being trained to digest economic theory and regurgitate it in exams, but never to question the assumptions that underpin it:
>
> *Tutorials consist of copying problem sets off the board rather than discussing economic ideas, and 18 out of 48 modules have 50% or more marks given by multiple choice.*

One of the co-authors of the manifesto summed up the problem by saying that 'Whenever I sit an economics exam, I have to turn myself into a robot.'

> **The problem**
>
> And in this lies the problem: unless you are free to suspend your judgement and start from the assumption that an explanation is uncertain and up for grabs, you cannot develop your higher cognitive abilities.

Once we accept something as certain, a fact, all discussion, analysis and creative thinking about alternative solutions come to an end. There is nothing more to discuss and, therefore, no opportunity to develop our thinking skills. As Paul Tillich once said, 'The passion for truth is silenced by answers which have the weight of undisputed authority.'[1]

And, obviously, if you don't use these abilities, you don't develop them. If you want to develop your backhand in tennis, play lots of backhands. If you want to improve your skills to discuss issues, discuss lots of issues.

The challenge of uncertainty

Our reluctance to suspend our judgement in this way to develop our thinking skills is due largely to the fact that it exposes teachers and students alike to the most challenging of all problems – uncertainty: a state we all seem to fear and avoid more than any other.

For centuries mathematicians believed they lived in a world of absolute certainty, as did priests, theologians and the laity. Today we still shelter from uncertainty beneath beliefs that promise the reassurance of certainty. We eagerly embrace authorities of all kinds, while the shelves of high-street bookstores buckle under the weight of books promising instant faith.

Yet, with the exception of formal subjects like mathematics and logic, in all other subjects and in all professions we cannot avoid uncertainty: empirical evidence will only ever take us so far. There is always an evidential gap between the facts and our convictions. To bridge this gap we have to make our own value judgement. As Arthur Koestler so eloquently put it, 'The ultimate truth is penultimately always a falsehood.'[2]

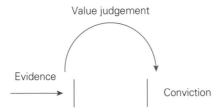

Refusing the challenge that uncertainty presents by sidestepping our responsibility to think for ourselves is merely a way of allowing someone else to make the judgement for us. In the process we turn our backs on the most exciting journey of our lives. By daring to surrender the illusion of certainty we accept the opportunity and the challenge of exploring for ourselves the amazing complexity of the world.

Indeed, understanding how to make decisions under conditions of incomplete information is one of the most urgent challenges we face. As teachers we should be doing for our students what Bertrand Russell believed philosophy could do for those who studied it: 'teach how to live without certainty and yet without being paralysed by hesitation'.[3]

Employability skills

Worst of all, for graduates trying to enter the world of work our failure to teach this has the most damaging consequences. Education systems around the world teach students certainties, yet when graduates leave to find employment they confront a world full of uncertainties. As a result, they lack the skills to think effectively in a world that is difficult to understand, where events are difficult to predict and where accidents and errors are a constant, daily reality. Students learn habits and orthodox frames of reference through which they interpret the present in terms of the past: nothing is new, nothing uncertain.

> Education systems around the world teach students certainties, yet when graduates leave to find employment they confront a world full of uncertainties.

It is not surprising, therefore, that graduates struggle to find jobs, while employers struggle to find employees with the right skills.

For instance. . .

The Confederation of British Industry's 'Education and Skills Survey' in 2011 found evidence of serious skills shortages with companies struggling to find suitable employees, while they were being inundated with applications from graduates with good degrees, but who lack the thinking skills that employers need.

The Chartered Institute of Personnel and Development (CIPD) found the same problem. Both emphasised the importance of the same range of creative skills. The CIPD survey made it clear that these 'higher level creative skills are key to our competitive future'.

And this is not just a problem in the UK. Worldwide, employers are finding the same problem. Graduates who have been trained in the lower cognitive skills are unable to think creatively, solve problems and make good decisions. The 2012 UNESCO background paper, 'Report on Skills Gaps', reviewed the literature on 120 employer surveys from developed and developing countries. It found that most employers described graduates as 'not employable', which is affecting all economies worldwide:

While the impact of skills shortages will be felt most heavily in the developed nations due to aging of the population, closing skills gaps is especially important for the world's young people aged 15–24, most of whom live in developing countries where only 10–20 per cent of graduates are considered employable by international standards. A chronic misalignment of the education system to the needs of the labor market is a global problem.

In India, for example, the World Bank reported exactly this problem in its working paper 'Employability and Skill Set of Newly Graduated Engineers in India'. It found widespread dissatisfaction with current graduates. Most notably it found that:

> 'Skills gaps are particularly severe in the higher-order thinking skills' and it recommended that education institutions should 'refocus the assessments, teaching-learning process, and curricula away from lower-order thinking skills, such as remembering and understanding, toward higher-order skills, such as analyzing and solving engineering problems, as well as creativity'.

Similarly, ManpowerGroup's '2012 Talent Shortage Survey', which researched the views of more than 38,000 employers in 41 countries and territories, found 'a substantial proportion of employers around the globe identify a lack of available skilled talent as a continuing drag on business performance'. As the report observes:

> That so many employers continue to identify talent shortages as a barrier to their business goals defies prevailing logic, especially when viewed against the high levels of unemployment in many economies – particularly among young adults.

The important employability skills

But what are these employability skills and why are they so important to employers? The following are the 10 most important skills:

1 **Communication skills** – verbal and written: the ability to express your ideas clearly and convincingly.
2 **Numerical reasoning** – the ability to carry out simple arithmetical operations and interpret and use data.
3 **Logical reasoning** – the ability to reason consistently.
4 **Conceptual thinking** – the ability to analyse concepts and arguments, to synthesise ideas into concepts and create new concepts.
5 **Teamwork** – working effectively and confidently with others.
6 **Planning and organising** – the ability to analyse a task, put together an effective plan and carry it out effectively.
7 **Creative thinking and problem-solving** – analysing problems, gathering information and using it creatively.
8 **Leadership** – the ability to form an effective team and motivate others.
9 **Flexibility** – the ability to adapt your thinking and the way you work to changing circumstances; not being rigid in your thinking.
10 **Initiative, self-motivation and self-awareness** – the confidence to act on your own initiative, to motivate yourself to come up with new ideas and solutions and to be self-reflective – able to identify your own weaknesses and areas in which you need to improve.

At the heart of these there is a core set of thinking skills that are the key to success in both your academic work and in your professional life. This book develops these core skills.

They produce the sort of thinker who is innovative, adaptable, open to new ideas and new ways of doing things, self-reflective and self-reliant. They are best found in the sort of creative thinkers who know how to analyse a problem, generate ideas, create solutions to problems and who have the confidence and courage to face the unexpected and make up their own minds, rather than relying on orthodox opinion and the judgements of others. They have the confidence to speculate and play devil's advocate, floating ideas that others would simply dismiss as fanciful. Above all, they are persistent: they don't give up easily.

Various studies have shown that creative thinkers have the following cognitive skills and capabilities:

1 They adapt successfully to special circumstances.
2 They recognise opportunities and possibilities.
3 They find order in chaos.
4 They cope well with new information.
5 They cross boundaries between subjects, recognising similarities.
6 They generate more ideas quickly, rather than just repeat conventional wisdom.
7 They analyse concepts and create new ones, seeing the abstract in the concrete, the general in the specific.
8 They synthesise disparate ideas in new and original ways to see problems from a different perspective.

These are the skills that employers most often say they need. But when they are inundated by applications from people who don't have them, they must do two things: test applicants to find those who do possess them and then train them to think to bring their skills up to the right level.

> **For instance. . .**
>
> Recently, the law firm Herbert Smith announced that applicants for their training contracts would be tested on their thinking skills. Those who succeed will then be trained how to think. One of the reasons for introducing the test is that too many students with a 'good degree' cannot 'think like a lawyer'. That is, they cannot think 'critically, analytically and conceptually'.

Psychometric tests

Many professions and an increasing number of companies and non-profit-making organisations test candidates in this way. It is estimated that up to 75 per cent of medium- to large-sized organisations and 95 per cent of the FTSE top 100 companies use them during the recruitment process. Beyond the economic benefits to an organisation, tests reduce the risk of making the wrong selection decisions and, arguably, are a fairer way of selecting people as everyone gets the same chance to do their best. The most frequently used tests are those for verbal reasoning, quantitative or numerical reasoning, abstract reasoning, inductive reasoning and decision analysis.

1. Verbal reasoning

The verbal reasoning tests are designed to assess candidates' ability to understand and analyse complex written arguments. Some involve comprehension passages that assess candidates' ability to read and think carefully about information presented in passages. The task is to read each passage carefully and then decide whether the statements listed follow logically from the information in the passage; whether they are true or false, or whether it is just not possible to say either way. Others involve choosing the closest synonym or antonym for a word.

2. Abstract reasoning

The abstract reasoning test assesses candidates' ability to understand and analyse visual information and solve problems without relying on language skills. Some questions involve identifying relationships, differences and similarities between shapes and patterns. You may be asked to form or identify a common concept from among different patterns.

3. Quantitative or numerical reasoning

Although the quantitative reasoning tests assess candidates' ability to solve numerical problems, they are less to do with numerical ability and more about problem-solving, that is to say, knowing what information to use by extracting it from tables and other numerical presentations and then manipulating it using simple calculations and ratios. They aim to measure reasoning using numbers as a vehicle, rather than measuring numeracy.

4. Inductive reasoning

In this test candidates are given qualitative and quantitative evidence and asked to draw relevant inferences. The evidence is incomplete and at times conflicting, so candidates have to match the strength of their inferences carefully to the strength and reliability of their evidence. In most questions you are given a list of inferences and asked to choose the most relevant and reliable. There is rarely a clear answer; instead you must use your judgement to come to the best decision in circumstances that are uncertain.

5. Decision analysis

The decision analysis test assesses candidates' ability to decipher and make sense of information. Candidates are presented with a scenario and a significant amount of information together with items that become progressively more complex and ambiguous. The judgements that are required cannot be based on logical deduction alone. This simulates decision-making in the real world, where decisions cannot always be made with all the information neatly accessible in one place.

There are other types of tests, like the spatial reasoning test, which is sometimes confusingly called 'abstract reasoning'. These are often used to meet the specialist demands of particular professions. The five we have listed are used more generally across professions. As you work through each chapter of this book, you will develop the skills you need to do well in these tests. You will also find examples on the website, so you can practise your skills.

Improving your skills

The most valuable assets in any organisation are its intellectual assets: the imagination and thinking skills of its employees. When the *New York Times* ran the story that Microsoft now had a market value greater than General Motors, it pointed out that the only real asset Microsoft has is the imagination of its workers. Whatever the organisation – large, medium or small business, charity, hospital or school – its success depends on the abilities of its workers to make good decisions and think creatively and conceptually. For this reason successful organisations work hard to recruit graduates who can think for themselves. This book will help you develop the skills you need to be one of those.

You will learn how to use and develop the skills you need to open up your enormous potential. In the process you will improve both your academic work and your employability skills. In particular, you will learn how to generate your own original ideas, how to create new concepts, how to solve the most difficult problem, assess risk, make the right decisions and cope with uncertainty. You will learn the techniques you need to do well in psychometric tests. But above all, you will learn how to crawl out from beneath the suffocating weight of someone else's authoritative opinion and think for yourself.

How good are we at thinking?

In this chapter you will learn. . .

- How our intuitions affect our thinking.
- How to distinguish between reliable and unreliable intuitions.
- The difference between System 1 and System 2 thinking.
- The importance of freeing ourselves from the influence of unreliable intuitions.

In Robert Pirsig's best-selling book, *Zen and the Art of Motorcycle Maintenance*, he describes 'the old South Indian Monkey Trap', which consists of a coconut, which has been hollowed out and chained to a stake. Inside there is some rice, which can be grabbed by reaching for it through a small hole. The hole is large enough to allow the monkey's hand to go through, but too small for him to take his clenched fist back out once he has grabbed the rice. He's suddenly trapped, not by anything physical, but by an idea. The principle 'when you see rice, hold on tight' has served him well, but has now turned against him.

We also find ourselves trapped by our ideas in exactly the same way. We struggle to accept climate change, because we are trapped by a certain idea of progress, which we can't let go even though it has turned against us. In the West it's difficult for us to free ourselves from ideas like competition and freedom from regulation, even when it's clear that they work against our best interests. As John Maynard Keynes put it, 'The difficulty lies not in the new ideas, but in escaping from the old ones.'[1]

For instance. . .

In the 1990s and 2000s companies in the banking sector were successful through their acquisitions. Buy an underperforming company on the cheap, ruthlessly strip it of costs and you create value with a more successful company that produces the level of profits that shareholders are looking for.

Yet in February 2009 Sir Tom McKillop and Sir Fred Goodwin, the former chairman and chief executive respectively of one of Britain's biggest banks, the Royal Bank of Scotland, both admitted to a select committee of the UK House of Commons that buying parts of the Dutch bank ABN Amro was a 'bad mistake'. The £48-billion deal not only wrecked RBS but threatened to bring down the whole of the British banking system. McKillop admitted that 'The bulk of what we paid for ABN Amro will be written off as goodwill.'

Similar stories could be told about Lehman Brothers, Lloyds Bank and others. These were experienced professional bankers with long careers in the business world, who went ahead with this and other deals at a time when the signs were that the credit crunch was already well under way. It wasn't as if this was an impetuous decision by the RBS board, which they regretted at leisure. They met to discuss it 18 times and still the directors were unanimous that the deal should go through. Like the trapped monkey, they relied on established patterns of expectations and applied a principle that had served them well, instead of analysing the evidence and taking a different course.

We are all trapped by ideas and unexamined intuitions, even when it's clear we are struggling to solve a problem and ought to find other ways of thinking.

Try this. . .

The Professionals

Simon, David, Clive and Justin are all professionals: one is a lawyer, one a dentist, one an accountant and one a teacher, although not necessarily respectively. What we want to know is what type of professional each of them is, given the following facts:

1 Both Justin and the accountant took courses taught by the teacher at the local college.
2 Clive has never heard of David.
3 The accountant, who got Simon out of serious financial trouble by reorganising his finances, is now going to sort out Clive's finances.
4 Clive and David were in the public gallery when the lawyer took on his first case in court.

This is a psychometric problem (we will come back to it later) that assesses our verbal logical reasoning. If you found it difficult, you are not alone. Most of us do. Like the monkey and the bankers we are not good at seeing beyond our established patterns of ideas and expectations.

Why is this?

At least part of the explanation lies in our evolutionary history. Over millions of years we have adapted to our environment to become routine, unreflective thinkers. For much of our existence our survival has depended on rules and patterns of behaviour well-tested by the thousands of generations before us. Learning to flee without thought in response to a certain pattern of colours and movement that signalled a predator was essential for survival. Our neural circuits have been designed by natural selection to solve the problems our ancestors faced:

- Is this a threat or an opportunity?
- Is everything normal?
- Should I approach it or avoid it?

Our minds are programmed for survival, not to seek out truth. As evolutionary psychologists are fond of pointing out, our modern skulls house a Stone Age mind.

> **Our modern skulls house a Stone Age mind.**

As a result, today we make decisions guided more by unchallenged rules and accepted patterns of behaviour than by sustained thought, analysis and reflection. Despite appearances, we are inveterately conservative. Most of us are blindly credulous and confident of the working assumptions we all seem to accept. Even our most systematic attempt to challenge the authority of the past with the rise of modern science in the seventeenth century is a comparatively recent development.

> **We are routine, unreflective thinkers guided by unchallenged rules and accepted patterns of behaviour.**

Intuitions

Most of what goes on in our minds is hidden from view. Consciousness is only the tip of the iceberg. We make judgements and decisions without being consciously aware of how or why we made them. Our intuitions determine how we use our thinking skills and how we select facts, reconstruct events and develop arguments. They can reshape experience to bring it into line with what we expect, again without us knowing.

> **Try this. . .**
>
> Read the following passage and see how well you understand it, even though the words in it appear to be largely unrecognisable.
>
> *Aoccdrnig to rseearch at an Elingsh uinervtisy, it deosn't mttaer in waht oredr the ltteers in a wrod are, the olny iprmoatnt tihng is taht the frist and lsat ltteers are in the rghit pclae. The rset can be a toatl mses and you can sitll raed it wouthit porbelm. Tihs is bcuseae we do not raed ervey lteter by itslef but the wrod as a wlohe.*

Our intuitions are rules of thumb, which on the whole work well, as in this case, but not in all. Our minds struggle to process statistics and calculate risk. We struggle with different forms of logical reasoning, analysis and mathematical judgements. Our intuitions seem overwhelmingly convincing, yet can be wrong and misleading.

> **Try this. . .**
>
> Think of a smooth planet, like the Earth, 25,000 miles around. Stretch a length of string around the equator to just fit. But then use a piece of string a yard too long.

Suppose we re-stretch it so that is stands out from the globe evenly all around. How far out from the surface would the string have to stand?

Now think about the same for the Sun (25 million miles around). How far out would this have to stand?[2]

Answer

Our intuitions tell us that the string would stand out much more from the surface of the Earth than the Sun. Yet the answer is 6 inches in both cases. Even though our intuitions give us a very definite idea about what is right, they are wrong. The surprise is that it doesn't depend on how big the globe is. Here's the formula, so you can try it for yourself.

C+36 inches = $2\pi(R+r)$

Not all intuitions are unreliable

Still, not all our intuitions are unreliable, so we need to know which ones we can rely on and which to abandon. In his best-selling book, *Thinking, Fast and Slow*, the Nobel Prize-winner Daniel Kahneman identifies four types that can be relied upon:

1 Those that evolved through adaptation with the environment.
2 Those developed in circumstances that are sufficiently regular to be predictable.
3 Those based on prolonged practice.
4 Those developed in circumstances where there is accurate and quick feedback.

1. Those that evolved through adaptation with the environment

As we have seen, we have inherited many of our intuitions from ancestors, who developed them over millions of years to ensure their survival. Today we have the same intuitions that are unerringly accurate. We know how to recognise signs, facial expressions and patterns of behaviour, and how to respond. Without these our ancestors would not have survived and we would not have been born. We can pick up facial expressions or hear the first word of a conversation and instantly know that someone is angry. We enter a room and know immediately that people have been talking about us.

For instance. . .

Have you ever wondered why it is that in westerns it is always the bad guys who get shot when they are the ones who draw first? Niels Bohr, the Nobel laureate and quantum physicist, was so intrigued by this that he came up with a theory: the one who draws second is faster because he draws without thinking. He then tested this by staging mock gunfights with his colleagues in his laboratory. Now researchers at Birmingham University have been able to show that the one who draws second is, indeed, 10 per cent faster.

2. Those developed in circumstances that are sufficiently regular to be predictable

In chess the pieces and the way we can move them never change, so it's possible for the player to make reliable predictions about what will happen if he makes a certain move. However, when these stable regularities do not exist, our intuitions and predictions are less trustworthy: unlike chess, it is not possible to develop the expertise needed.

For instance. . .

In his book, *The Black Swan*, Nassim Taleb asks us to imagine how little our understanding of the world in 1914 would have helped us guess what was about to happen. The same could be said about the financial crash in 2007/8. Recently the Bank of England released the minutes of its meetings before the crash, which reveal that its senior economists had no idea what was about to happen. The same must be true about similar recent crises in 1982, 1987, the early 1990s and in 1998.

Professions, like bankers and investment advisers, who deal with the future, base their predictions on an unrepeatable past. Consequently, they have an 'expert problem', because they are plagued by 'Black Swans': 'unknown unknowns'. As Taleb argues, Black Swan logic dictates that what you don't know is far more relevant than what you do know. The problem with bankers and investment advisers is that they don't know what they don't know.

For instance. . .

After examining eight years of the records of wealth advisers, Daniel Kahneman came to the conclusion that the results resembled what you would expect from a dice-throwing contest. He concluded that in their annual bonuses firms were rewarding luck, believing it was skill.

Definition
Black Swans: unknown unknowns – we don't know what we don't know.

3. Those based on prolonged practice

In contrast, reliable intuitions are often developed by those who have worked in a stable area for a number of years – doctors, nurses, fire-fighters. These intuitions give them an uncanny ability to see things obscured to the rest of us. Presented with just a few symptoms, a doctor can make a complex diagnosis. A fire-fighter suddenly senses danger but might be hard pressed to explain what exactly it was that alerted him.

For instance. . .

It is estimated that to become a chess master we would have to play for around 10,000 hours: that is more than six hours a day, five days a week, for six years. With that sort of experience, studying thousands of patterns of play, it is said that a chess master can walk past a game and, at a glance, reliably predict mate in two or three moves.

4. Those developed in circumstances where there is accurate and quick feedback

Feedback, too, is important to confirm or deny whether your intuition is worth relying on. Chess players get instant feedback, which hones their intuitions. The same is true of some professions, like anaesthesiology, where practitioners get good, quick feedback, so they can see how trustworthy their intuitions are. However, in others, like radiology, where they obtain little information about the accuracy of their diagnoses, or where their predictions are long-term, it is more difficult to develop reliable intuitions.

How to recognise unreliable intuitions

Intuitive thinking plays an important and valuable part in our thinking; so we need to know when we can rely on our intuitions and when we need to think more reflectively. This distinction is reflected in Daniel Kahneman's description of two types of thinking:

System 1 thinking – fast, intuitive thinking
System 2 thinking – slow, reflective, more deliberate thinking

When we realise that our intuitions are likely to produce unreliable answers, we resort to System 2 thinking. So what intuitions should we look out for?

1. The narrative fallacy

Although we live in an uncertain world, we tell quite a different story. In our attempts to understand unfamiliar experience and dispel our anxieties we are inclined to create persuasive stories, compelling narratives composed of recognisable behaviour, which tie the events into a sequence of causes, using concrete, rather than abstract terms. In our normal lives we are familiar with such stories, featuring individuals with recognisable traits, intentions and personalities. Familiar and predictable, they make it easier for us to understand unfamiliar, disturbing events.

This is System 1 thinking. Its primary role is to make sense of things by reducing them to the familiar. It is strongly biased towards stories, in which the elements are causally linked. But it is weak at the sort of thinking that involves discrete facts, like statistics, where there is no causal glue to bind the elements together and no familiar personality traits.

The illusion of predictability and control

Even more important, narratives like this give us a sense of predictability and certainty: a sense that we know how things happened, that we can control them and predict their occurrence. As a result, we tend to underestimate the many ways in which luck and Black Swans affect the outcome.

For instance. . .

Breakthroughs in science are frequently unpredictable, yet to make them understandable we rationalise them after the event, giving them the illusion of inevitability as if there was a simple logic to their discovery. Indeed, even among scientists, the suspicion is that such rationalisations of the scientific method reflect less what scientists actually *do* and more what they think they *should* be doing.

Sir Peter Medawar, an immunologist and Nobel Prize-winner, argues that such talk is 'simply the posture(s) we choose to be seen in when the curtain goes up and the public sees us'.[3] It only seems to be logical in character because 'it can be made to appear so when we look back upon a completed episode of thought'.[4] In fact scientific discovery is a much more creative, messy process of false starts, dead ends and sudden insights.

Luck, Black Swans and uncertainty

However, this is not to say that there are no causes; there are. It is just that System 1 thinking has a tendency to oversimplify and ignore evidence in its search for a simple, causal narrative. Rationalisations after the event give us the illusion that we're in control and that there are no uncertainties. We underestimate the many ways in which luck affected the outcome. Nassim Taleb makes the point that

> History and societies do not crawl. They make jumps. They go from fracture to fracture, with a few vibrations in between. Yet we (and historians) like to believe in the predictable, small incremental progression . . . we are just a great machine for looking backward . . . humans are great at self-delusion.[5]

- System 1 thinking makes sense of things by reducing them to the familiar.
- These are persuasive stories with recognisable characters and traits.
- They give us the illusion of certainty, predictability and control.

The ultimate test

Of course, the ultimate test of any explanation is how well we could have predicted the event in advance. By creating these compelling stories of why things happened System 1 thinking gives us the security of knowing that we can predict events and prepare for them, when in fact that is frequently not the case.

> **For instance. . .**
>
> Remember Taleb's example of how little our understanding in 1914 had prepared us for the events that were to follow. Prior to the war most people had in mind a dynamic war of valour and glory with fast-moving troops battling it out over open territory, not the war of attrition with millions fighting over just a few yards, living in trenches full of mud and water, and dying in bomb craters in the middle of no man's land surrounded by tangled barbed wire.

If anybody should be able to predict events that affect us all, it should be those in power. But in 2007, on the eve of the financial crash, neither the Prime Minister Gordon Brown, nor the opposition leader David Cameron, had any suspicions of what was about to happen. Gordon Brown declared that, as a result of the ingenuity and creativity of bankers, 'A new world order has been created': we have the privilege of living in 'an era that history will record as the beginning of a new Golden Age'.

Similarly, at the time, when there were clear signs that the banking system was in trouble, David Cameron was confidently declaring that, largely as a result of the bankers' efforts, a new world economy had been created. The Left's misguided belief in regulation had been thoroughly discredited, he claimed, 'Liberalism' had prevailed and the world economy was now more stable than for a generation.

Unreliable intuition

As this shows, the narrative fallacy affects the way we assess risk and probability. We feel confident in the reassuring causal stories we create and it is difficult for us to doubt that the future is not predictable. Few of us can resist the intuition that what we can make sense of in hindsight, we could predict at the time. But System 1 thinking merely fills us with subjective confidence in the coherence of our story, which is no substitute for rational analysis and evaluation of the problem.

> Unreliable intuition: what we can make sense of in hindsight, we could predict at the time.

2. Simplifying heuristics

Many of our most unreliable intuitive responses come from substituting one question for another. Instead of thinking reflectively about a problem and analysing its implications, we tackle an easier one. In experiments, subjects who were asked to assess the probability of an event, make forecasts, estimate the frequency of something occurring or assess the reliability of a hypothesis, ignored relevant statistical information. Instead, they relied on a familiar heuristic or principle that they had formed from experience, which simplified the problem.

2.1 Representativeness

One form of this is to substitute for a complex question the simpler one that asks whether it resembles something familiar. Stereotypes are a typical example. We hold assumptions about a particular group and, at least tentatively, we accept that these are facts about every individual who is a member of that group.

Try this. . .

You see someone on a bus reading a copy of *Mind*, a quarterly review of philosophy. Which of the following is the better bet:

1   She has a PhD.
2   She doesn't have a degree at all.

Most of us are likely to choose 1, because it is more representative of the stereotype we have of someone who would read a journal containing scholarly articles on philosophy. But a better bet is 2, because there are many more non-graduates than PhDs, so we are likely to meet more of the former than the latter on a bus.

Try this. . .

Read the following description and then rank the eight propositions below, starting with the most probable and ending with the least probable.

   Linda is 31 years old, single, outspoken and very bright. She has a degree in philosophy. As a student she was deeply concerned with issues of discrimination and social justice, and also participated in anti-nuclear demonstrations.

a)   Linda is a teacher in elementary school.
b)   Linda works in a bookstore and takes yoga classes.
c)   Linda is active in the feminist movement.
d)   Linda is a psychiatric social worker.
e)   Linda is a member of the League of Women Voters.
f)   Linda is a bank teller.
g)   Linda is an insurance salesperson.
h)   Linda is a bank teller and is active in the feminist movement.

Now check to see if you placed *h* higher than *f*. If you did, you're not alone. When Tversky and Kahneman gave this problem to undergraduates at the University of British Columbia, 92 per cent did so. They also gave it to graduates at Stanford University Business School; 83 per cent of them did likewise, even though all of them had taken advanced courses in probability and statistics. Undergraduates at several major universities did the same: 85 to 90 per cent of them ranked *h* higher than *f*.

   This is also an example of the 'Conjunction fallacy': we have judged the conjunction of two events to be more probable than one of them. The conjunction rule says that the probability of two events occurring together is less than the probability of either one of them occurring separately. As you can clearly see from the Venn diagram below, this makes obvious sense.

A = Bank tellers
B = Bank tellers active in the
    feminist movement

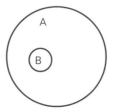

The set of feminist bank tellers is wholly contained in the set of bank tellers; therefore, the probability that Linda is a feminist bank teller must be lower than the probability that she is a bank teller, quite simply because there are more bank tellers than there are feminist bank tellers. It shows that the more you specify an event by giving it more detail, the lower is its probability.

Resemblance is a very strong intuition. We choose the answer that combines the most personality traits to produce the most coherent, plausible story. This is much easier than calculating probability. But it's the wrong answer. As you can imagine, substituting plausibility for probability in this way can produce the most serious miscalculations in forecasting, particularly when it involves the criminal law and jury deliberations.

- We substitute for a complex question a simpler one.
- Rather than ask how probable, we ask how familiar something is.
- Conjunction fallacy: we judge two events to be more probable than one.

2.2 Belief bias – shared assumptions

In the same way, we all carry around certain beliefs and assumptions through which we interpret and make sense of our experience. They provide the basis on which we decide what's probable and what's not. Scholars in a particular field will share the same basic assumptions. Social scientists share a view of human nature that is rarely questioned, in which the individual is conceived as rational and self-interested.

> **For instance. . .**
>
> In his famous book, *The Structure of Scientific Revolutions*, Thomas Kuhn describes scientific progress as a series of revolutions as one powerful theory, a paradigm, triumphs over another. The new paradigm sets the basis upon which research is to be conducted, defining its broad assumptions: its goals, the problems to be worked on and the methods to be employed.
>
> Scientists then settle down to what Kuhn describes as 'normal' science. Taking the truth of the paradigm for granted, they make no attempt to falsify it, but to confirm it by concentrating on the questions it defines as relevant and guarantees to have a solution.

This often affects our ability to reason deductively. In one study[6] participants were given two statements and then asked if a certain conclusion could be logically deduced from them.

Try this. . .

In each case assume the statements are true and ask yourself whether or not the conclusions must therefore be true.

No police dogs are vicious.
Some highly trained dogs are vicious.
Therefore, some highly trained dogs are not police dogs.

No nutritional things are inexpensive.
Some vitamin tablets are inexpensive.
Therefore, some vitamin tablets are not nutritional.

No addictive things are inexpensive.
Some cigarettes are inexpensive.
Therefore, some addictive things are not cigarettes.

No millionaires are hard workers.
Some rich people are hard workers.
Therefore, some millionaires are not rich people.

Answer

The first two are valid deductive arguments, but the last two are invalid.

If, like many, you are surprised by this, you have probably fallen foul of the belief bias: your prior beliefs weighed more heavily than your concern for the logic of the arguments. The conclusions of the first and third are believable, but those of the second and fourth are not. The researchers found that when validity was at odds with believability there were more wrong answers. Arguments that were valid, but had unbelievable conclusions, were only accepted by 55 per cent. When the argument was invalid, but the conclusion was believable, it was accepted by 70 per cent.

- Our prior beliefs dictate our answer, not the logic of the argument.
- They form the basis on which we judge whether something is probable.

2.3 Anchoring effect

Like our prior beliefs, if we have a preconceived impression of the quantity of something and we are then asked to estimate the quantity, our estimate is drawn to the figure we had in mind. System 1 thinking does its best to create a world where our preconceived figure, the anchor figure, is the true figure.

For instance. . .

Estate agents, who were asked to value a house, were given a pack of information, including the asking price. Half of them were given a substantially higher 'anchor' price and half a substantially lower price. They were then asked to set a reasonable price.

When they were asked what affected their judgement, not one mentioned the asking price. They insisted that they ignored it, relying instead on their professional expertise. But the average price set by those who were given the lower asking price was only 41 per cent of the price set by those with the higher asking price. It seems not even professional training insulates us from the effects of this.

- Our preconceptions heavily influence our estimate, regardless of other factors.
- System 1 thinking influences our judgement to conform to the anchor figure.

2.4 Availability bias – ease of recall

When we are asked to estimate the frequency of something, often we find the answer by retrieving from our memories instances of it happening. The ease with which we can do this determines how high we judge the frequency to be: if we can easily retrieve instances of it happening, then the number is likely to be high. Again, we substitute one question for another: instead of estimating the frequency of something we report our impression of how easy it was to retrieve an example from memory.

> **For instance. . .**
>
> There are not many of us who can say truthfully that our judgement as to the safety of air travel has not been affected by the dramatic reports of a plane crash. Extensive coverage of it in the media and newspapers temporarily affects our assessment.

The same can be said of our estimate of the safety of our streets. We read alarming stories of mugging in our area and we're apprehensive going out at night. What we need, of course, is to mobilise our System 2 thinking to counter our intuitions and reassess these estimates.

> **For instance. . .**
>
> RBS had undertaken several successful takeovers of other small banks, therefore the availability bias no doubt made them overconfident when they decided to acquire ABN Amro. Failure didn't come easily to mind so they underestimated the risk.

- The ease with which we can recall instances of something, influences our judgement of how frequently it happens.
- We substitute an easy question for a difficult one.

2.5 Affect heuristic

This is, perhaps, the most familiar of all heuristics. Like the others, we substitute an easy question for a more difficult one. In this case a simple emotional response serves as the answer to difficult judgements and decisions. We refer to our gut feeling, liking and disliking, with little deliberation or reflection.

For instance. . .

A student is trying to make up her mind whether to apply to a university. She asks herself, 'Do I think the University of Durham is a good university?', but instead answers the question, 'Did I enjoy my visit to Durham?'

This type of response is probably more common that we think. Even trained professionals at times rely on their emotional responses to answer difficult questions. Ranjana Srivastava, a medical oncologist, describes how, 'Extraordinary calls get made in hospitals because something "just feels right" to one doctor.'

- An emotional response serves as an answer, rather than reflective thought and deliberation.
- Such System 1 thinking favours our gut reactions, what we like and dislike.

Unreliable intuitions

1 The narrative fallacy
2 Simplifying heuristics:
   2.1 Representativeness
   2.2 Belief bias
   2.3 Anchoring effect
   2.4 Availability bias
   2.5 Affect heuristic

Together these unreliable intuitions act as a barrier to smart thinking. We get locked within their systematic routines, unable to free ourselves. As a result, we struggle to think logically, process statistics, assess risk and probability, and use our imagination to create our own unique ideas and solutions. In short, they trap our enormous potential.

In the following chapters you will learn how to release this potential. In particular, you will learn how to use your System 2 thinking to generate more of your own ideas, to think conceptually and creatively, to assess risk and probability, and to make sound, well-reasoned decisions.

Summary

1 For the most part we are routine, unreflective thinkers.
2 We struggle to process statistics, think logically and assess risk and uncertainty.
3 Not all of our intuitions are unreliable.
4 The narrative fallacy makes sense of things by reducing them to the familiar.
5 The five simplifying heuristics work by substituting a simple question for a complex one.

What's next?

Like the monkey in the trap, we need to release our grip on ideas and mental routines that are trapping our thinking, so that we can release and develop our enormous potential. In the next chapter you will learn what smart thinkers do, how they think, and what you need to do to become one yourself.

Companion website

On the companion website you will find examples of psychometric problems similar to those in this chapter that you can use for practice. www.he.palgrave.com/smart-thinking

What is smart thinking?

In this chapter you will learn. . .

- The difference between thinking and reasoning.
- The key elements of smart thinking.
- How to become a smart thinker.
- What smart thinkers can do.
- How to use smart thinking skills to solve psychometric problems.

The great German philosopher Immanuel Kant describes enlightenment as 'man's emergence from his self-imposed nonage', which he defines as 'the inability to use one's own understanding without another's guidance'. He then challenges us 'Dare to know!':[1] dare to have the courage to think for ourselves.

Living with uncertainty has always been a daring challenge for individuals and societies. Much of our history has been dominated by those who have been certain that their race is the chosen people and their religious beliefs, even their sect within that religion, represent the unquestionable word of God. For these reasons they believe they are charged with the sacred duty of eliminating all uncertainty, all those beliefs and ideas that are in conflict with theirs.

Today we still find ourselves sheltering within reassuring certainties, but now it is the warring ideologies of left and right raging within all modern societies that free us from Kant's challenge to think for ourselves. While professing to be free thinkers and open to new ideas, as Aldous Huxley once said, 'Most of one's life . . . is one prolonged effort to prevent oneself thinking.'[2]

For instance. . .

In one study, subjects were asked to sit in a chair and do nothing but think. So difficult did some people find it to be alone with their own thoughts that, just to break the tedium, they took the opportunity to give themselves mild electric shocks, which they had earlier said they would pay to avoid. Of the men, two-thirds gave themselves painful jolts during a 15-minute spell of solitude. One gave himself 190 shocks. Of the women a quarter gave themselves shocks. In more than 11 separate studies researchers found that people hated being left to think, regardless of age, education, income or the amount they use smartphones or social media.

In contrast, the real intellectual giants of our age seem to do nothing else but seek the solitude in which to think for themselves. John Nash, the American mathematician and the subject of the movie *A Beautiful Mind*, read little and spent most of his time just thinking. He could always be found walking the corridors of the college, lying on a desk or table, or just sitting by himself, oblivious to the presence of anyone else. As one of his colleagues remembers, 'He was always buried in thought . . . Nash was always thinking . . . If he was lying on a table, it was because he was thinking. Just thinking.'[3]

What is thinking?

But what exactly is thinking? As we can see from Nash's example, the first thing we must avoid is confusing thinking with the mere acquisition of knowledge.

1. Thinking and the acquisition of knowledge

If there is one thing that geniuses have in common it is a profound dislike for merely absorbing knowledge and an overwhelming desire to learn by doing and thinking. To put aside your original thoughts and pick up a book instead, they believe, is the ultimate betrayal of your mind.

In our professional lives learning just knowledge and accepted ways of doing things not only leaves us poorly prepared, but may actually be harmful as we cling to ways of doing things that events are rapidly making obsolete. We are left relying on what has been done before, tackling tomorrow's problems with yesterday's methods. The modern world is changing at an unprecedented pace. Our knowledge has an ever-decreasing half-life, that period in which 50 per cent of it becomes obsolete.

For this reason it is not enough just to learn a bank of templates, patterns of behaviour, which we can draw upon to meet the demands of any situation. As the financial crisis shows, there are rare events and genuine uncertainty for which there are no templates of behaviour. Worse still, this can trap us within received patterns of behaviour, unable to think for ourselves.

- The best thinkers learn by doing and thinking.
- Mere acquisition of knowledge leaves us poorly prepared in a rapidly changing world.
- We are trapped within received patterns of behaviour unable to think for ourselves.

Although knowledge and the skill to recall it accurately are important, even more so are the skills needed to take advantage of new opportunities and unexpected problems: the skills to think for yourself, speculate, experiment, explore and innovate.

2. Thinking and reasoning

Reasoning, too, is often mistaken for thinking. When we use the word we mean a method of arguing logically: deductively or inductively. When we reason deductively we argue from our premises to a conclusion in a series of logically valid steps. When we reason inductively, instead of starting with premises, we start with empirical evidence from which we draw inferences.

Hence, although we often argue loosely that a rational person is one who is guided by her reasons, rather than emotions, strictly speaking it means someone who is logical: someone who creates consistent arguments that develop through a series of logically valid steps. When we talk about how rational a person's beliefs and preferences are, the only real test is how consistent they are deductively or inductively.

For instance. . .

Thousands of people believe that they have been abducted by aliens or that the vapour trails we see lining the sky are really evidence that governments are secretly seeding the atmosphere with chemicals to control our behaviour. You may think these beliefs are unreasonable, but they are still rational as long as they are consistent with all their other beliefs. Rationality dictates that our beliefs are logically consistent, irrespective of whether they are reasonable or not.

Reasoning on its own, though, does not embrace all we mean by thinking. You may be reasoning about something, putting together a consistent, perfectly valid argument that moves from one logical step to another, but still you may not be thinking about the ideas you are using. Otto Frisch, one of Niels Bohr's colleagues, recalls that Bohr 'never trusted a purely formal or mathematical argument. "No, no," he would say, "You are not thinking; you are just being logical."'[4]

3. Thinking

Thinking, then, involves more than just reasoning. It is a generic term embracing reasoning, along with non-rational mental processes like creativity, problem-solving, analysis, synthesis and evaluation, most of which only appear rational after the event. But still there is more to it. There is a dynamic component: to say that you are thinking means that you are actively processing ideas, whereas acquiring knowledge or thinking logically can be done passively, almost as if the thinking part of you is not there. This is the point Bohr is making. Thinking means going beyond what you know, or what you can show logically, to discover something new.

For this reason the concept of thinking also embraces certain affective characteristics that good thinkers seem to share. You could say that they insist on control; they are never happy just to let something happen in their thinking without having evaluated and accepted it on their own terms. They reflect on their thinking, they monitor it. Although this suggests thoroughness and persistence, they are also flexible and adaptable. They are usually captivated by novelty and eager to explore new ideas: they are curious and adventurous. But perhaps above all, they have the courage to speculate, even when there is a danger that their ideas might be dismissed as unworkable and naïve.

Thinking involves. . .

1 Reasoning
2 Non-rational processes
3 Active processing
4 Discovering new things
5 Self-monitoring
6 Thoroughness and persistence
7 Flexibility and adaptability
8 Curiosity and adventurousness
9 Courage to speculate

What is smart thinking?

This lays the foundation for what we mean by 'Smart Thinking', to which there are two core elements:

1 Metacognition
2 Counterintuitive thinking

At the centre of the lives and work of all great thinkers, from Newton to Hawking, from Dostoevsky to Virginia Woolf, there you will find these two elements.

1. Metacognition

As you work through this book you will lift your thinking onto a higher level, where you are able to cope with greater complexity and uncertainty. For this we need to develop our higher cognitive skills: to generate ideas, create and analyse concepts, synthesise ideas to see problems differently and to design solutions to difficult problems.

But, just as important, we need to place ourselves at the centre of things, monitoring our thinking, making changes where they are needed, experimenting with different ideas and different mental processes, and making unexpected connections between ideas. All of this means metacognition: the confidence and the ability to think about our thinking while we think, changing it where it needs to be changed. It means conscious self-reflection and self-monitoring.

Definition
Metacognition: thinking about our thinking while we think.

What to monitor

Even though metacognition involves constantly monitoring our thinking while we're thinking, we can learn to recognise those moments when we need it most – when we need to be on our guard:

1 When our intuitions are likely to be unreliable.
2 When we make complex decisions.

1.1 Unreliable intuitions

We saw in chapter 1 that in many situations there is no substitute for our intuitive thinking. Many of our judgements and decisions are made by routine intuitions before we know it. This leaves us vulnerable to the sort of routine mistakes we saw in chapter 1:

1 The narrative fallacy
2 Simplifying heuristics:
    2.1 Representativeness
    2.2 Belief bias
    2.3 Anchoring effect
    2.4 Availability bias
    2.5 Affect heuristic

It's important, therefore, to recognise when we're likely to make these mistakes, so that we can use our System 2 thinking to reflect on the problem and decide whether to allow, modify or suppress our intuitive answers.

Try this. . .

A bat and ball cost £1.10.
The bat costs £1 more than the ball.
How much does the ball cost?

Answer

Most of us answer 10p. But it is wrong. A little reflection would have revealed the error. Many thousands of students have given the wrong answer, including over 50 per cent of those who took the test at Harvard, MIT and Princeton, and over 80 per cent at other universities. The error appears to come from having too much confidence in our intuitions and failing to recognise when they are likely to make errors.

This is a 'cognitive reflection test'[5] designed by Shane Fredericks to check how good we are at metacognition and at recognising when we should use our System 2 thinking to reflect on the problem.

Try this. . .

Determine as quickly as you can whether the following argument is logically valid. Does the conclusion follow from the premises?

All roses are flowers.
Some flowers fade quickly.
Therefore some roses fade quickly.

Answer

Most students endorse the conclusion, but it is in fact invalid. As you can see from the Venn diagram below, it is possible that no roses are among those that fade quickly:

F = Flowers
S = Some flowers that fade quickly
R = Roses

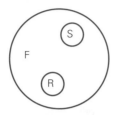

It would have been better for us to have recognised that in cases like this we are likely to make mistakes, so we ought to allow System 2 thinking to check our intuitive answer. This is an example of the 'belief bias': once we believe in a conclusion we're likely to ignore the logic and assemble those arguments that appear to support it. We're even more prone to this when our emotions are involved. Our emotional attitude to climate change, tattoos, hunting or nuclear power might drive our beliefs as to their benefits and risks.

1.2 Complex decisions

Nevertheless, much of the time we can rely on our intuitions, if we have developed them over sufficient time and tested them against reliable feedback.

> **For instance. . .**
>
> Many aspects of daily medical practice eventually become routine. Indeed, this is vital if quick decisions are to be made to save lives. Managing diabetes, repairing fractures and administering antibiotics all become simple routine procedures after a time.

However, some problems cannot be solved by resorting to this type of routine, intuitive thinking. If we were to do so, we could easily find ourselves sweeping aside careful deliberation about, say, a serious moral dilemma, on the grounds that our intuition about it 'just feels right'. To solve these we must resort to the more deliberative, reflective System 2 thinking.

> **For instance. . .**
>
> Throughout the medical profession serious ethical dilemmas face doctors: gender selection, whether to refuse to insert a feeding tube to bring about a dignified death, when to give up working on a patient so that his organs can be 'harvested' safely or when to turn off a ventilator support.

For all of these difficult dilemmas intuitive System 1 thinking cannot be relied upon. As Ranjana Srivastava observes, a new kind of doctor is called for:

one who can make quick decisions where required but who also possesses depth, sagacity and the ability to acknowledge when a case moves into a blurred ethical space.

Metacognition

1 Smart thinking places us at the centre of our thinking.
2 We have to learn what to monitor: our unreliable intuitions and complex decisions.

2. Counterintuitive thinking

Of course, once we have realised it isn't safe to let our intuition solve a problem or make a decision, we must revert to System 2 and do some serious smart thinking. But what sort of thinking is this? Well, it isn't the routine logical kind that we can do with little personal investment. As we have just seen, our thinking must involve self-awareness and self-monitoring. We must be present in our thinking. By definition it must also be counterintuitive: it must challenge our normal responses, think the unthinkable, generate ideas and make connections between them that we would not otherwise have thought about.

2.1 Conceptual thinking

Let's say you have a problem that you can't solve, what do you do? The first thing is to redefine it, to sharpen it up so that you can clearly see all its implications. To do this we would need to analyse the key concepts in the problem.

Analysis

Often the most difficult problem resists all our attempts to solve it because we haven't seen all the implications hidden within the concepts we use to describe it.

For instance. . .

Most teachers have to work on very limited budgets. Over recent years commercial organisations have seen in this an opportunity to get their message across to the next generation of consumers while helping teachers with the funds they need to improve the quality of education. Large corporations, like Exxon, have sponsored educational materials to be used by children in schools, while others have given vending machines and equipment, all in return for some commercial exposure in the school.

Let's say you are a teacher and your school has been offered a grant from a large fast food company in return for which you will be expected to use the teaching materials they provide. You must make a decision: are you willing to accept this or refuse it? Where do you start? Of course, you realise that at the heart of this lies your 'duty of care', but what does this entail, how far does it go? To solve your problem you will have to analyse this concept to get a clearer idea of the responsibilities it entails.

You're clear about your responsibility to protect your students from physical harm, but does it extend farther? Do you have a responsibility to protect them from intellectual harm? The company literature might try to persuade them to believe something that might not be true, or might make an emotive appeal that bypasses their intellectual capacity to evaluate what they are being told.

Synthesis

Alternatively, you may have a problem that can only be solved by synthesising, rather than analysing, ideas: pulling ideas together into a new and original synthesis, so that you can see a problem in a new, interesting way. We often struggle to solve problems, because we cannot produce original ideas when the material for these ideas is all around us. All we have to do is to pull these ideas together.

For instance. . .

Thirty years ago to talk about a 'telephone' meant referring to a large, heavy object sitting in the corner of a room tethered to the wall. Making a call away from your home or office meant first checking to see if you had the right change and going in search of a public call box, usually occupied and often vandalised.

But then someone synthesised a few ideas that were available to us all. New technology was making phones smaller and all around us there were mobile appliances, like radios, even televisions. So was born the mobile phone. Think of any modern product, website or technology and you will find most originated from synthesising ideas that were familiar to us all in our everyday lives.

For instance. . .

In 1948, like most people, Edwin Land was frustrated that whenever he shot a roll of film in a camera he had to take it to a technician to have it processed and then wait for the results. Why not have a camera that would process its own pictures on the spot? So, he brought the existing technology together and invented the Polaroid camera. Everyone knew that the technology existed, but only Land synthesised the ideas into this original concept.

Smart thinkers can. . .

1 Analyse complex concepts into their constituent ideas.
2 Synthesise disparate things into a whole, where others only see parts.
3 See new things in old ideas.
4 Bring ideas together in new and original ways.
5 Create and adapt concepts.

2.2 Generating original ideas

Alternatively, you may think that the reason you can't solve a problem is that you just need more or different ideas. You need to free yourself of the limited ideas thrown up by your intuition and think counterintuitively. We all find it difficult to escape these limitations and generate ideas that we would never have thought of otherwise. Yet it is possible. Later in this book, you will learn a simple method that you can use whenever you want to step outside of your initial ideas and think differently.

Smart thinkers can. . .

1 Step outside their normal mental structures and generate unexpected ideas.
2 Ask themselves naïve questions.
3 Immerse themselves in ideas.

2.3 Creative thinking

But often it's not a question of having enough ideas or even having the right ideas; it's the connections we make between them. Our intuition is not naturally creative: it is conservative, wedded to routines. So we need to draw inferences from our ideas and create hypotheses and possible solutions to problems that would not otherwise have occurred to us.

Try this. . .

Go back to the psychometric problem in chapter 1 (page 10). Tackling this sort of problem involves drawing all those inferences we think can safely be drawn from the facts we are given and then plotting them systematically on a structure or grid, gradually eliminating options on the structure so that we are left with the answers.

1. Lay out all the facts

First, enter on the structure all the facts that the question might give us. This one gives us facts about relationships, so we will have to rely on our inferences from these to start plotting what we know.

	Teacher	Lawyer	Dentist	Accountant
Simon				
David				
Clive				
Justin				

2. Drawing inferences: Making connections

2.1 Divergences

From (1) we know that Justin is neither the accountant nor the teacher, so we can put crosses in the boxes opposite his name under the columns for these two professions. From (3) we can see that the accountant is neither Clive nor Simon, so again we can put crosses in the appropriate boxes. And from (4) it's clear that neither Clive nor David is the lawyer, so we can put crosses in those boxes too.

2.2 Convergences

Having plotted these on our structure we can now draw inferences from the convergences that we are left with. As we now know that Justin, Clive and Simon cannot be the accountant, this leaves just David. We can therefore put Xs in the other columns alongside David's name. So now we know that according to (1) David has studied a course taught by the teacher, while (2) tells us that Clive does not know David. Consequently, Clive cannot be the teacher and thus, by elimination, he must be the dentist. This means we can now complete the dentist's column. As a result there are three crosses in Justin's boxes, so he must be the lawyer. And this leaves Simon as the teacher.

	Teacher	Lawyer	Dentist	Accountant
Simon	O	X	X	X
David	X	X	X	O
Clive	X	X	O	X
Justin	X	O	X	X

As you can see, the problem is more straightforward than you might have thought. Our confusion is magnified by the fact that our immediate response is to engage our System 1 thinking with all its intuitive responses. When each of these fails to produce a solution we are left with the wreckage of these failed attempts cluttering up our thinking. But if we can learn to engage our System 2 thinking straightaway, we can make better use of our thinking skills. In this case we were able to organise our thinking rationally, laying out as clear as possible everything we knew, so that we could use our deductive thinking to fill in the gaps and find a solution.

Counterintuitive hypotheses

Like many problems, this one immediately engages our intuitive thinking, which then hits a deadend. At this point we seem to have nowhere to go. Our intuition points us in one direction, when the answer lies in another. So we need counterintuitive ways of thinking about the problem that will generate different possible solutions, which we would not otherwise have seen. In chapter 12 you will learn how to use four different methods of doing this. One of these is to approach the problem from a different direction.

Try this. . .

You are organising a tennis tournament. Your first job is to arrange the timetable of matches. You have 80 entrants, so how many matches will there be?

Answer

Our intuitions calculate the number of matches by adding up the victors from each round until we get to the final. But a more direct and simpler method is to start from the opposite direction and work with those who lose. As 79 out of the 80 lose, there must be 79 matches.

Smart thinkers can. . .

1 Simplify complex things, making clear what would otherwise remain obscure.
2 Analyse information and ideas to see how to use them in novel ways.
3 See connections between ideas others don't see.

2.4 Decision-making under uncertainty

When our decision-making is determined by our intuitive thinking we often make unwise and irrational choices. Our intuitive preferences consistently violate the rules of rational choice. Nowhere is this more obvious than in our assessment of risk. We are aware that there are uncertainties, but we are poor at calculating how great these are, which is surprising in view of the evolutionary advantage in having an intuition that calculates risk and probability accurately.

Try this. . .

What is the likelihood of two people out of the 23 (including the referee) on a football pitch sharing a birthday?

Answer

Most of us say that, given there are 23 on the pitch and there are 365 days, the likelihood is anything between 6 and 7 per cent. But in fact it is just over 50 per cent: it is more likely than not. The problem is that our intuition works in single people, where, in fact, what matters is the number of ways people can be paired. With 23 people there are 253 possible ways (the first person can be paired with 22; the second with 21; the third with 20 and so on). This makes the odds of a shared birthday much higher.

With such unreliable intuitions, it is not surprising that bookmakers and gamblers are able to exploit the unwary. To guard against these intuitive failings, we need to think counterintuitively. We need a systematic, step-by-step method through which we can

Smart Thinking

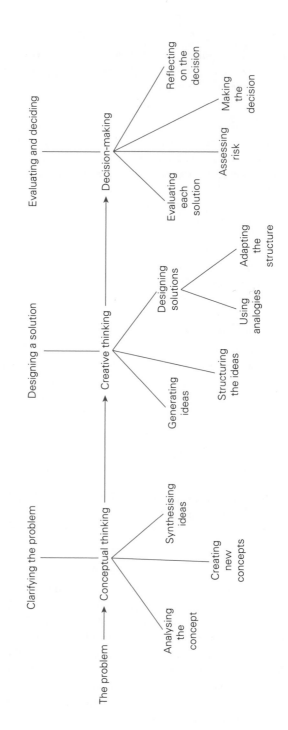

harness our System 2 thinking, evaluate each option rationally, calculate risk accurately and come to the best decision. In the last stage of this book you will learn just this in a simple 4-step method.

Smart thinkers can. . .

1 See what others miss.
2 Think again, when something seems obvious.
3 Cope with doubt and uncertainty.

How to become a smart thinker

It is claimed that the American psychologist William James once said, a great many people think they are thinking when they are merely rearranging their prejudices. This applies to us all to some degree. We may not be rearranging our prejudices, but we all think we are original thinkers when in reality we are just reorganising the same ideas we have expressed a hundred times. So how can we avoid this and become smart thinkers? Whenever we learn something new, it helps to have a few markers, a few 'dos and don'ts'. The following set of 'dos' will chart your way to becoming a smart thinker.

1. Suspend your judgement

As we have seen, smart thinkers question their own thinking and ideas. They accept with humility that they may have got the answer wrong or only have part of it. They are also aware that answers come from the most unlikely sources. So they hang a question over everything and suspend their judgement. For many of us this is unsettling; we find it difficult to admit uncertainty. But good thinking rarely occurs where there are answers that carry the weight of undisputed authority.

2. When you think something is obvious, think again

To help you do this, remind yourself that most complex problems need careful reflection and delayed judgement, not instant decisions modelled on established patterns. Smart thinkers go deeper than the surface and the deeper you go the more excitement and creative energy you will generate.

3. Forget about yourself

Then, as you begin to think, do two things. First, forget about yourself in your thinking. Smart thinkers realise they must forget about what they might wish will be the case in any situation, before they can see what the situation itself requires. In contrast, those who are ruled by their ego have something to protect: their own image of themselves. They are likely to become defensive and no longer open to new ideas, the possibility of being wrong and of thinking differently:

- Smart thinkers can forget about themselves in their thinking.
- By empathising with others they develop wider sympathies and sounder judgement.

Smart thinkers learn to empathise with others, vicariously experiencing what others in a particular situation might feel, believe or prefer. Consequently, they see more and tend to make better decisions. Curious about the lives and experiences of others, they are more effective at trading places to see what they would do or feel in similar situations. They hypothesise more, experience more things and develop the ability to create more structures through which to process and understand more things. As a result they develop wider sympathies and sounder judgement.

4. Step outside the routine structures that organise your thinking

Second, detach yourself from your routine patterns of thought. Smart thinkers are good at applying seemingly unrelated mental frameworks to a problem. They learn not to be afraid of making the most unlikely connections between ideas. In this way they liberate their minds from the narrow grooves in which they might otherwise be trapped, allowing themselves to scan a wide range of possible answers.

Definition
Smart thinkers detach their minds from routine patterns of thought.

5. Make space for good ideas to come through

But to do this effectively we must make space for new ideas. Our minds are so interested in things that they make connections when we least want them to. For much of the time they are full of meaningless static: conversations are recalled and justifications rehearsed again and again until we have no room for anything else. It takes most of us a lifetime to realise that there is no room for serious thought in such a cluttered mind. The thoughts may be there, full of insight and vision, but we can so easily pass through life without even knowing that they are there at all. In order to let good thoughts come through, we must clear a space for them. There must be no irrelevant preoccupations prowling around, hijacking the mind.

6. Ask naïve questions

Then, as you think, get into the habit of asking naïve questions. The Ancient Greek philosopher Socrates maintained that wisdom begins with the recognition of one's own ignorance. Reading his famous dialogues you realise how important this is for training the mind's eye to see what needs to be seen, but is so often missed. The solutions to many of our problems are hidden in plain view, so asking naïve questions is the key to seeing them. Even more important, life becomes endlessly fascinating as a result: there is always something to explore, new ideas to uncover.

7. Be persistent

And, equally important, be persistent. Most smart thinkers learn the value of allowing themselves to become obsessed by an idea, so that it never gives them rest. To find the answer to a complex problem we may need to keep it in our minds for days, weeks, even years on end. From Sir Isaac Newton to Andrew Wiles the British mathematician, who spent nine years working alone proving Fermat's Last Theorem, the value of such persistence is a common theme.

> **For instance. . .**
>
> When asked how he went about his work Einstein answered, 'I think and think, for months, for years, ninety-nine times the conclusion is false. The hundredth time I am right.'[6] And when Sir Isaac Newton was asked how he discovered the law of gravitation he answered, 'By thinking about it all the time.'[7] He explained, 'I keep the subject constantly in mind before me and wait 'til the first dawnings open slowly, by little and little, into a full and clear light.'[8]

8. Reject the fear of failure

And, along with persistence, be confident that you will ultimately succeed. When we fear failure we play it safe: we revert to the lower cognitive skills and merely recall what we know. Smart thinkers learn to be optimists: they are motivated by the hope for success, rather than the fear of failure. Optimists appear to progress farther, because they have a clearer vision. They see fewer obstacles blocking their path.

9. Allow for reverie

After sustained work allow yourself time for reverie. This may seem like idleness, but our minds need the time to answer questions, to process and order our ideas, and make new connections between them. While we are thinking about nothing in particular, it is generating our most perceptive ideas.

10. Organise yourself to catch ideas whenever they appear

Finally, we need a good system to catch our ideas. Coming up with good ideas is a continuous, unbroken process. Good or bad, they breed other ideas. When we think about a problem we may produce an idea that clearly wouldn't work, but it is very likely to produce other ideas out of which solutions are likely to come. They are seeds that will bear fruit, so we must have a system of notebooks and journals to catch them whenever and wherever they appear.

How to become a smart thinker

1 Suspend your judgement.
2 When you think something is obvious, think again.
3 Forget about yourself.
4 Step outside your routine structures that organise your thinking.
5 Make space for good ideas to come through.
6 Ask naïve questions.
7 Be persistent.
8 Reject the fear of failure.
9 Allow for reverie.
10 Organise yourself to catch ideas whenever they appear.

How To Become a Smart Thinker

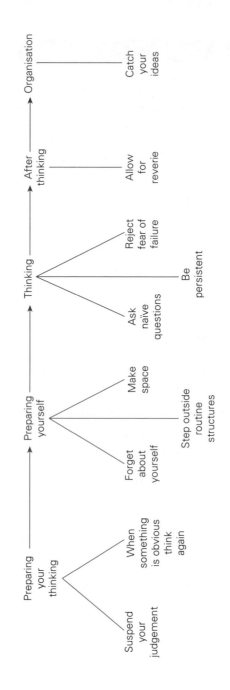

Summary

1 The best thinkers learn by doing and thinking.

2 Smart thinking goes beyond what we know or can demonstrate logically to discover something new.

3 Smart thinking has two core elements: metacognition and counterintuitive thinking.

4 Metacognition involves thinking about our thinking while we think.

5 Counterintuitive thinking challenges our normal responses, generating new ideas and creating connections between them we would not have thought about.

What's next?

Perhaps our most serious obstacle to becoming smart thinkers is that we live in a culture that has excessive confidence in what it knows and is reluctant to acknowledge its own uncertainty. For all our talk of innovation and our eagerness to embrace progress we are inveterately conservative in our thinking, timid about change and fearful of uncertainty. In the following chapters you will not only learn how to overcome this, but the methods and techniques that will unlock your enormous potential to become a smart thinker.

Companion website

On the companion website you will find examples of psychometric problems similar to the one in this chapter that you can use for practice. www.he.palgrave.com/smart-thinking

Conceptual Thinking

According to the World Bank's report, *The Changing Wealth of Nations*, 80 per cent of the developed world's wealth lies in human capital. When Philip Morris bought Kraft in 1988 for $12.9 billion, physical assets represented less than $2 billion; the rest were intellectual assets – the ideas and creativity of its staff.

This is amazing by itself. But it is even more so when you consider the type of asset that ideas are. Economists describe them as 'non-rival assets', in other words they can be shared and used by more than one person at a time, unlike the traditional assets of land, labour and capital. If I have a mechanical digger and I let you use it, only you can use it. Moreover, it will inevitably suffer diminishing returns: gradually it will wear out; it will become less efficient and will need to be repaired and serviced more often. In contrast, ideas produce increasing returns. If I share with you an idea, both of us now have it: we can both develop it, add other ideas to it and make it even more valuable.

Now go one step further and think about concepts, the most dazzling of all the stars in the firmament of ideas. They are the source of all our understanding and power over our world: our most effective means of interpreting it, reducing the confusion of life and giving us the capacity to shape our environment.

Concepts are general classifications or universals that we create from our experience of particular things. We group all those things that share particular characteristics under one idea or principle, giving us the ability to go beyond the particulars of our world and extend our understanding in ways that would otherwise be impossible, indeed, in the strict sense of the word, 'inconceivable'. Each time we use them we bring our understanding gained from past experience to bear on the present and to shape our future.

However, so influential are they that for much of the time we are unaware of the way they manage our thinking: our conclusions and judgements may be influenced in ways over which we have little control. We may wonder why a problem is so difficult to solve, when all along it is our concepts and the way they direct our thinking that prevents us finding a solution.

So we need to think about our thinking (metacognition): to analyse these concepts and reveal the way in which they shape the patterns into which our ideas are organised, so we can redesign them, create new concepts and find new ways of releasing our boundless imagination. This is what we will do in this stage.

What is conceptual thinking?

In this chapter you will learn. . .

- How you can learn to think differently.
- How to define a problem clearly.
- The difference between conceptual and other forms of thinking.
- What makes conceptual thinking such a powerful agent of change.
- The sort of psychometric tests that are used to assess our conceptual thinking skills.

If university education is about any one thing it is about developing our ability to think conceptually: to lift ourselves above our normal dialogue and examine it from a distance; to question our use of concepts and how they influence our thinking. We step back from our arguments and ask ourselves, 'Have I seen all the implications of using this concept in this way?', 'Can I synthesise these ideas and bring them together under one concept to see something I haven't seen before?' and 'If I use this concept in this way, will it be pushing my arguments in a direction I don't want to go?'

Being pulled the other way

Unfortunately, there are powerful forces pulling us in the other direction. An important part of learning any academic subject is accepting its language and concepts. To understand the arguments that are developed in texts and journal articles, or by our teachers, we must first accept the concepts they use to develop their ideas.

The same applies if we want to enter a particular profession. To be a lawyer we must learn to think like a lawyer as we must learn to think like a doctor, teacher, architect, scientist or economist, if we want to enter any of these professions. But we also need to learn how to escape this network of concepts and explanations, when we search for alternative solutions to difficult problems, particularly when they appear to call for a new type of solution that lies beyond these conventional approaches.

The problem is, of course, that when we have doubts about what is being said or want to question the underlying assumptions of the leaders in our field, like the economics students who walked out of the lecture at Harvard in November 2011, it is as if we are behaving recklessly and turning our backs on a community of scholars, to which we have worked so hard to belong.

- To study any academic subject or enter any profession we must first learn how to think this way.

- But we must also learn to escape the network of concepts and explanations that dominate them.

Finding new answers

This is exactly the challenge faced by those who have made the most significant scientific breakthroughs over the last 500 years. Their education and training had prepared them well in the established ways of approaching a problem in science, but still the problem holding up progress in their field persisted unresolved. So, the only solution was to try to think differently about the problem.

But how was this to be done? We are never taught to think this way. Our education focuses on the principles and procedures that have received the widest possible acceptance within our subject or profession. We are told that we must immerse ourselves in the literature of our subject. Accordingly, our education teaches us to think in one direction, when the problems may only be solved by thinking in another. For this reason it has been said that genius is the capacity for productive reaction against one's training.

Genius is the capacity for productive reaction against one's training.

How to do this

The most interesting thing about this is that these revolutionary breakthroughs came about not because researchers had new or better data, but because of the quality of their thinking and the concepts they created. In many cases, faced with problems that defy solution, the answers only finally came as a result of being able to think outside of the concepts they used everyday. Once they revealed the structure of these concepts and the way they were shaping their understanding, they could then adapt them, synthesise ideas in new ways or create new concepts to find the answers they were looking for.

In this way the problem could be portrayed differently. Like a crime novel, the answer then appeared, as if it had been hidden in full view all the time. After the event, some of the most stunning breakthroughs appear to be almost prosaic, yet the thinking that produced them is pure genius, as the work of scientists, like Copernicus, Galileo, Darwin and Einstein, illustrates.

For instance. . .

Galileo and Copernicus both questioned the assumption, which seemed obviously true to all sane people, that the Earth was stationary and the universe rotated around it. Einstein questioned the deeply held intuitions of absolute space and time to arrive at his theory of special relativity, which overthrew Newtonian physics that had dominated thinking for two centuries.

Examples like these show that it's not the quantity of information alone that yields good decisions, but the quality of our thinking and the type of concepts we use. We hear a lot about the 'information age' and how important it is for us to be kept constantly up to date. But more important is how we use this information. If we fail to question the concepts we use, we might flatter ourselves that we are up to date and on the cutting edge, yet we might only be coming to conclusions that repeat the mistakes of the past.

- Answers to the most difficult problems only finally came as a result of thinking outside of the concepts used everyday.
- We hear a lot about the importance of being kept constantly up to date, but more important is how we use this information.

What sort of a problem is it?

So what is the first thing we must do? Whenever we are presented with a problem the first thing to do is analyse it to see what sort of questions it asks. Then we can see more clearly what we need to do to make progress. The problem is that as our minds are quick to look for order in our ideas, they leap at the first sign of organisation. Once they have done this, other lines of thought are closed, while we gather the material we need to shore up our first thought. Like scientific paradigms, this restricts what we can think and the direction in which our research can go.

For instance. . .

When George Stephenson was constructing the Manchester–Liverpool Railway in the late 1820s, he had to decide what rail gauge to use. He chose 4 feet 8 ½ inches, a size he is said to have arrived at by finding the average axle width of 100 carriages. Others say its origin is to be found in the coalfields of North-East England, while some even suggest that it dates back to the rutted roads marked by chariot wheels during the Roman Empire.

Whichever it is, the question he seems to have asked was, 'What is the most common gauge?' Instead, he could have posed perhaps a better interpretation of the problem: 'What would be the ideal gauge for passenger comfort?' This would have produced a wider, more comfortable gauge, rather than the narrow gauge that is now the standard for most of the world's railways.

The eighteenth-century French writer and philosopher Voltaire is said to have insisted that we should judge a man by his questions, rather than by his answers. The best minds see in any problem several distinct and interesting questions. They are good at defining them and analysing their internal elements.

Clear answers depend upon clear questions. Otherwise our minds will see only what they are prepared to see; what they always see. What we take to be the problem, might turn out not to be the problem at all, just a symptom of the real problem. By asking a clear question we point ourselves in the right direction to find the ideas and evidence we need: we set the controls on our thinking that will determine what's relevant and what's not. The clearer the question we set ourselves, the more dominant and effective are these controls.

> **The best minds are good at seeing several, interesting questions and then analysing them clearly.**

The first important thing to know is what type of question it is that we are asking. Is it a question of fact, value or concept? If we confuse one with another, we can find ourselves producing a bewildering solution that fails to address the important issues.

For instance. . .

A few years ago a local health authority decided to withdraw the dialysis treatment from a patient, who lived in a hostel for the homeless. Medical resources are limited, so these decisions have to be made.

But the type of reason that is to count as a good reason depends on the type of question you ask. Unless you identify and separate the different types of questions involved, you could easily find yourself searching for one type of answer to a problem that really needs another: you might treat a problem as, say, a question of fact, when it is, in reality, a question of concept.

Try this. . .

Listed below are the sorts of statements that were made to explain the decision. See for yourself the kind of traps we could easily fall into. Can you identify which are statements of fact, value and concept, and which are mixed? Can you see what they are a mixture of?

1 The patient is rude.
2 He is aggressive.
3 He has poor quality of life.
4 He should be denied treatment.
5 He is unemployed.
6 He lives in a hostel for the homeless.
7 The treatment should be given instead to someone else.
8 He is rootless.
9 He has no family.
10 He makes a mess which the nurses have to clean up.

Answer

Mixed

A. Fact/concept 8, 9, 10
B. Fact/value/concept 1, 2
C. Value/concept 3

Unmixed

4, 5, 6, 7

Fact/concept

In group A clearly these are statements of fact, but what is meant by 'rootless', 'mess' and 'family'? One person's mess might be another's everyday disorder; something that it is just not worth getting worked up about. As for 'rootless', the patient might not have a family, but he might have rich personal relations with his friends in the hostel. Even 'family' raises problems. He might not have many close blood relatives, but he might have many close friends he likes to regard as 'family'.

Fact/value/concept

As for group B words like 'rude' and 'aggressive' are not just descriptions of a way of behaving, they are also evaluative: we usually don't approve of such behaviour. But then there are also questions of concept raised by these words. What do we mean by 'rude' and 'aggressive'? Do they just convey personal prejudices or is there an objective standard by which we can judge such behaviour?

Value/concept

Similar questions can be raised about the one statement in group C. Clearly there is a question of value here with the use of the word 'poor', but we can also raise a question of concept about the 'quality of life'. We need to analyse this carefully before we allow ourselves to apply it to this sort of case.

1. Facts and values

It's not inconceivable that some people might argue, 'Of course his treatment should be withdrawn. He lives in a hostel!' To them it seems a simple question of fact. But, as you can see, it's more complex than that. Obviously, it is a matter of fact that he lives in a hostel, but the implication of this is that, as a result, his quality of life is not good enough to justify the treatment. So on this simple statement of fact hangs also a question of concept as to what is a satisfactory quality of life, and a question of value, that the failure to reach this standard justifies the judgement to remove the treatment from him.

The most obvious difference is that between a fact and a value. Put simply, a fact is a statement about what *is* the case, whereas a statement containing a value judgement is about what *ought* or *should* be the case. One is *descriptive*, the other *prescriptive*. A statement of fact purports to represent the way the world is and, therefore, it is subject to rational criticism: we can assess it in terms of its truth or falsehood as to whether it succeeds in representing the world accurately. In contrast, a statement of value is concerned about how the world should be. It does not purport to represent the way the world is and, therefore, cannot be assessed in terms of truth or falsehood.

Fact	Value
A statement about what *is* the case.	A statement about what *ought* or *should* be the case.
Descriptive	Prescriptive

Statements like 'He is unemployed' and 'He lives in a hostel for the homeless' are clearly statements of fact that can easily be proved true or false. Whereas statements like 'He should be denied treatment' and 'The treatment should be given instead to someone else' state what *should* happen to the patient and his treatment. If we disagree with any of these judgements, unless we can show that they are based on inconclusive or contradictory evidence, or there is an inconsistency in the argument, we will be faced with a non-negotiable value judgement, a prescription, which is simply different from our own.

Try this. . .

As we will see later, many psychometric problems are designed to assess your ability to understand complex arguments. They include questions that ask you to distinguish between a fact and a value: between those words that express a value judgement and those that are neutral or express some other state of mind, like the following:

1 Explain the differences between, and any ambiguities in, the questions: 'Will we buy tea or coffee?'; 'Should we buy tea or coffee?'
2 Give the *neutral* term or the term of *approval* that corresponds to each of the following: enemy, babble, secret, reckless, plotting, notorious, fawning, accomplice.
3 Distinguish between: 'I ought to apologise', 'I intend to apologise', 'I am trying to apologise', 'I want to apologise', 'I promise to apologise', 'I am willing to apologise'.

Although the difference between a fact and a value is not difficult to understand, it is still very easy to introduce a value into an argument without really knowing it. Often, when words are used in a different context or for different purposes, they become mixed, both fact and value. Words, like 'honesty', 'promise', 'heroism' and 'cowardice', used in a particular way in a particular context represent both a description of the facts and a value judgement.

> **For instance. . .**
>
> The statement 'John promised to pay Sarah £30' is a simple statement of fact. But the word 'promise' means more than just an undertaking to do or to refrain from doing something. It also means it is 'good' to keep such an undertaking and 'bad' not to. In other words, there are both prescriptive and descriptive elements to the meaning of the word. Consequently, from the statement of fact that 'John promised to pay Sarah £30', we can deduce the value judgement that 'John *should* pay Sarah £30'.

2. Concepts

Questions of concept can also hide unnoticed within a simple statement of fact in a similar way. In each case where concepts are used we're asking a unique sort of question: 'Yes, but what do you mean by X?' In a probing, self-reflective way we are questioning our own use of these quite ordinary words. We are saying that these can no longer be taken for granted; that there are implications to our argument that are concealed by our use of these words.

In some discussions we have to step back and ask questions like these. In the statements about the dialysis patient we would have to ask, 'What do we mean by 'rootlessness', 'aggression' or even 'family'?' Often our discussions turn on the meaning of such concepts. What seems like a discussion over a difference of fact turns out to be a difference of concept with both sides using it in different ways.

> Conceptual thinking involves a unique type of questioning: one that is self-reflective, probing the way we use quite ordinary words.

What is conceptual thinking?

Now that we know the conceptual problem we must tackle, how does this type of thinking differ from any other?

- Learning to think conceptually involves learning to lift ourselves above our normal discourse, so that we can examine it from a distance, like someone who has never heard of these things before.
- It involves thinking naïvely about the concepts we use, free of all the assumptions that condition us to accept them uncritically.
- It means thinking about our thinking – metacognition.

By distancing ourselves from our normal understanding of concepts in this way we can analyse them into their constituent ideas to reveal the patterns into which these ideas and their connections are organised. Then we can create new patterns by synthesising these ideas in different ways so that we can see new ways of approaching a problem or create new concepts by merging two or more patterns together.

- We can **analyse** them into their constituent ideas and reveal the patterns into which they are organised.

- We can **synthesise** ideas to create new patterns, so that we can see new ways of approaching a problem.
- We can **create** new concepts by merging two or more patterns together.

The importance of conceptual thinking lies in the fact that, beyond the simplest operations, thinking is all about creating these sorts of connections between ideas. On their own, ideas have little value or significance; it is only when we make connections with other ideas that they become useful.

For instance. . .

Although the idea, 'The object in front of me is red', makes sense, it has very limited value or significance.

But connect it with other ideas, like 'The object is a person' and 'The red is blood', and it becomes altogether more significant.

This illustrates an important point: that the quality of our thinking is determined not by the strength of our ideas but by the significance of the relations we find and the connections we make between them. In making these connections we create patterns or structures of ideas and these shape our thinking, often without us even knowing. It is these patterns that lie at the heart of concepts.

> The quality of our thinking is determined not by the strength of our ideas, but by the significance of the relations we find and the connections we make.

The structure of our ideas

So, unless we learn to think conceptually and analyse the concept to reveal the underlying pattern of ideas, we can find ourselves being led repeatedly down the same route into the same dead ends as we doggedly try to solve a problem. We can find ourselves going round and round in circles, trapped by the same ideas. Unless we can learn to think differently, we will never make progress. To do this we must learn to analyse them, so that we can create different connections and patterns that have a better chance of revealing the solution.

Out of our experience our minds create patterns of behaviour reflecting our beliefs, values and preferences. From these we retain only those that have been successful in dealing with the routine situations we confront. They act as mental shortcuts designed so that we can avoid having to make lengthy and involved calculations every time we have to decide what it would be best to do.

Over the years our thinking has been extensively programmed in this way. We use these patterns of behaviour routinely and without deliberation to help us navigate the immense space of possibilities open to us. In this way we can interpret experience, reduce our confusion to manageable levels and predict what is likely to happen if we choose one thing rather than another.

For instance. . .

As consumers we are presented with a bewildering range of choices. We cannot hope to evaluate each and every one before we decide. Instead, we take shortcuts: we form patterns into which we organise our beliefs, values and preferences, which then act as standard operating procedures to guide us routinely as we make these decisions.

We solve most of our problems in exactly this way. We take the same route to work each day and each time we go to the supermarket we have in our minds the same list of things we need, representing the pattern of our consumption habits. Faced with a bewilderingly large number of TV channels we program into our receiver a template of our favourite channels.

Unfortunately, the most familiar patterns are not always the most useful. And in most cases we're not likely to be aware of this. Once they're formed we tend not to second-guess them. To do so would be to sabotage them. We choose what we have become used to choosing, because it is easier to navigate the immense space of possibilities that way. Accordingly, we tend to ignore anything that might seem to contradict and throw into doubt our choices and established patterns of behaviour.

For instance. . .

In the 1950s, studies of cognitive dissonance found that consumers would continue to read advertisements for a new car after they had bought it, but would avoid information about other brands, fearing post-purchase misgivings.

Humour and crossword puzzles

These patterns are the scaffolding of our understanding: they lie at the heart of almost everything we do. Without them we would struggle to see the point of a witty or humorous comment and we couldn't even start to tackle a crossword puzzle without recognising, comparing and adapting them.

Try this. . .

How would you answer the following crossword clue?

'Savings book' – seven letters

Answer

Like many clues, this is split in two with both parts leading to the same word. As you compare the structure of ideas represented by both words your aim is to find a similarity, which points to the answer. The answer is, of course, 'Reserve'. Your savings are a reserve and you can book or reserve a table in a restaurant or a seat on a train.[1]

As for wit and humour, Sir Peter Medawar in his book, *Induction and Intuition in Scientific Thought*, gives us this one. He explains:

> *The Rev. Sydney Smith, a famous wit, was walking with a friend through the extremely narrow streets of old Edinburgh when they heard a furious altercation between two housewives from high-up windows across the street. 'They can never agree', said Smith to his companion, 'for they are arguing from different premises'.[2]*

As he points out, in this and similar examples there is a real or apparent structural similarity between two or more schemes of ideas and it is this that makes it witty. We instantly recognise that the word 'premises' can be used in two ways.

Insight

More significant, when this similarity between structures of ideas is real, we experience those wonderfully insightful moments of sudden clarity, when we understand a difficult principle or idea for the first time. A teacher might give you an analogy, which suddenly makes a difficult subject clear. This sudden insight and the clarity it brings comes from instantly apprehending the structural similarity between the two sets of ideas: the subject and the analogy.

> **Insight is the sudden recognition of the structural similarity between two sets of ideas.**

Mapping the interrelations between ideas

To make sense of isolated facts and ideas, then, we must reveal the connections between them and map out their interrelations. The two most effective means of doing this are by analysing the causal and conceptual relations between ideas.

Structuring ideas

1 Causal relations
2 Conceptual relations

In chapter 10 we will examine how we map out our ideas using causal relations. In the next three chapters we will learn how to map them using their conceptual relations by learning how to create new concepts, analyse their meaning and synthesise our ideas into new patterns. In the process we will learn that this is central to almost everything we do.

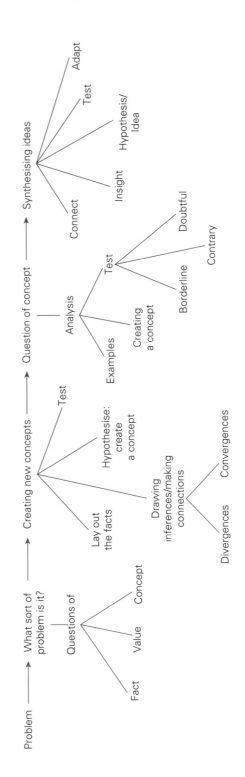

Conceptual Thinking

Problem → What sort of problem is it? → Creating new concepts → Question of concept → Synthesising ideas

Questions of
- Fact
- Value
- Concept

Lay out the facts

Hypothesise: create a concept

Test

Drawing inferences/making connections
- Divergences
- Convergences

Analysis
- Examples
- Creating a concept
- Test
  - Borderline
  - Doubtful
  - Contrary

Connect

Insight

Hypothesis/Idea

Test

Adapt

Conceptual thinking and psychometric tests

Unfortunately, at university few of us are taught these skills. We learn something about them in those rare moments when we see our tutor analyse a concept or pull ideas together into an original synthesis to create a new way of looking at a problem. If we are able to recognise the significance and meaning of what has happened – and, sadly, most of us don't – we might have a chance of retaining a small inkling of what went on so that we can try to do the same ourselves.

Failing that, most of us fill the gap in our skills by copying the sort of adversarial debating skills taught in so many schools and college debating societies and played out everyday in the media between the competing ideologies of political parties. However, this simplified model of thinking stunts our abilities to think conceptually and creatively. Our thinking is constrained by the need to manipulate opinion and win the argument, rather than reveal the truth by confronting all the issues honestly and presenting the evidence accurately, irrespective of whether it supports our opinion.

> The adversarial discourse of modern politics stunts our abilities to think conceptually and creatively.

Verbal reasoning tests

And, of course, this leaves us poorly prepared for the sort of psychometric tests used by employers to see if we have developed just these skills. The main aim of these tests is to assess our ability to understand and analyse complex written arguments. This involves interpreting and distinguishing between complex concepts that are very similar. To cope with these questions successfully we must be able to analyse the subtle implications of the concepts, otherwise we may miss the point of the whole passage.

As you work through the following three chapters you will develop the skills you need to tackle successfully these and similar problems. For now, try the following tests so that you can assess your skills.

Word differentiation

This type of question assesses your ability to differentiate between the meanings of similar words.

Try this. . .

1 Distinguish between the following. . . .
   1.1 Indifferent, impartial, disinterested
   1.2 Revoke, recant, abjure, renounce
   1.3 Obedient, obsequious, servile, submissive, obliging
   1.4 Telling lies, misleading, failing to inform, breaking a promise, breaking an agreement

2 What is the difference between the following pairs of words?
   2.1 Infer, imply, flout, flaunt, simple, simplistic
   2.2 Sensual, sensuous, militate, mitigate, sympathy, empathy
   2.3 Bravado, bravery, hope, optimism, generosity, munificence
   2.4 Rational, reasonable, illusion, delusion, correct, true

Comprehension and word meaning

These questions involve comprehension passages, which assess your ability to read and show that you have understood the subtle implications of the words used in the passage.

> ### Try this. . .
>
> In the second half of the nineteenth century as labour and information swept across borders, new pressures for change were generated, bringing with them unprecedented social and cultural fragmentation. Towns grew at **inconceivable** rates into vast cities drawing workers in from the countryside to interact with the foreign labour flooding in from all over Europe. Here a new cosmopolitan culture developed, **fuelled** by rising literacy and a popular mass press. The revolution in communications alone was fuelling forces for uniformity in tastes, culture and fashion that touched just about every European society that engaged in commerce. Except where they were consciously **protected**, national styles slowly faded. With the impact of dance music, the cinema, the wireless and cheap recreational literature drawing its inspiration from the US, it was clear by the 1930s that the social and cultural identity of many, once a source of patriotic pride and a sense of **belonging**, was disappearing beneath a uniform, cosmopolitan culture that was constantly changing.

1 Which of these words is closest in meaning to the word 'inconceivable' in the second sentence?
   a) Unimaginable
   b) Unprecedented
   c) Impossible
   d) Improbable
   e) Incredible
2 Which of these words would best replace the word 'fuelled' in the third sentence?
   a) Inspired
   b) Influenced
   c) Built
   d) Prepared
   e) Sustained

3 Which of these words means the same as 'protected' in the fifth sentence?
   a) Defended
   b) Insulated
   c) Secured
   d) Screened
   e) Supported
4 Which of these words means the opposite of 'belonging' in the last sentence?
   a) Irrelevant
   b) Independent
   c) Alien
   d) Impertinent
   e) Discretional

Answers

a, a, a, c.

The logic of the passage

This type of question assesses whether you have understood the logic of the passage by getting you to identify parts of the arguments developed in it, like conclusions and the reasons used to support them. Usually, some of the questions can be answered by more than one choice, so you are instructed to choose the best answer that most accurately and completely answers the question. You are also warned not to make assumptions that are superfluous or incompatible with the passage.

> ### Try this. . .
>
> Some telephone companies have diversified their businesses by combining into one package line rentals, broadband and TV. Consequently, they are no longer providing the same quality of service to their original telephone customers. Therefore, if they want to keep their customers, they must concentrate exclusively on one of these different markets.
>
> For this argument to be logically valid, it must make which one of the following assumptions?
>
> a. Most customers do not want a package that includes all three things: line rental, broadband and TV.
> b. If a telephone company specialises exclusively in the provision of line rentals, then it will be successful.
> c. The primary responsibility of a telephone company is to be a successful business.
> d. If a telephone company is to be successful, it must serve its customers well.
> e. None of these three elements – line rentals, broadband and TV – have much in common.

Answer

d

Summary

1 The first thing we need to do is define the question clearly.

2 Conceptual thinking involves lifting ourselves above our normal discourse and asking naïve questions.

3 The quality of our thinking is determined by the significance of the connections we make between our ideas.

4 Our thinking is extensively programmed by patterns of ideas we rarely question.

5 Many of our most important breakthroughs in our understanding have come about as a result of thinking conceptually.

What's next?

We began this chapter by arguing that if university education is about any one thing it is about developing our ability to think conceptually. No matter what the academic subject, no matter what the profession, the ability to create concepts, analyse their implications and synthesise ideas into new patterns has been the source of the most remarkable insights that have generated new ways of explaining things and new visions of what is possible.

From relativity to plate tectonics, from the Renaissance to the Enlightenment, from railways to the Internet, new concepts have changed our world beyond recognition. In the next chapter we will learn a simple method of creating our own original concepts.

Companion website

On the companion website you will find examples of psychometric problems similar to those in this chapter that you can use for practice. www.he.palgrave.com/smart-thinking

How to create concepts

In this chapter you will learn. . .

- What a concept is.
- How concepts help us think more creatively.
- How to create concepts using a simple, practical method.
- How to tackle verbal logical reasoning tests.
- About the importance of reverie to our conceptual thinking.

Most of our thinking goes from the general to the specific: from the abstract to the concrete. This is the way we find explanations for things. We're told that an argument between two people on the side of the road is an incident of road rage and we understand. In this chapter we move in the opposite direction: from the specific to the abstract. If the first direction is the way we find explanations for things, this is the way we come to understand them. We do this either by creating a new concept out of specific ideas or, as we will see in chapter 6, by synthesising them in a new way.

Our minds think in patterns, many of which are represented by concepts. Each time we gather ideas we search for patterns that will help us interpret the ideas and make sense out of them. But often, as our ideas come together, we see them form a configuration that we cannot describe using any existing concept, so we have to invent a new way of representing that pattern of ideas – a new concept.

What is a concept?

A concept is a general classification of particular things. It is a universal: it groups 'all' things that share particular characteristics under one idea or principle. The philosopher Bertrand Russell explains, 'Awareness of universals is called *conceiving*, and a universal of which we are aware is called a *concept*.'[1] Underlying these concepts or general classifications are patterns of ideas, through which we group and organise experience, and which allow us to see things in a particular way.

These patterns give us the capacity to interpret the world, to reduce the confusion of life to manageable levels. They give us the ability to think beyond the mere particulars of our world: we can generalise about things and come to conclusions that extend our understanding in ways that would be impossible otherwise. Concepts represent our most effective means of doing this. Each time we use them we bring the understanding we have gained from past experience to bear on the present and shape the way we act in the future.

As we saw in the last chapter, the process of forming such patterns is conceptual thinking: we step back from the ideas, facts and information we have assembled and we structure and classify them into general terms revealing the relationships between them.

For instance. . .

All occupations that share particular characteristics are grouped together and classified as 'professions'. This concept represents a pattern of ideas to which individual examples must comply. To be a professional we must possess certain characteristics: we must be non-amateurs, proficient, have a mastery over a body of knowledge and skills, and we must commit ourselves to a distinctive ideal of service, which imposes on us ethical obligations, to which other members of the community are not subject. In return we enjoy a licensed monopoly and operate a professional organisation to which we restrict entry.

Effects on our thinking

But still, in practical terms, how does learning to create concepts help our thinking? How will this help us think more creatively, to see things we would not otherwise have seen, generate innovative ideas and solve the most difficult problems?

1. Organising and retrieving information

On the simplest level these powerful instruments serve a similar function to that of a modern library's classification system by giving us instant access to impressive amounts of useful information we have stored under them. Indeed our survival in the past has depended on this. Recognising that a certain configuration of colours and movement represents a dangerous predator has been the difference between life and death.

For instance. . .

In the famous 1944 film *Double Indemnity* the claims assessor, played by Edward G. Robinson, tells his boss how mistaken he is to assume that a man's death is due to suicide from falling off the back of a train. He quickly runs through the concepts that make up the general classification system for organising the actuarial evidence for every type of suicide to locate rapidly the evidence that shows the man's death could not have been the result of suicide by this means.

---

2. Interpreting and evaluating information

But concepts do more than just give us instant access to an impressive amount of information. Using these powerful tools of thought, helps us process complex material and come to our judgements almost effortlessly.

3. Being more creative

Even more impressive is the creative potential of concepts. Each time we create a concept we lay out clearly in a structured form all the possibilities of a situation that are open to us. From here we can begin to think imaginatively about what to do; not just about what is at present a fact, but about how things might or should be.

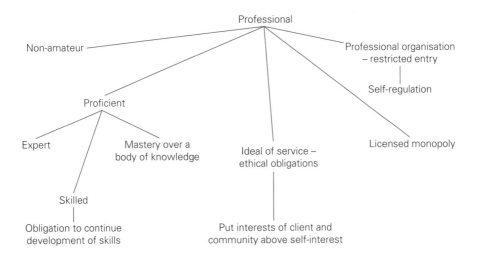

When we think conceptually we abstract the general concept or principle, which applies to all circumstances (past, present and future), and divorce it from the concrete circumstances embedded in the present. As a result, we display before us all the creative potential of a situation freed of all the specific details, which might otherwise clutter up and obscure our vision of the possibilities.

4. Predictive power

In turn this gives us the power to predict the likely effects of doing one thing rather than another. By creating patterns that map out the environment in this way, we can predict what is likely to happen. With this we are in a much better position to solve even the most difficult of problems.

For instance. . .

In the middle of a recession a government might consider investing in infrastructure projects to create growth and increase income and employment. But, to avoid inflation, it will need to know by how much to stimulate the economy. What is needed is a concept that maps out the environment in which this type of decision is made. The 'Multiplier', a concept created in 1931 by Richard F. Kahn, one of Keynes's students, does just that.

It gives economists a way of predicting the likely effects, so they can calculate accurately how much to stimulate the economy without increasing inflation. Investing in an infrastructure project will increase incomes for those who produce it, which will then flow onto other producers and retailers as workers and companies spend their new income. These producers and retailers will take on additional staff and purchase additional material, which, in turn, creates new income for more companies and employees. In this way, the ripple effect of the initial investment flows outward through the economy, creating new income and increasing the demand for goods and services.

The only limit to this stimulus is the amount that is siphoned off into taxes, savings and other withdrawals. The multiplier makes clear that the lower the marginal propensity to save – to siphon off in this way – the greater the multiplier effects. In fact, the multiplier is the equivalent to the inverse of the marginal propensity to save. So, if a tenth of the stimulus is taken out in withdrawals, then the multiplier will be 10, which means, if a government invests £2.5bn in infrastructure projects, it can predict that this will stimulate the economy by £25bn.

Concepts

1   Organising and retrieving information
2   Interpreting and evaluating information
3   Being more creative
4   Predictive power

Creating concepts

Although creating concepts sounds a complex, even mysterious, process, we can all learn to do it. From those in PR and advertising, who think up novel ways of promoting a product, to inventors and designers, who create new types of product or service, like those who first thought about ways of helping people find new friends by creating networking sites on the internet, all are attempting to design new concepts. It starts with evidence of individual behaviour and moves to the general: from the particular to the universal.

> **For instance. . .**
>
> In a chilling scene at the start of Stanley Kubrick's 1968 Oscar-winning film *2001: A Space Odyssey*, an ape picks up a bone from the bleached skeleton of an animal and strikes the skull, smashing it into pieces. Then, in the moments that follow, quiet and motionless, with the bone held in both hands high above his head, he forms a concept. This is no longer just a bone to smash this bleached skull before him, but a 'weapon' to strike all the skulls of all his enemies.

In the same way, we see ideas come together to form a pattern. We search for an existing concept that might fit the pattern. Finding none, we create a new concept that represents this pattern of ideas.

> ***Try this. . .***
>
> ## Psychometric test – Abstract reasoning
>
> The following is an example of abstract reasoning, which tests our ability to understand and analyse visual information without relying on language skills. In this example you are asked to identify the differences and similarities between shapes and then form a common concept from among them.

Some people protest that they have no idea how to do this, yet even with the briefest of acquaintances with these shapes, after confronting just four or five examples, most are quite clear about the core characteristics of the concept. Indeed, they can be surprisingly dogmatic as to what is and what is not an example of it, just minutes after declaring they knew nothing about it and had no idea how to create and analyse it.

The advantage of using abstract shapes in this way is that they liberate us from any preconceptions that might have been raised if we had used familiar language. We are not tempted to let others do the thinking for us by referring to what some authority might have to say about them. The concept is ours to form without assistance from anyone else.

Examine in turn each of the figures below. As you do, you will see a concept emerge, which I have called an 'olic'. Not all of the figures are olics, so you will have to form your idea of the concept and then use it to distinguish between the olics and non-olics. Once you've done this, answer the following:

1 Which of the figures are olics?
2 Analyse the concept of an olic and list three of its core characteristics.

1

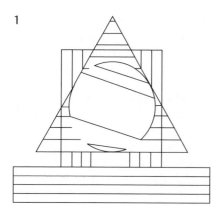

2

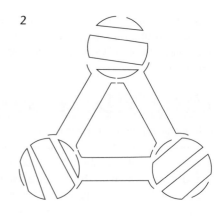

3

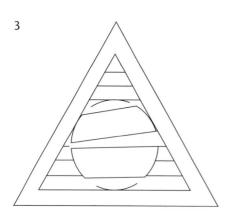

4

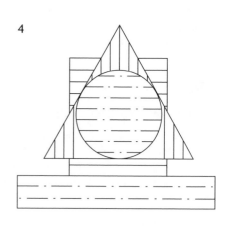

5

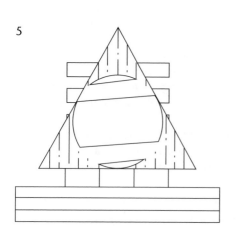

6

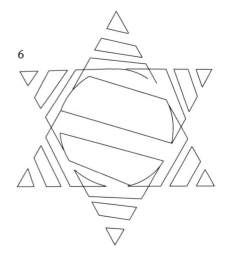

7

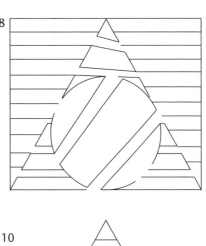

8

9

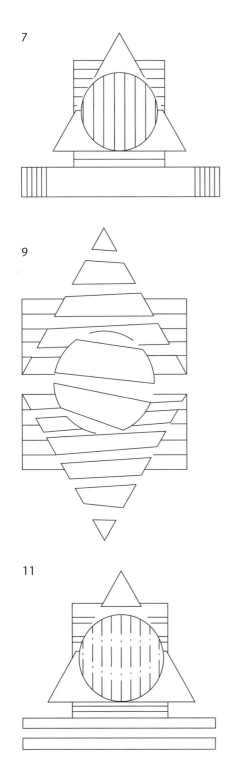

10

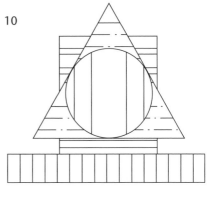

11

12

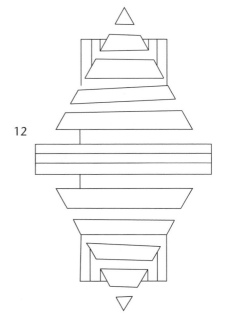

Answers

1 1, 4, 5, 7, 10, 11
2 You could have chosen your three characteristics from any of the following:
   2.1 Long rectangular base.
   2.2 A circle at the centre.
   2.3 A triangle surrounding the circle.
   2.4 A rectangle surrounding the circle and intersecting the triangle.

Even though you haven't come across an olic before, the concept emerges, leaving you in no doubt about its core characteristics.

Try this. . .

Now try a similar test using language instead of abstract shapes. This is a 'Category combination problem'. You are asked to do the same as you did with the olics: create a concept, in this case a category, which embraces all of the examples. You are given the following three sets of things:

A. Table; chair; bench; wardrobe.
B. Banana; pineapple; orange; peach.
C. Railway timetable; search warrant; marriage certificate; property contract.

Instructions:

1 Identify the categories for each group.
2 Combine these categories to create a new super-category for all of them.
3 Provide a label for the new category and write a brief, one-sentence description of it.
4 List as many additional examples of the super-category as possible.
5 List additional features linking the examples combined in the new category.

Possible answers

   1 Furniture; fruit; printed documents.
   2 Products of trees.
   3 'All the furniture could be made of wood, all of the documents of paper made from wood, and fruit and wood come from trees.'
   4 and 5. The answers to these questions are much less constrained, so I have left these to your own imagination.[2]

Connecting ideas

As you can see from these two tests, we all have the ability to create concepts. But most of us lack the skills to use these abilities, to unlock our potential. Often we simply don't see the connections between ideas that point to a new concept. Take the following example and ask yourself whether you would have seen the connection that resulted in a very successful business idea.

For instance. . .

In 1995 a story appeared in *People* magazine and on TV shows, like *Oprah, NBC Dateline* and *Good Morning America*, about two mothers who had noticed something interesting in the behaviour of their children: their babies liked watching the smiling faces of other babies. They then extended their thinking from this specific observation to the universal and created a new concept.

In other words, they argued that, if their children react in this way, then the chances are that everyone's children will do the same. And, as all mothers at times find themselves in unfamiliar situations, where their babies feel agitated and they have to find some way of settling them down, this may be the answer. So they created *Baby Mugs*, a 27-minute video featuring 85 laughing children's faces set to music. They then set about selling it to clinics, day-care centres, even normal households, and in a short time they were selling over 35,000 units every month.

Like so many good ideas, this one starts from the ability to think counterintuitively. In particular, they were not willing to let what was obvious pass them by unnoticed. With open minds, accepting nothing on trust, they asked themselves naïve questions. As a result, they found something interesting in quite normal events and created something that all parents need, but was hidden in full view.

> **Think counterintuitively and ask naïve questions.**

Of course, you may think that *Baby Mugs* doesn't sound like such an insightful idea. Looking back after the event it may appear to be the result of a simple process of rational deduction. But start the other way around with no connections drawn and it is far from obvious. As we have said, even the thinking behind some of the greatest scientific discoveries and innovations seems prosaic in retrospect. *Baby Mugs* is no different. But then what could be more obvious than an internet site where people could communicate with their friends? Yet, it was only Mark Zuckerberg and Aaron Greenspan who appear to have come up with the idea of **Facebook**.

A practical method

We began this chapter by saying that underlying all our concepts are patterns of ideas, through which we group and organise experience, and which allow us to see things in a particular way. So, creating new concepts like *Baby Mugs* – indeed all creativity – involves the ability to form these patterns by making connections between our ideas. As we said in the last chapter, the quality of our thinking is determined not by the strength of our ideas, but by the significance of the connections we make between them. New connections produce new concepts that give us a new way of seeing the world. As Steve Jobs once said:

> Creativity is just connecting things. When you ask creative people how they did something, they feel a little guilty because they didn't really do it, they just saw something. It seemed obvious to them after a while.[3]

So we have to learn the skills involved in making connections – unexpected, insightful connections. Unfortunately, our minds are not naturally creative. The overwhelming influence of System 1 intuitions means that we only see what we have been prepared to see. We can look at all the facts without ever seeing the pattern of connections that would lead to a new concept or solution. It just seems irrelevant from the perspective of our established patterns of ideas.

Moreover, our System 1 thinking works too fast, so we miss things, we make unexamined assumptions and skip stages in our thinking. As a result, we fail to notice the concept, the insightful idea, hidden in full view.

- Our minds are not naturally creative.
- We see what we are prepared to see.
- Our System 1 thinking works too fast, so we miss things.
- We fail to notice the concept, the insightful idea, hidden in full view.

However, we can learn to create new connections by using a simple method that teaches us to think more deliberately about our ideas, so that we don't take things for granted. Working through these steps slowly gives us more opportunity to think counterintuitively.

Four simple steps

1 Lay out all the facts
2 Drawing inferences: making connections
  2.1 Divergences
  2.2 Convergences
3 Hypothesise/Create a concept
4 Test

1. Lay out all the facts

First, we need to lay out systematically all the facts we know about the problem. If you think back to the olics question, there we were *given* the material we needed. Now we have to generate it ourselves, taking care not to take anything for granted. Unfortunately, it's easy to convince ourselves that we are aware of everything, so there is no point in deliberately listing all we know. As a result, we fail to think through all the possibilities.

Therefore, in laying out the facts think naïvely. Some of the most stunning insights, that have broken a logjam to progress, have come from researchers asking the most obvious questions about things that others regarded as just common-sense. Such questions seem unnecessary and trivial. So, slow yourself down and question those assumptions that may seem obvious. Take nothing for granted.

2. Drawing inferences: Making connections

The obvious way to search for connections and inferences is to look for **divergences**, those things that clearly contradict one another, and **convergences**, those that are supportive. A convergence may be an idea that supplements another, revealing more clearly its implications; it may be a logical extension of a point; or it may just offer evidence of a point.

To keep track of the connections you make and the inferences you might be able to draw, set them down in a clear structure: a matrix, as we did in chapter 2 (page 32), or any form of pattern notes that allows you to see at a glance the connections between the ideas. If you're not sure what is meant by pattern notes, look at the examples in the next chapter. In some cases, having laid it out in this way, the solution will be clear.

3. Hypothesise/Create a concept

Whether we are creating a new concept or designing a hypothesis that will solve a problem we are doing the same thing: making connections between ideas. Having laid out clearly all that we know and can infer, these patterns of connections will now be much clearer. As a result, you will find it's not difficult to create the concept you're after or find two or three possible solutions to a problem you want to solve, as we will see in the following example.

4. Test

Having done that, you will need to test them with examples and situations in which they appear not to work. In the next chapter, you will learn a method of testing your concept using borderline, contrasting and doubtful examples.

Psychometric problems

The best way to illustrate the method is to try it on the sort of verbal reasoning problem that we worked through in chapter 2 (pages 31–2).

Try this. . .

A Murder Case

A recent murder case involved six men: Collins, French, Gooch, Haigh, Moran and Walker. In no particular order these were the victim, the murderer, the witness, the police officer, the judge and the executioner. These were the facts of the case. The victim had died instantly from a gunshot at close range. The witness did not see the crime committed, but testified that he had heard an altercation followed by a gunshot. At the end of the trial the murderer was convicted, sentenced to death and the sentence carried out.

From the following facts decide what role was played by each of the men.

Moran knew both the victim and the murderer.
During the trial the judge asked Collins to give his account of the shooting.
Walker was the last of the six to see French alive.
The police officer testified that he picked Gooch up near the place where the body was found.
Haigh and Walker never met.

1. Lay out all the facts

First, enter on the structure all the facts that the question might give us. Like the problem we examined in chapter 2, this one gives us facts about relationships, so we will have to rely on our inferences from these to start plotting what we know.

2. Drawing inferences: making connections

First we must draw all those inferences we think can safely be drawn from the facts we are given and then plot them systematically on the structure. Once we have done this we can create hypotheses, which we then test, gradually eliminating options on the structure, so that we are left with the answers.

1 Divergences

Moran knew both the victim and the murderer.

Inference: *Therefore, he cannot be the victim or the murderer.*

2 Convergences

In court the judge asked Collins to give his account of the shooting.

Inference: *Therefore, Collins must be either the police officer, the witness or the murderer.*

Walker was the last of the six to see French alive.

Inference: *Walker is either the executioner or the murderer, because he was the last to see French alive.*

Inference: *French is either the victim or the murderer.*

The policeman testified that he picked up Gooch near the place where the body was found.

Inference: *Gooch is either the witness or the murderer.*

Each of these inferences allows you to put a cross in the squares that no longer apply to that particular person.

	V	M	W	P	J	E	
Collins	X				X	X	= P or W or M
French			X	X	X	X	= V or M
Gooch	X			X	X	X	= W or M
Haigh							
Moran	X	X					Knew V + M
Walker	X		X	X	X		Last to see French alive

3. Hypothesise/Create a concept

Now we can create hypotheses from what we know.

1 Facts

Haigh and Walker have never met. We know that Walker is either the executioner or the murderer, because he was the last to see French alive. French is either the victim or the murderer.

2 Hypothesis

If Walker is the executioner, then Haigh has to be the victim, otherwise they would have met, along with every other character.

4. Test

Let's say Walker is the murderer:

If Walker is the murderer, then he would have met all the characters, including Haigh. Therefore Walker must be the executioner and Haigh must be the victim.

Let's say Walker was the executioner:

If Walker was the executioner, then Haigh has to be the victim, otherwise they would have met.

Therefore, Walker is the executioner and Haigh is the victim.

Fill out the structure

We can now put crosses in all those squares that no longer apply to Walker and Haigh and 'O' in those that accurately label the characters. In the column for the judge this leaves only one square available: the one alongside Moran. This leaves only one space in the column for the police officer, alongside the name of Collins. This, in turn, leaves only one space available in the column for the witness, alongside the name of Gooch. This, finally, leaves just one space in the column for the murderer, alongside the name of French.

	V	M	W	P	J	E	
Collins	X	X	X	O	X	X	= P or W or M
French	X	O	X	X	X	X	= V or M
Gooch	X	X	O	X	X	X	= W or M
Haigh	O	X	X	X	X	X	
Moran	X	X	X	X	O	X	Knew V + M
Walker	X	X	X	X	X	O	Last to see French alive

Try this. . .

Now try the following question on your own. You'll find the answer and explanation on the companion website at www.he.palgrave.com/smart-thinking.

The Engagement Party

Diana, Jessica, Virginia, Bryan, James and Tom are old friends, who have known each other since childhood. Recently, they all left university at the same time and got themselves jobs. Even though they are in full-time employment they still see each other regularly. For some time it has been clear that each of them has paired off and formed a stable heterosexual relationship with another member of the group. Now they have decided to get engaged and to announce their engagements at the same time to the rest of their friends at a party.

From the following information decide what engagements were announced at the party.

Tom, who is older than James, is Diana's brother.
Virginia is the oldest girl.
The total age of each couple is the same although no two of them are the same age.
Jessica and James are together as old as Bryan and Diana.[4]

Reverie and insights

Although this is a simplified illustration, it demonstrates the importance of laying out what we know, so that we can then create the connections between our ideas that form the basis of new concepts, here represented by the hypotheses we create. However, there will be times when clarity doesn't come, when the sudden insight, the concept that lights up the way forward, just doesn't appear. At times like these, when you have thought hard about a problem, but cannot find a solution, you have to learn to abstain from conscious effort and do something else.

For instance. . .

In one study participants were told, 'You are given four separate pieces of chain that are each three links in length. It costs 2 cents to open a link and 3 cents to close a link. All links are closed at the beginning of the problem. Your goal is to join all 12 links of chain into a single circle at a cost of no more than 15 cents.'

All participants worked on it for half an hour. In the first group only 55 per cent solved it. Those in the second group took an hour break in which they did other things. Their success rate was 64 per cent. A third group took a four-hour break. Their success rate was 85 per cent.[5]

This shows the effectiveness of the subconscious in organising and structuring our ideas. Writing about the creative process in her legendary book, *Becoming a Writer*, Dorothea Brande describes the subconscious as 'the great home of form'.[6] It is quicker to see patterns than our conscious mind:

Far behind the mind's surface, so deep that he (the writer) is seldom aware . . . that any activity is going forward, his story is being fused and welded into an integrated work.[7]

Therefore, she argues, we must learn to trust this 'higher imagination'[8] to bring aid to our ordinary thinking. We need to come to terms with this 'enormous and powerful part of (our) nature which lies behind the threshold of immediate knowledge'.[9]

The subconscious

'the higher imagination'
'the great home of form'

Out of this process the connections are made and the insight appears almost effortlessly compared with the sustained work that preceded it. The lines of thought converge, the clues cooperate and we see the solution as one complete whole in which all the parts fit. Peter Medawar believes such insights share three characteristics:

1   the suddenness of their origin;
2   the wholeness of their conception;
3   and the absence of conscious premeditation.

And this is no accident, as the Gestalt psychologist Wolfgang Köhler insists: it is not as if we have just stumbled on the solution by stabbing in the dark. In fact, this is a common experience, widely reported by some of the greatest thinkers of our time. Henri Poincaré the French mathematician, August Kekulé the German organic chemist, and Albert Einstein, all described similar experiences. Although their sudden, brilliant insights might seem effortless and spontaneous, they were, in fact, born out of the sustained work that preceded them. After they had stopped working, when they were no longer thinking about it, the solution would come when they were doing something else or just daydreaming.

For instance. . .

One day in his early years at the patent office Einstein was daydreaming at his desk when he saw a builder on the rooftop opposite his window. A sudden inspiration came to him as he imagined the man falling off the roof. This he described as 'the happiest thought of my life'. He realised that the man would not feel his own weight, at least not until he hit the ground. It was the clue he needed to extend relativity to gravity. Max Born later described this as 'the greatest feat of human thinking about nature, the most amazing combination of philosophical penetration, physical intuition, and mathematical skill'.[10]

Beneath all these experiences there is a systematic, step-by-step method. Working through the steps described in this chapter will bring you to the point where insights are born, solutions found and concepts created. Consciously or unconsciously, your mind will deliver you at the point where you are able to see things that you were never able to see before.

Summary

1   Concepts influence every aspect of our thinking from retrieving and evaluating information to being creative.
2   Underlying them are patterns consisting of connections between our ideas.
3   The most successful ideas that have shaped our world have come from people creating concepts by seeing connections between ideas that the rest of us miss.
4   Using the simple 4-step method we can learn to see more of these connections.
5   However, when the answer refuses to come, we must learn to abstain from conscious effort and trust our subconscious.

What's next?

In this chapter we have seen how we can create concepts that give us new insights and ideas. However, we have also learned that they have a hidden nature, a pattern of ideas that can dictate our thinking, persuading us to think and act in particular ways without us making any deliberate choice. It's important to learn, therefore, how to analyse them to reveal their influence. In the next chapter you will learn a simple technique to unlock your abilities to do this.

Companion website

On the companion website you will find examples of psychometric problems similar to those in this chapter that you can use for practice. www.he.palgrave.com/smart-thinking

How to analyse concepts

In this chapter you will learn. . .

- The importance of analysing concepts for every aspect of our thinking.
- How the meaning of concepts depends on the context and purpose for which they are used.
- How to distinguish between open and closed concepts.
- How to uncover the pattern of ideas at the heart of a concept.
- How to test your concept using borderline, contrasting and doubtful cases.

Towards the end of his life, Albert Einstein said that he went into his office every day 'just to have the privilege of walking home with Kurt Gödel',[1] the famous Austrian logician and mathematician. In his book, *A World without Time,* Palle Yourgrau explains that, using relativity, Gödel calculated how a spaceship could travel into the past or the future. But then, by analysing the concept of time, he dropped a bombshell on physics.

He pointed out that if we travel into the past, then time never really passed and 'a time that fails to pass is no time at all'.[2] Einstein realised what this meant: time was not just relative, it was an ideal, it did not exist. In effect, Gödel had proved that in a world ruled by the theory of relativity, time simply cannot exist. By analysing the concept of time, he had produced a revolutionary notion: a world without time.

Lifting the bonnet

Gödel had done what we all do when we analyse a concept: he had lifted the bonnet to look at the engine beneath. It is this that drives and directs our thinking in ways over which we would otherwise have little control. We may wonder why it is so difficult to understand something or why we struggle to solve a problem, not knowing that the problem is created by our own concepts. The moment we lift the bonnet and see the pattern of ideas beneath, we see new ideas in exactly the way that Gödel saw the implications of relativity.

Lift the bonnet to see the pattern of ideas beneath.

In our academic work

In our academic work the importance of doing this is all too obvious. In history we need to be aware of the implications of using concepts like 'revolution'; in literature concepts like tragedy, comedy, irony and satire; in politics concepts like freedom, ideology, equality, power and authority; in law concepts like punishment, obligation and the difference between law and morality; in business the difference between bribes, commissions, gifts, incentives and tips.

In our professional work

Although we might think all this talk of analysing concepts seems only relevant to academics and intellectuals, none of us escape the need to lift the bonnet to see the way concepts influence our work. We live in second-hand worlds: the quality of our thinking is determined by meanings we have received from others. To be a good teacher, nurse, dentist, optician or physiotherapist, you will have to stand back from your concept of the role of someone in your profession and ask yourself, 'What is this sort of professional supposed to do? Can I do more for my patients or clients?'

For instance. . .

The concept of a local doctor has changed over the last 50 years, almost beyond recognition. She is no longer responsible just for her patients individually, but for the prevention of illness generally in the community by promoting healthier lifestyles, even influencing planning decisions that might adversely affect the environment in which her patients live.

There will be concepts at the heart of your work that you are constantly wrestling with to make sure you do a good job. A nurse, a doctor and a hospital administrator, all will have to be clear about their concepts of 'patient care', 'quality of life' and 'patient autonomy'. A teacher will have to be clear about the concept of 'duty of care': where it begins and ends. A journalist and an editor will have to know what's meant by 'privacy' and 'public interest' and at what point one can no longer be an excuse for invading the other.

In business

The concepts we use not only determine the way we interpret and organise experience, but form the basis on which we advocate a certain type of action. At the heart of a concept is a readiness to respond in certain ways rather than others. Many organisations ignore this and get trapped in their own culture, believing that, as this is the way they've always done things, they ought to keep doing it this way. As a result, they train their staff for yesterday's work, preparing them for the past, rather than the future.

> **At the heart of a concept is a readiness to respond in certain ways rather than others.**

The way to avoid this is to start thinking conceptually, so we can rise above the day-to-day administration and think strategically. This means analysing the concepts we use to understand our environment so we can see the patterns of ideas they represent. Then we can use our imagination to reveal the range of possibilities that are open to us.

For instance. . .

A businessman trying to find a niche for his service, an advertising executive searching for new ways to promote her client's product or an engineer with a ground-breaking invention or design; they are all analysing concepts to see how they can place their work to meet the strongest demand.

We all need the ability to analyse the concepts that affect our understanding and behaviour. To do this we must get used to standing back from them and asking the sort of question that Gödel asked: 'What do we mean by time?', 'What do we mean by revolution, bribery or privacy?'

Analysing concepts

The problem is that analysing the concepts we use every day in this way just seems unnecessary. So we have to learn to ask that characteristically philosophical question, 'Yes, but what do we mean by X?' In a probing, self-reflective way we are questioning our own use of these quite ordinary words, which can no longer be taken for granted.

This sort of questioning was famously developed over 2,400 years ago by Socrates, who railed against the self-serving simplifications of traditional debate and rhetoric. Carefully probing the pronouncements of authorities and the arguments of his students, he began by taking nothing for granted, asking the simplest and most naïve questions. In this way he was able to reveal their confused use of words, the concealed implications of their arguments lying unnoticed in concepts they had taken for granted, and the self-contradictory beliefs obscured by their confident rhetoric.

- Ask probing, self-reflective questions about ordinary words.
- Ask naïve questions about the concepts you take for granted.

The first step is to realise that words have more than one meaning, depending on the context and purpose for which they are used. They have no meaning in their own right. Therefore, our concern should be for their actual and possible uses. If we were to look up their meaning in a dictionary, we would find just somebody's picture of what they mean in a particular context, or a mere snapshot, a still in the moving reel of images, each one recording what the concept meant at a particular time and how it has changed and is still changing. Our task, therefore, in analysing a concept is to map out all the different ways in which it is used.

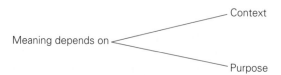

Most of the concepts we use are constantly changing, both because of cultural and social change and because the purposes for which we use them change. The meanings of concepts, like 'progress', 'success', 'luxury', 'necessity', 'poverty' and 'prosperity', are all relative to who uses them and the context in which they are used.

> **For instance. . .**
>
> We might be able to agree that in the absolute sense the concept of poverty means someone who has no means of sustenance or permanent shelter from the elements. But in its relative sense it means different things in different circumstances to different people. In some societies today poverty is more like being without a colour TV, a refrigerator or even a second car.

Open and closed concepts

1. Closed concepts

Even so, with some concepts analysing them is, indeed, as straightforward as looking up the word in a dictionary. They are what you might describe as 'closed concepts'. They usually have an unchanging, unambiguous meaning. Words like 'bicycle', 'bachelor' and 'triangle' each have a structure to their meaning, which is bound by logical necessity. We all agree to abide by certain conventions that rule the meaning of these words. So, if you were to say, 'This bicycle has one wheel' or 'This triangle has four sides', no one would be in any doubt that you've made a logical mistake and you would run the risk of not being understood. When we use them according to their conventions we are, in effect, allowing our understanding of the world to be structured in a particular way.

> Closed concepts: their structure is bound by logical necessity.

2. Open concepts

But with 'open concepts' it's the reverse: our experience of the world shapes our concepts. Their meaning is not governed by a complex set of formal rules, like closed concepts, so they cannot be pinned down just by looking them up in a dictionary. Their meaning responds to, and reflects, our changing experience. As we saw above with the concept of poverty, they change through time and from one culture to another.

Closed and open concepts

1 Closed concepts are governed by complex sets of formal rules, while open concepts adapt to changing circumstances and experience.
2 Closed concepts structure the way we understand our experience, while open concepts are structured *by* it.

Our concern, therefore, is rarely with the words and their dictionary definition. If I say about the dialysis patient that, 'He has a poor quality of life', you know the meanings of the words I use, yet you can still ask, 'But what do you mean by "poor quality of life"?' Though we understand the words, the question of the concept remains.

For instance. . .

The word 'family' is not difficult to understand, but the concept can be. In some societies and at some times 'family' and its related concepts, like 'aunt' and 'uncle', have fairly unambiguous, unchanging meanings: narrow definitions exclusively grounded in relations by blood and marriage. But in other societies they are more open, encompassing not just relatives in the strict sense, but also older, long-standing friends of the family.

This is likely to be a reflection of the social practices prevalent in different societies and at different stages in their development. A predominantly rural society with limited social mobility might use them in the narrow sense. In contrast, in a society undergoing industrialisation, with greater social mobility and less permanent communities, the concepts are likely to be applied more loosely to close friends of the parents of a child. A young family, which has recently moved to a city some distance from their parents' homes, may seek to reconstruct the security of an extended family by including close friends as aunts and uncles to their children.

In fact, some open concepts seem more open than others: there seem to be no core elements at all to the concept, even though all the examples we come up with we still call by the same name.

For instance. . .

In *Philosophical Investigations,* Ludwig Wittgenstein cites the example of 'games' and concludes that there is no core set of characteristics: nothing that you can say that is common to them all. As you move from one type of game to another some common features appear, while others drop out. Some involve competition, while others involve just one player. Some require skill, while others only require luck. All that we have, he argues, is just 'a complicated network of similarities overlapping and criss-crossing'.[3]

Try it for yourself. List every game you can think of and try to find a core set of characteristics that is common to them all.

Try this. . .

Which of the following are closed and open concepts?

1 Mammal
2 Deduction
3 Miracle
4 Depression
5 Deprivation
6 Harm
7 Necessity
8 Freedom
9 Motive
10 Fruit

Answers

Open concepts – 4, 5, 6, 7, 8
Closed concepts – 1, 2, 3, 9, 10

Conceptual analysis – the three-step technique

The significance of this distinction lies in the fact that thinking based on the properties of open concepts produces more creativity, more novelty, than that based on closed concepts, which allow only simple departures from the normal. Open concepts have more permeable category boundaries, which allow us to build new complex structures of ideas. In the last chapter we created a new concept, the olic, and we tackled a category combination problem (pages 63–6), which involved creating new complex structures of ideas. This sort of thinking lies at the heart of our creativity.

> Open concepts are permeable, allowing us to be more creative.

Given this, no matter what our business, profession or academic discipline, it's clear that we all need to develop the skills to analyse concepts to reveal the underlying structure of our ideas. Normally, when we use a concept, we allow one or more of these ideas to dominate our thinking. So, by analysing the structure we can start at a different point, with a different idea, and with this make new connections with other ideas. We can work with the structure, adapting and changing it to create new concepts and solutions to problems.

In what follows you will learn a simple three-step technique, which you can use routinely. As you work through it, think about the concepts you come across in your own work, concepts like 'equality', 'authority', 'privacy', 'needs' and 'revolution', and ask yourself 'What do we mean by this?'

Step 1: Gather your typical examples

First, spend some time gathering the evidence: say, five or six examples of the way you use the concept in your everyday life. Try to make them as different as possible. In this way you'll be able to strip away their differences to reveal more clearly their essential similarities.

Try this. . .

We often hear the concept of 'tragedy' used in contexts that leave us wondering whether the concept means more than we think. It leaves us almost as perplexed as the word 'hero', when we hear it used to describe footballers, athletes, even celebrities.

Someone might describe the failure of their football team to get to the final, or the loss of their mobile phone, as a 'tragedy'. This seems to devalue the concept, particularly when it is compared to an earthquake or hurricane that kills hundreds, even thousands, destroying family homes and sweeping away all their belongings.

So, what do we mean by the word 'tragedy'? We start by summoning examples of situations in which we might use the concept. Then we can analyse these to abstract their core characteristics as we did with the olic and the category combination problem. There are, of course, the well-known Greek and Shakespearean tragedies, like the following:

Oedipus

Although Oedipus is warned by an oracle that he will kill his father and marry his mother, despite all his attempts, he does just as the oracle says. When his true identity is revealed, his mother commits suicide and Oedipus blinds himself with her brooch.

Macbeth

Driven on by his lust for power and his wife's ambitions, Macbeth destroys everything he loves, his best friend, his wife and finally himself.

Othello

Although he loves Desdemona, Othello allows Iago to work on his love and turn it into jealousy. He then murders her believing that she has been unfaithful with Cassio. When Othello realises his tragic mistake, he commits suicide.

Romeo and Juliet

After falling in love, Romeo and Juliet marry secretly. But then Romeo is banished from the city and Juliet, who is about to be married to Paris against her will, takes a sleeping potion to bring on a semblance of death. Having heard of her death, Romeo returns and drinks poison at Juliet's tomb. When she awakes a few moments later to find him dead, she stabs herself to death.

Then there are commonplace examples of events that we would describe as tragedies, like the following:

> **Accidental death**
>
> A man backs his car out of his garage, but, unknown to him, he runs over and kills his young son, who is playing in the drive behind the car.
>
> **The burglar**
>
> A man wakes up in the middle of the night after hearing a sound, which he suspects is a burglar. He sees a figure moving about the house and shoots him, only to discover he has shot his son.
>
> **Fund-raiser**
>
> A cyclist sets off on a fund raising trip from Land's End to John O'Groats, but he is hit by a lorry and dies two weeks into the trip.

If you find it difficult to come up with examples, ask yourself these three questions.

1. How do I use the concept?

First, 'How do I use the concept – do I use it in more than one way?' If you find you do, then you have a structure emerging: each way needs to be explored and its implications unwrapped. The prepositions we use with concepts are in many cases a very useful indicator of different meanings. For example, we use the concept 'authority' in two different ways when we say that someone is 'an' authority and when we say they are 'in' authority.

> **For instance. . .**
>
> The same can be said about the concept of freedom. We tend to talk about being free *from* things, like repression, constraints and restrictions of one form or another. I might say with some relief that I am finally free from pain having taken tablets for pain relief, or that a political prisoner has at last been freed from imprisonment. In both cases we're using the word in a negative way, in that something is being taken away, the pain or the imprisonment.
>
> But we also use the word in what we might describe as a positive way. In this sense the preposition changes from being free *from* something to being free *to do* something. We often say that, because a friend has unexpectedly won a large amount of money, she is now free to do what she has always wanted to do – to go back to college, or to buy her own home. Governments, too, use the concept in this way, arguing that the money they are investing in education will free more people to get better, more satisfying, jobs and to fulfil more of their dreams.

2. What sort of thing am I referring to?

If this doesn't help, ask yourself a second question, 'What sort of thing am I referring to when I use the concept?' This means recalling simple everyday situations in which you might find yourself talking about a 'bribe', 'need' or 'privacy', even if you don't actually use the word. So, when you refer to a 'tragedy', what sort of thing do you have in mind?

3. How does it differ from similar things?

To help you with this question it's often useful to ask a third: 'How does it differ from similar things?' When I use the word 'bribe' how does it differ from other things, like commissions, gifts, tips and incentive bonuses? When I use the word 'authority', how does it differ from things, like power, force, legitimacy and influence? In the case of 'tragedy', how does it differ from an accident, a disaster or a catastrophe?

Questions

1 How do I use the concept – do I use it in more than one way?
2 What sort of thing am I referring to?
3 How does it differ from similar things?

Step 2: Analyse your examples

Now, using these examples, create your concept: use your conceptual skills to abstract the general from the concrete, just as you did when you created the concept of olic and when you tackled the category combination problem. In other words, identify the common characteristics in each of your examples, isolating them so that you can then put them together to form the concept. In this way, by recognising the common pattern of characteristics that each example possesses, we visualise what the concept might look like that underlies all the examples.

Sometimes you may find you have, say, seven examples, four of which have the same core characteristics, while the other three fail to match them in some respects. That's okay, in these cases you need to corral the four similar examples, using these to create your concept, and then use the remaining three to test it.

Creating your concept – pattern recognition:

1 Identify the common characteristics in your examples.
2 Isolate them and put them together to form the concept.

For instance. . .

From the examples of tragedy listed above I concluded that the concept has five core characteristics.

1 It describes an event involving death, injury or destruction.
2 It also seems to be a self-defeating event, in which, ironically, without meaning to, by pursuing one thing, we destroy all our hopes and desires.
3 It involves the loss of something that is irreplaceable.
4 It seems to come about as a result of circumstances that are beyond our control, either because of a flaw in our character, or because our actions are influenced by strong, uncontrolled emotions.

> **5** Finally, in cases like this we seem to act without knowing all the facts: there is a hidden undisclosed element. Our strong desires might blind us to the eventual outcome, which is clear to everyone else. This is what is often called 'tragic irony'.

Of course, you may not have the same points in your analysis, but they are likely to be very similar. Remember, there are no right answers to this, just a concept whose meaning changes according to different contexts and purposes.

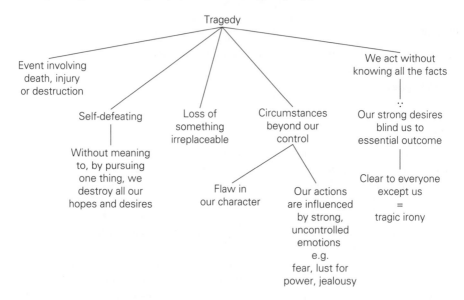

Step 3: Test your concept

In most cases you will find you have the overall structure right, but there may be details or subtle distinctions you haven't seen. So, by testing your concept you will identify those characteristics that are essential, while you ditch those that are only accidental to it. In the process you will sharpen up your understanding of the core characteristics.

To test it in this way you need only take some simple, but quite deliberate steps. Our aim is to set up mental experiments to test our concept first against those examples that are borderline cases of it, then against contrasting cases and, finally, against doubtful cases. At each stage we will refine it until we have it right.

1. Borderline cases

First, with your structure in front of you try to think of a borderline case, an example of your concept that doesn't fit comfortably within your structure. It may lack features that are in your structure, or have other features that are absent from it. Then analyse its characteristics. You may find there's more to this example than you first thought and it does, in fact, fit within the structure. Alternatively, after thinking through all the possibilities, it may become clear that, although it is a good example of the concept, it doesn't fit, so you will have to make adjustments to your structure to take account of it.

> **For instance. . .**
>
> On 10 June 1981 a 6-year-old Italian child, Alfredo Rampi, fell into a very narrow, deep well. When rescuers arrived he was about 36 metres below ground level. A parallel shaft was dug, but the drilling caused him to slip down another 30 metres. The drama was broadcast live, non-stop throughout Italy as the rescue attempts became ever more desperate, but he only slipped down further. After many hours, it was clear that Alfredo's voice, which was relayed by microphone, was getting weaker. Eventually he is thought to have died at around 6.30am on 13 June.

5. We act without knowing all the facts

This is undeniably a tragedy, yet it doesn't seem to fit the characteristic that 'We seem to act without knowing all the facts', when the outcome is clear to everyone else. It's true that the rescuers acted without knowing the likely effects of their actions, which resulted in Alfredo's falling still further. And, of course, as time passed their desperation to rescue him grew stronger. But it is difficult to see how this includes tragic irony: the eventual outcome wasn't clear to everyone else, except, perhaps, to those who might have argued that they knew that fate or destiny had doomed the rescuers' attempts from the start.

So, with this characteristic we have two choices: we can abandon the element of tragic irony that failure was clear to everyone, except those involved in the tragedy, or we can retain it and include the influence of destiny or fate as the overpowering force that all those who were not involved were aware of.

Whatever your decision, you will find that you have sharpened up your concept considerably as a result. You will either have shaken out an accidental feature that we need to discard or sharpened up a core characteristic that was not sufficiently clear in your original analysis.

2. Contrasting cases

As a result of this test you will probably feel more confident that you have now got it just about right. So it's time to put this confidence to the sternest test you can find, this time by imagining an example that presents a clear contrast to your concept. Think of the strongest example you can find that clearly doesn't fit within the structure of your concept. The best examples fail to share one or more of the core characteristics of your structure. Again, test your structure against this example to see if you need to make any adjustments to the characteristics and the way they interrelate.

For instance. . .

September 11, 2001

Terrorists destroyed the twin towers of the World Trade Centre in New York by flying two passenger aircraft into them with the loss of those on board and nearly 3,000 in the towers. Aware of what was taking place, many on board the planes made last-minute phone calls on their mobile phones to say goodbye to their loved ones.

---

1. Event involving death, injury or destruction

This, too, seems to be an obvious tragedy, but there are many events that involve death, injury and destruction on an enormous scale that we would not describe as a tragedy, so why do we describe this as one? In other words, what is the difference between a tragedy and a disaster, like the Boxing Day tsunami in 2004 that killed 230,000 in 14 countries, destroying many coastal communities?

The difference might be that such events are not seen as tragedies until we learn something about the people involved: until we can relate to them. At that point it has a sobering impact on us, changing the way we view the world. If this is the case, we need to sharpen up our first characteristic to make this clear.

2. Self-defeating

It seems we will also need to make changes to the second characteristic. It is clearly not the case that those who boarded these planes were themselves the architects of their own deaths. So we will either have to drop this characteristic or redefine it, perhaps more generally as the 'Destruction of all our hopes and desires'. This could include those who suffered as a result of, what we could describe as, 'evil fortune', in that they were unlucky enough to book a seat on this flight, and those who suffered as a result of their own actions.

4. Circumstances beyond our control

This characteristic also needs to be sharpened up in line with this example. Clearly circumstances were beyond the passengers' control, but this was not due to either of the two reasons on our structure, so we need to add a further reason: the influence of others, as in this case, or of natural forces.

5. We act without knowing all the facts

Clearly, unknown to the passengers, their fate was sealed the moment they took off, but it was not their own strong desires that blinded them to their eventual outcome, nor destiny or fate, but the actions of others, in this case terrorists. So we need to add a further reason to our structure.

Both of these two tests will probably have brought you to a point where you now know the core characteristics of your concept and the structure that defines their interrelations. If you are not this certain, you will have to test it with one or more additional contrasting examples, but it will rarely take more than this. In most cases you will have identified the core characteristics fairly clearly by now.

3. Doubtful cases

If this is the case, it's time to move to the next stage and test the consequences of adopting these as your core characteristics. We need to imagine an example that would make it difficult for you to accept these consequences. Either this is not, after all, an example of the concept, or we have missed something.

Unlike the previous stages, in this one we are neither identifying core characteristics, nor others that we need to ditch because they are merely accidental to the concept. We have our core characteristics now and their interrelations that define the concept. In this stage we are refining the distinctions that are in our analysis, so we get a clearer, sharper understanding of the core characteristics and their interrelations. As a result we inject more subtle shades of meaning into our distinctions.

> **For instance. . .**
>
> Despite his enormous talent and influence on modern art, particularly on Expressionism, Van Gogh only painted for a few brief years. He began painting in the 1880s, but his life was stricken by mental instability and, after spending some months in a mental institution, he took his own life in 1890 at the age of just 37.

Although we would regard this as a tragedy, it doesn't fit comfortably into every characteristic on our structure.

2. Self-defeating

By taking his own life he knew he would be destroying the thing he valued most, his artistic ability, and therefore we can presume he meant to do it. Nonetheless, we can still question how aware he was of the significance of what he was doing, given his mental instability. So we have to decide whether to discard this as an example of a tragedy, or amend our structure to take account of it, perhaps by rewriting it as 'without *being aware of it* we destroy the thing we value most'.

Contrasting Case

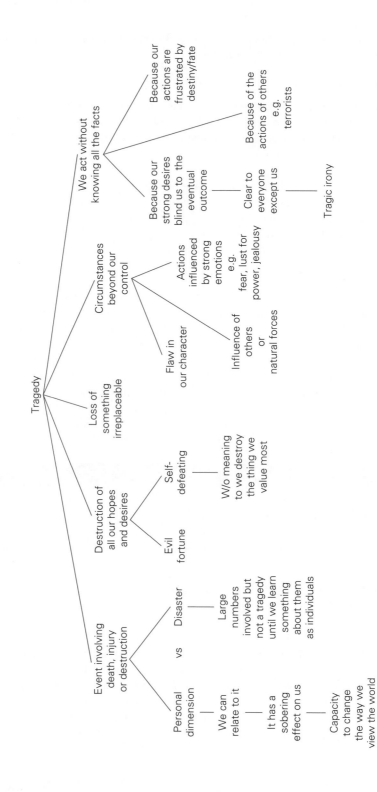

Doubtful Case

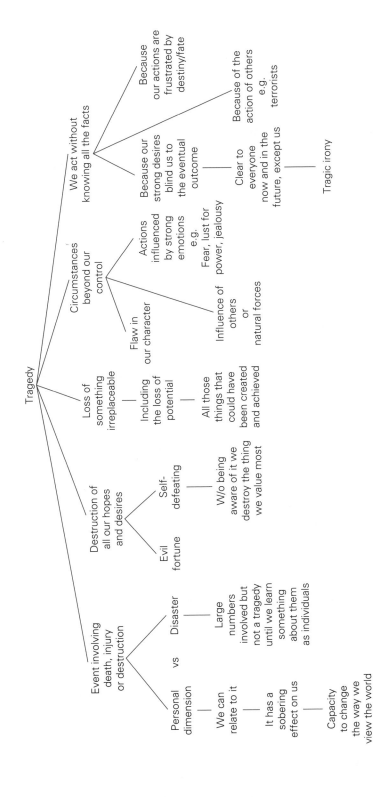

Tragedy

- Event involving death, injury or destruction
  - Personal dimension vs Disaster
    - Personal dimension
      - We can relate to it
      - It has a sobering effect on us
      - Capacity to change the way we view the world
    - Disaster
      - Large numbers involved but not a tragedy until we learn something about them as individuals

- Destruction of all our hopes and desires
  - Evil fortune
  - Self-defeating
    - W/o being aware of it we destroy the thing we value most

- Loss of something irreplaceable
  - Including the loss of potential
  - All those things that could have been created and achieved

- Circumstances beyond our control
  - Flaw in our character
  - Influence of others or natural forces
  - Actions influenced by strong emotions e.g. Fear, lust for power, jealousy

- We act without knowing all the facts
  - Because our actions are frustrated by destiny/fate
  - Because our strong desires blind us to the eventual outcome
  - Because of the action of others e.g. terrorists
    - Clear to everyone now and in the future, except us
    - Tragic irony

3. The loss of something irreplaceable

There is no doubt that this represented the loss of something irreplaceable. But, unlike other examples, it represents the waste of all his 'potential', all the things he could have created and achieved, rather than the loss of existing things. This suggests that we need to adjust this characteristic to take account of this difference.

5. We act without knowing all the facts

The tragic irony in this characteristic rests on the assumption that everyone knows the significance of the eventual outcome, except the individual involved. In Van Gogh's case this can only be maintained in retrospect: looking back we all know how significant his contribution was to modern art, but he didn't. So, if we include Van Gogh as an example of tragedy, we will have to amend this characteristic to take our retrospective assessment into account.

The result of this test can go in one of three ways: you will have confirmed that your doubtful case is not an example of the concept; or that it is and it does fit into your structure after all; or that it is and it doesn't fit, which means that you will have to adjust your structure. Whichever is the outcome, you will have a clearer understanding of the core characteristics and their interrelations.

Table

As we have worked our way through each of these stages we have deliberately asked awkward questions to test and refine the distinctions we made in our original analysis. In the table below you can see each stage clearly set out, so you can use it step by step in your own work.

The Three-step Technique

Activity	Objective
Step 1: Examples List five or six of the most typical examples that are as different as possible	To get material that will illustrate similarities and differences
Step 2: Analyse Pattern recognition – identify the common characteristics and their interrelations	To form the hypothesis: the prototype concept
Step 3: Testing **1. Borderline cases** Compare our concept with an example that either lacks features that are in our structure, or has others that are absent from it	To identify all those features in our structure that are merely accidental

2. Contrasting cases	
Compare our concept with an example that doesn't share one or more of the core characteristics of our structure	To identify the core characteristics and their interrelations
3. Doubtful cases	
Test the core characteristics by examining a case in which it would be difficult to accept their consequences	To refine the distinctions in our our analysis to get a clearer, sharper understanding of the core characteristics and their interrelations

Psychometric problems

In chapter 3 (pages 54–6) we saw the range of questions that are set to test our verbal reasoning in psychometric tests. Developing your skills to analyse concepts will help you to create your concept quickly and effectively under timed conditions, even though you won't have time to test it with borderline, contrasting and doubtful cases.

Try this. . .

Once you have analysed a few concepts, test your skills to create a concept as you did with tragedy and olic by answering the following word differentiation questions:

Distinguish between the following. . .

1 Extravagant, liberal, lavish, prodigal, improvident.
2 Exceptional, eccentric, outlandish, abnormal.
3 Astute, cunning, crafty, subtle, shrewd.
4 Impersonate, mimic, imitate, caricature, parody.
5 Taciturn, reticent, laconic.

Summary

1 We need to learn to lift the bonnet so we can see the pattern of ideas that drive the concepts that structure our thinking.
2 At the heart of a concept is a readiness to respond in certain ways.
3 Closed concepts structure the way we understand the world; open concepts are structured by it.
4 Open concepts are permeable, allowing us to be more creative.
5 The three-step technique allows us to explore beneath our concepts and think more creatively.

What's next?

We began this chapter with Kurt Gödel and the bombshell he dropped on physics. If there is one thing that all original thinkers have in common, it is the courage to question those ideas they and others have long accepted, no matter how unsettling and disturbing this questioning may be.

In this chapter we have learned how we can all do this by analysing the key concepts involved in a problem, deliberately and imaginatively, step by step, using the three-step technique. Once we have done this we can reveal new insights and new ways of looking at a problem by synthesising these structures of ideas into new concepts that often surprise us in their originality. In the next chapter we will learn how to do this.

Companion website

You will find other examples of concepts that have been analysed on the companion website. www.he.palgrave.com/smart-thinking

How to synthesise ideas

In this chapter you will learn. . .

- The four different types of synthesis.
- The three rules that govern the way we manage concepts.
- How to engage our System 2 thinking so that we think counterintuitively.
- The five-stage method for synthesising our ideas.
- How to tackle 'Insight' psychometric problems.

The next time you spill some salt, before you sweep it away, take a good look at it. You may be looking at one of the fundamental organising principles in the natural world. The stability of the pile is the product of each grain acting and reacting in response to other grains, generating a complex pattern of interrelations, until the pile self-organises into a stable system. This is a complex adaptive system at the edge of chaos where all complex systems go to solve complex problems. One more spilt grain and it could tip over into an avalanche of chaos, until it again self-organises into a new stability.

The most interesting aspect of this is that the secret of its stability lies not in the characteristics of each isolated grain, but in its organisation, its collective properties. Complex systems with all their emergent properties and their collective behaviour are nonlinear: they are greater than the sum of their parts. What's more, they can be found everywhere, from simple organisms to whole species, from the human mind to entire cultures, societies and economies.

For instance. . .

In an economy millions of individual decisions to buy or not to buy can reinforce one another to produce a recession or a boom. And, in turn, this can feed back on itself to affect the very buying decisions that produced it in the first place.

Above all, they demonstrate that synthesising individual entities can produce the most surprising results. In the same way, you can bring two unpromising ideas together and suddenly you have an idea of surprising potential. The properties of the whole cannot always be predicted from the parts. This is what creative people can do: they can bring order to chaos by structuring ideas; they can synthesise ideas from different areas of thought and expertise to produce the most surprising results.

Synthesising two or more ideas can release surprising potential.

Types of synthesis

In an earlier chapter, I argued that if university education is about any one thing it is about developing our skills to think conceptually. Yet despite its importance, we are never taught these skills, even though at universities students are routinely assessed on the basis of them. At best, we learn them in passing, if we know what we are looking for and we are perceptive enough to recognise it when it happens.

In your own studies you may be able to recognise examples of the different types of synthesis that we are routinely called upon to do. There are, in fact, four different types:

1 Creating new concepts;
2 Reformulating patterns of ideas;
3 Gathering ideas under an existing concept;
4 Synthesising two or more concepts.

1. Creating new concepts

In chapter 4 we learned how to move from the specific to the general to create new concepts.

2. Reformulating patterns of ideas

In the last chapter we learned a simple three-step technique to analyse concepts, revealing the patterns of ideas they represent. Once we have done this we can reformulate these ideas in new ways or simply place the emphasis differently within the concept. In this way we can use concepts in a new and interesting way to see things we have never seen before.

For instance. . .

Now that we have analysed the concept of tragedy, we know that there are five principles that make up the pattern of ideas that the concept represents. Placing the emphasis on any of these we are likely to see aspects of an event that we would have missed otherwise. As a result, we are likely to see it in quite a different light.

We might start by emphasising the importance of the personal element, or the tragic irony in the event, or the fact that it is self-defeating, that without meaning to we destroy the very thing we value most. Whichever it is, we suddenly see the event in a richer, more interesting way, containing insights that we would otherwise have missed.

In chapter 12 we will learn four simple strategies we can use in this way to design the most inventive solutions to difficult problems.

3. Gathering ideas under an existing concept

The third type of synthesis occurs when we gather our ideas under an existing concept, often one that we would not usually associate with these ideas. As a result we see things in a new and insightful way. This is the source of some of our richest insights as we will see. Indeed, many of them come as a result of importing a concept from another discipline or profession entirely.

> **For instance. . .**
>
> After its emergence in the 1930s and 1940s historians were able to import the concept of totalitarianism from the social sciences and use it to re-examine different periods in history. With the leader's mesmeric influence on crowds and the masses, they began to wonder how significant the crowd and a leader's capacity to manipulate collective sentiment had been in previous periods with leaders, like Napoleon. And with this was born a new area of historical study: the crowd in history.

The problem is that when we create a concept it's generally easy to recognise that this is what we have done, but synthesising ideas under a concept often isn't. Later in this chapter we will learn a simple method of doing this, which will make the thinking process more deliberate, so that we can do it more consciously.

4. Synthesising two or more concepts

The fourth method involves combining two or more concepts: merging their patterns of ideas to create a new way of looking at a problem. This has produced some of the most surprising and successful ideas that have transformed some disciplines, opening up new avenues of research, while others have formed the basis of new business opportunities.

> **For instance. . .**
>
> Consider the unique classifications of human beings invented by creative thinkers in the past. In the nineteenth century William James the American psychologist and philosopher classified people as 'tough-minded and tender-minded'. The Swiss psychiatrist Carl Jung invented the now common classification of people as 'introverts and extroverts'. Developments in psychology and behaviourism brought us 'convergent and divergent' thinkers.

New classifications like this, and the questions they evoke, can completely change our attitudes and thinking. But then combine them and you get structures for generating all sorts of unexpected, interesting ideas and ways of freeing us from routine, predictable responses. We can now talk about 'divergent introverts', 'divergent extroverts', 'convergent introverts', and 'convergent extroverts'; classifications that can help us explain all sorts of behaviour, which we would otherwise find difficult to explain.

> **For instance. . .**
>
> Recently, researchers at Cornell University examined the attitudes of hotel guests. They broke them down into four research categories by combining four concepts: 'satisfied' and 'dissatisfied' and 'stayers' and 'switchers' to get 'satisfied stayers', 'dissatisfied

stayers', 'dissatisfied switchers' and 'satisfied switchers'. Of course it would have been obvious to think about satisfied stayers and dissatisfied switchers, but without combining the concepts in this way it would have been difficult and counterintuitive to think there may be dissatisfied stayers and, even more, satisfied switchers.

The way it works – three rules

One of the reasons we find this sort of thinking so mysterious and difficult is that we are burdened with too much baggage. We have all read the legendary accounts of scientists who tell us how they came to make their ground-breaking discoveries. It all seems a perfectly logical, even mechanical, process. But this misrepresents the practical problems involved in thinking of any kind.

Indeed, even among scientists themselves, the suspicion is that such rationalisations of the scientific method reflect less what they actually *do* and more what they think they *should* be doing. As we saw in chapter 1, Peter Medawar argues that such talk is 'simply the posture(s) we choose to be seen in when the curtain goes up and the public sees us'.[1] It only seems to be logical in character, because 'it can be made to appear so when we look back upon a completed episode of thought'.[2]

However, even though it is not a simple logical process, we can learn how to do it better. There are three rules that govern the way we manage concepts and the patterns of ideas they lend to our thinking. The first we know already; the other two describe the way we synthesise and create new concepts.

The three rules

1 Knowledge is expressed in the form of mental structures or patterns. These act like rules that determine how we think and process ideas.
2 These patterns are in competition. Experience causes useful patterns to grow stronger by adapting to new ideas, while less useful ones grow weaker.
3 Plausible new patterns are generated from the combination of old ones. We make connections between them to create new patterns.

Together these rules explain how we generate new insights and arrive at solutions to our most difficult problems. As the first indicates, we organise our knowledge into stable patterns. Then, when we are presented with a problem, we search among our stock of patterns – each one triggered off by a concept – to see if the evidence before us exhibits one of these patterns. If it doesn't, we search for a solution by adapting and synthesising our ideas as the second and third rules indicate.

A practical method

The problem we all face is that we don't have a method for doing this. So we fall back on our familiar System 1 thinking with all its routine intuitions. However, these are not designed to produce new ideas and insights, so we struggle to be creative. Our minds are designed merely to act as they have always acted, in accordance with well-rehearsed intuitions that have worked well in the past.

So, we need a method that will help us engage our System 2 thinking so that we can think counterintuitively. This is how many of the most important breakthroughs in our thinking have occurred. The brightest ideas have developed out of systematic work and simple routines. In fact, they appear to emerge out of almost pedestrian, predictable thinking. In what follows you will learn a simple, practical method of five stages that you can use routinely to generate ideas and concepts that are surprisingly interesting and full of potential.

Synthesising ideas – a practical method

1 Connect
2 Insight
3 Hypothesis/idea
4 Test
5 Adapt

1. Connect

The distinguishing characteristic of intelligence is not what you know, but what you do with it: the ability to identify relevant connections and put together what ought to be conjoined. As we have learned already, the quality of our thinking is determined not by the strength of our ideas, but by the significance of the relations we find and the connections we make between them. This is the starting point of all creative thinking. As Steve Jobs pointed out, 'Creativity is just connecting things . . . creative people . . . [are] able to connect experiences they've had and synthesise new things.'[3]

In this first stage just take a pattern of ideas, a concept that you have analysed or a pattern of ideas you have put together about a topic you're interested in. Then, relate this to another pattern of ideas, again a concept or a set of ideas you have put together, and start to identify connections between them. You can do this by searching for different things, but it helps if you can do it in a systematic way. Carefully work through the following list searching for:

1 Contrasts,
2 Contradictions,
3 Causes,
4 Similarities,
5 Seeing parts of the whole,
6 Seeing the whole from the parts,
7 Seeing extensions of ideas, like logical inferences.

As you explore each one you will see connections between the ideas. In chapter 4 we looked at how to make connections through convergences and divergences. Here the method is broadly the same, except you have more tools at your disposal. The important thing is not to take anything for granted: ask the most naïve questions.

For instance. . .

Psychometric problems – Insight questions

The answer to this sort of question depends upon asking naïve questions about those things we take for granted. In this way we reveal everything we know about the problem. Try this question:

A landscape gardener is given instructions to plant four special trees so that each one is exactly the same distance from each of the others. How is he able to do it?

It's not difficult to see how he could plant *three* trees the same distance from each other, forming the three points of an equilateral triangle. But how could he do this with *four* trees? The key lies in questioning the assumption that we're inclined to take for granted: that he is planting on level ground. It could be done, if he were planting on a mound of earth forming an equal-sided pyramid.

As well as asking naïve questions, concentrate on another part of the pattern of ideas represented by the concept that you don't normally consider. Now that you have analysed a concept you will know that there are different parts to the pattern of ideas it represents. By seeing alternative interpretations of the concept in this way you can make new connections with other ideas.

Try this. . .

In 1905 Niels Bohr, who won the Nobel Prize for physics in 1922, was sitting an exam at the University of Copenhagen. One of the questions was how can you measure the height of a building using a barometer. As a barometer measures air pressure the expected answer was to measure the pressure at ground level, then at the top of the building and then calculate the height from the difference between the two. Although Bohr knew the answer, he wasn't satisfied with it and began to think up different ways he could answer the question. How many different ways of using a barometer to measure the height of the building can you see?

Answer

1   Bohr's answer was to tie a piece of string to the barometer, lower it down to the ground, and then add the length of the string to the barometer.

He failed on the ground that his answer showed insufficient knowledge of physics, but on appeal he was given five minutes to answer the question again. He then suggested a number of answers all displaying knowledge of physics.

2   Throw it off the roof and count the seconds until it hit the ground. Then calculate the height.

3   Measure the length of the barometer and of its shadow and calculate the ratio. Then measure the length of the shadow of the building and multiply it by the ratio.

4 Tie a piece of string to the barometer and set it swinging as a pendulum. Time the pendulum at ground level and at the top of the building. Then calculate the height of the building from the difference between the two.

5 Use the barometer to calculate the difference in air pressure at ground level and at the top of the building – the correct answer.

Finally he had given the answer the examiners wanted, but he wasn't finished there:

6 Climb the fire escape marking off the height of the building in barometer lengths. Then add up the number of barometer lengths.

7 Offer the janitor the barometer as a bribe to reveal the height of the building.[4]

The mark that Bohr received is not known, but it illustrates how you can generate new unexpected connections between ideas once you start to think about the different ways you can interpret the pattern of ideas represented by a concept. This has been the source of some of the most dramatic breakthroughs in our understanding.

> **For instance. . .**
>
> In his attempt to understand the nature of energy Einstein took the two concepts, mass and energy, both seemingly unlike, and thought about the connections he could make between them. Then he related them to the things and ideas around him with which he was familiar.

In a moment we will look at how Einstein used this shift in perspective to reveal new insights into the nature of energy, but first,

> **Try this. . .**
>
> ## Tragedy and freedom
>
> In the last chapter we analysed the concept of tragedy and in the process discovered that there was more to the concept than we first thought, in particular that it involves destroying the thing we value most. So take this aspect of the concept and see what connections you can discover with the other concept we briefly analysed – freedom. We found that we talk about two types of freedom: freedom *from* something, a negative type of freedom in which we are released from restrictions, and a positive type of freedom *to do* something, to have the means of developing our abilities and of achieving what we want to.
>
> The question we need to ask, therefore, is can this type of positive freedom result in tragedy in the sense of destroying the thing we value most. Positive freedom can give us the opportunity to develop our skills to earn more and do what we most want to do; to be what we want to be and set our own goals. So, is there anything self-defeating in our response to positive freedom?
>
> One obvious connection here is that, with positive freedom, which comes from developing our skills so we can take advantage of greater opportunity, some people

will choose a job because it pays the most only to find themselves trapped and deeply frustrated in a job that is not fulfilling. Eventually, they end their working lives realising that they failed to do what they really wanted to do and defeated their own purpose.

2. Insight

At this point, having compared two things from perspectives that we would not normally adopt, we often experience an insight, that shaft of light that sheds the sort of clarity that leaves us wondering where on earth it came from. In *The Structure of Scientific Revolutions*, Thomas Kuhn explains that the shift from one paradigm to another is not the result of a cumulative process, but a sudden transition, a gestalt, that 'emerges all at once, sometimes in the middle of the night, in the mind . . . deeply immersed in crisis'.[5]

Principle

Insights come from comparing two things from perspectives that we would not normally adopt.

A similar thing occurred in chapter 4 (pages 63–6), when we compared the abstract patterns, out of which the concept of olic suddenly appeared. This may seem commonplace, but the certainty and clarity of vision are the same.

For instance. . .

Einstein had the same experience. He analysed and compared the two concepts of mass and energy from a different perspective, as if energy could behave like a solid object. He then experienced the sudden insight that 'Matter is frozen energy'. It is locked even within the smallest fragment of matter: a piece of paper, a stick of wood, an iron filing or a small piece of uranium.

When the subatomic particles that make up the object become unfrozen, they can become enormously powerful as in a nuclear reactor or in the energy released by the sun. Einstein explained this hoarded energy with an analogy: 'It is as though a man who is fabulously rich (i.e. mass) should never spend or give away a cent (i.e. of its energy); no one could tell how rich he was.'[6]

Einstein's greatest insights came from just this type of thought experiment, fuelled by these unusual comparisons of ideas and the most naïve questions. He was a top-down thinker: his work contained few, if any, references to the research of others. The theory of relativity developed out of an image that had haunted him since he was 16, imagining himself racing a light beam: 'What would it be like to sit on a beam of light?' he asked himself. It led to the revelation that the speed of light was the one constant in the universe; everything else was relative to the position and speed of the observer.

***Try this.* . .**

Tragedy and freedom

If the connection we have made doesn't lead to the dawning of an insight, think about examples of people you have known to be in this situation and distil the essence of it: what lies at the heart of it? This is asking you to do what you did when you identified the essence of an olic from the abstract diagrams. You are looking for a generalisation that lies at the heart of all these examples.

From this an insight might suddenly force itself upon your thinking in the form of two concepts: extrinsic and intrinsic value. You could argue that those who pursue the high paying job, because it will bring them wealth and possessions, are pursuing those things that have 'extrinsic value', whereas those who pursue the type of job that they find deeply fulfilling are pursuing those things that have 'intrinsic value'.

The more you probe the more you realise that the value of those things that have extrinsic value, like property and wealth, lies not in what they are, but *in what they can bring*. They offer us a promissory note with which we can buy other things.

In contrast, those things that have intrinsic value are of value *in and of themselves*. You realise that these are the sort of things and events we long remember. They give us a deep sense of well-being: a good book in front of a roaring fire on a cold winter's night; an evening spent with old friends; an unexpected kindness. So, if we were to find intrinsic value in a job, it is likely to give us a similar deep sense of fulfilment.

3. Hypothesis/idea

From the insight that we have generated we can now begin to create a hypothesis, which we can test and then adapt.

For instance. . .

Einstein's insight that matter was frozen energy gave him what he needed to develop his most famous equation in his theory of special relativity:

$E = mc^2$ *(Energy = mass x speed of light squared)*

***Try this.* . .**

Tragedy and freedom

In the same way, we now have to use our insight as the inspiration for an idea, a hypothesis. Of course, the fundamental question that arises from this insight that we would all want to ask ourselves is 'What sort of job should I be choosing that will bring me the sense of fulfilment that intrinsic value brings?' But before that, we need to test the hypothesis, 'If I pursue extrinsic value, I am likely to find myself trapped in a job and a lifestyle that are deeply dissatisfying.' In other words, we would destroy the very thing we value most: our own personal happiness and fulfilment.

4. Test

The last two stages are in many ways a lot more straightforward. Our aim is not just to test our hypothesis to see if it works, but to reveal whether and in what ways we need to adapt it.

> **Try this. . .**
>
> ### Tragedy and freedom
>
> To test this hypothesis we might use the evidence of surveys that assess whether people feel more fulfilled, or at least happier, after having experienced an increase in their wealth over a long period. For example, the University of Chicago's National Opinion Research Center found that the proportion of Americans describing themselves as 'very happy' has consistently hovered around one-third since the 1950s, despite the astonishing growth in affluence in post-war America.[7]
>
> We could also look for personal testimony from those who have successfully pursued careers that have brought them extrinsic value in terms of wealth. For example, in an interview, Donald Trump explained that it is rare to find anyone who achieves this kind of major goal that brings them significant wealth and doesn't then immediately feel sad, empty and lost. Indeed, he admitted that he only has to look at himself to know this is true.

5. Adapt

If the idea you were testing related to an academic subject, you may need to adjust the emphasis or qualify it in some way. However, if you were developing a new product or an enterprise to fill a niche market, you might need to do more to adapt it to meet the demand.

> **For instance. . .**
>
> When Edwin Land unveiled the first commercial Polaroid camera in 1948, it was only after a long developmental period in which he played a pivotal role converting his idea into a working camera and developing instant film.

In fact, in many cases there is a prolonged process of iteration between the testing and adaptation stages as the final version of the idea begins to emerge.

> **Try this. . .**
>
> ### Tragedy and freedom
>
> In this case, however, you may not need to adapt your conclusion, although you may want to stand back from the results and use them to reflect on what type of

job you ought to be looking for: 'What can I learn from this to ensure that my work
has the intrinsic value that will make it fulfilling?'

You might conclude that your job must give you three things: pleasure, meaning
and excellence. In other words, you must enjoy it; it must have significance, a
meaning for you that will never leave you wondering whether the work you do is
worthwhile; and it must be suited to your skills, so that you are constantly
reminded that you are good at what you do.

A practical example

Now that you have worked through each of the stages of the method, tackle the
following problem yourself before looking at the answer below. You won't be able to
match the solution that was developed detail for detail, particularly in the last two
stages, but you should be able to follow the first three stages.

*The city of Bangalore has 8.5 million residents, who generate more than 4,000 tonnes of
solid waste every day. Around 90 per cent of this ends up in landfills, despite being largely
recyclable, and the problem is getting worse. Although the city has made waste
segregation compulsory, without a costly system of enforcement it has had little effect.
Moreover, these foul-smelling, unhealthy landfills attract large numbers of waste-pickers,
who scavenge through the heaps of garbage everyday in search of items that are
recyclable, from which they can earn something. How would you solve the problem?*

Answer

1. Connect

Our task is to find connections between two patterns of ideas:

a)   There is an increasingly large volume of recyclable waste going into
     overflowing landfills;
b)   These foul-smelling, unhealthy sites attract large numbers of waste-pickers,
     who are condemned to poverty and an unhealthy lifestyle.

We can bring together these two ideas, represented by the waste-generators and the
waste-pickers, in two ways:

1   We can bring the waste-generators (the residents) to the landfill sites, where
    the waste-pickers are;
2   Or we can bring the waste-pickers to the beginning of the waste supply chain
    where the residents are.

2. Insight

As in many cases, once you have laid out and connected the two patterns of ideas
the insight is all too obvious. As soon as we realise that there are problems with both
of these options, an insight forces itself upon our thinking. In retrospect it appears
obvious: bring them together in one place – a website. The idea is simple, but then
so too was the Polaroid camera and **Facebook**.

3. Hypothesis/idea

At this point it often appears that the real work begins. You may have the insight 'All As are Bs', but it is not until you have converted this into the hypothesis 'If A, then B' that you have something you can test and then adapt if necessary. So we need to convert this insight into a practical idea that will deal with the problems, how will this website be created and how will this collaboration work?

The first problem was solved with a cloud-based platform called **I Got Garbage**. As for the collaboration, the waste-pickers were organised into franchises and apartments hire a waste-picker franchise in a 'pay-per-kilo' system. It works by waste-pickers collecting the segregated waste from the apartments, selling recyclable dry waste to scrap dealers and then composting the wet waste at the apartments or sending it to government-run composting centres. The residents are discouraged from making too much reject waste by charging them for it. They use the website to hire the services of waste-pickers, while the waste-pickers use it to increase their efficiency and income.

4. Test

The initial results of the collaboration were encouraging with the 5,251 waste-pickers almost doubling their average monthly income from $80 to almost $150 and with 2,350 tonnes of waste recycled.

5. Adapt

However, certain improvements were introduced to give more accurate feedback about what was happening, so that everyone could see how to make the system more efficient. The residents were asked for volunteers to become waste auditors, so they could track their carbon footprint, and even take day-long trash trails to educate them about the route that their trash takes to landfills.

As for the waste-pickers, mobile applications have been introduced to help them track their trash flow and collection routes. Waste-pickers can use them to connect to the nearest scrap-dealers, who then become the first sale point, thereby reducing the distance they have to travel each day.

In this problem much of the value lies in the last three stages as the idea was developed, tested and adapted, whereas with Einstein's discovery the value lay largely in the work done in the first two stages. The same is the case with the sort of psychometric tests that are set on these skills: some rely more on the initial insight, whereas others call for more development.

Psychometric tests – insight problems

Although the following problems may seem distant from the sort of problems we have been examining in this chapter, they aren't. You start as we did by analysing the patterns of ideas you are dealing with. **Pin down clearly the ideas you have been given, miss nothing out**. Some things will be stated; others will be implied, leaving it up to you to make the relevant inference. Just as important as determining what you *do* know is realising what you *don't* know, so don't take anything for granted, challenge your assumptions.

Once you've done this, **look for connections**. With the ideas clearly organised, concentrate on a part of this that you would normally not consider. As we have discovered, only by seeing alternative interpretations of the problem beyond your normal expectations can you make new connections with other ideas. This will open up different perspectives and help you see connections with other ideas. As you work systematically through these the **insight** is likely to come. From this, **develop the hypothesis**, the solution, which you then **test**. If it doesn't answer the problem completely, then you will need to **adapt it**.

Try this. . .

The triangle below points to the top of the page. Show how you could move three circles to get the triangle to point to the bottom of the page.

The ideas we have been given, stated and implied, seem to be:

1   Circles have to be moved out of the row of four circles.
2   The single circle in the first row must move: it would involve moving too many circles to convert this into a row of four circles, leaving none that could be moved to convert the others.
3   Therefore, row three must remain the same.
4   This leaves row two containing two circles to be converted into a row of four circles.

To do this we must move the outside two circles on the row containing four up to the second row, making this into a row of four. Then the single circle on the first row must be moved down to form the point of the triangle below the row that now contains two circles.

Now try these. You will find the answers on the companion website.

1   A man bought a horse for $60 and sold it for $70. Then he bought it back for $80 and sold it for $90. How much did he make or lose in the horse-trading business?
2   A woman has four pieces of chain. Each piece is made up of three links. She wants to join the pieces into a single closed loop of chain. To open a link costs 2 cents and to close a link costs 3 cents. She only has 15 cents. How does she do it?[8]
3   In the days before watches were invented, clocks were valuable possessions. A man living in a remote area had one that kept very good time. However, he woke

up one day to find it had stopped, so he had no idea of the correct time. He decided to walk to the next valley to visit his friend, who also had a clock that kept good time. He chatted with his friend for a while and then made his way home. He didn't know the exact length of the journey before he started. How did he manage to set his clock correctly when he got home?

4 You are standing outside a light-tight, well-insulated closet with one door, which is closed. The closet contains three light sockets each containing a working light bulb. Outside the closet, there are three on/off light switches, each of which controls a different one of the sockets in the closet. All switches are off. Your task is to identify which switch operates which light bulb. You can turn the switches off and on and leave them in any position, but once you open the closet door you cannot change the setting of any switch. Your task is to figure out which switch controls which light bulb while you are only allowed to open the door once.[9]

Summary

1 Synthesising two or more ideas can release surprising potential.

2 There are four types of synthesis.

3 By just placing the emphasis on a different part of the pattern of ideas represented by a concept we can see things we have never seen before.

4 There are three rules that govern the way we manage concepts and the patterns of ideas they represent.

5 Insights come from comparing two things from perspectives that we would not normally adopt.

What's next?

As we have seen so often in this chapter, insights can at times seem obvious once we have seen them, but then the best and most successful ideas often do. This doesn't make them any easier to discover in the first place. It's what makes invention and creativity so intriguing: there are astonishing ideas out there waiting to be discovered, but so few of us have developed the skills to see them. Working through the stages of this practical method will help you develop these skills.

Once we have developed our conceptual skills, we have at our fingertips the most powerful means that we know for shaping and understanding our world. Armed with this we can now tackle the most baffling problems. In the next stage we will develop our creative thinking skills. We will learn how to generate our own ideas, structure them, use analogies to find solutions and design solutions to problems.

Companion website

You will find similar examples of the sort of psychometric problems shown in this chapter on the companion website. www.he.palgrave.com/smart-thinking

How will this improve my grades and employability?

In this chapter you will learn. . .

- How conceptual thinking can help you achieve the highest grades in your essays.
- That it is the key to identifying an original, interesting topic for your dissertation.
- How important it is for the structure and organisation of your dissertation.
- About the significance of conceptual thinking as an employability skill that all employers are looking for.
- How much easier it is to cope with psychometric problems once you have learned the methods and skills of conceptual thinking.

In the last four chapters we have seen the extraordinary power of concepts. On the one hand they can lift us above our normal discourse, allowing us to see new insights and ways of approaching problems that would otherwise have been obscured to us. By analysing them we can reveal the inner structure of an issue or problem so we can approach it differently; we can see new ways in which we can recombine its elements to create things that nobody has seen before.

On the other hand, while they liberate us by opening up all sorts of possibilities in this way, they can also trap us in the comfortable predictability of routine thinking. They can influence our behaviour quite independently of our rational evaluation by setting off a train of thought which we follow routinely. We interpret experience in a particular way, organise it and advocate a certain type of action as a result, without being conscious that the concepts we use obscure alternative lines of thought and interpretation.

Examiners

These are the things that most interest examiners, whether you are being assessed in your academic work or in the psychometric questions that test your employability skills. Examiners want to see how well you can deal with these problems.

1 Can you analyse and use concepts imaginatively?
2 Can you demonstrate that you are sensitive to all their hidden subtleties and implications?
3 Can you use them to open up new ways of thinking that will bring new insights and ways of approaching problems?

Academic work

Now that you know how to analyse concepts, create new ones and synthesise ideas you can bring all the power of concepts and conceptual thinking to your academic work.

1. Essays

This is clear the moment an examiner begins to read your essay. The first concern of all examiners is can you think conceptually? As they set about reading your essay they will be looking for two things:

1 Have you seen the point of the question; have you unravelled its meaning clearly?
2 Then they will want a clear indication of the strategy you are going to adopt to answer it. This means showing that you have a clear structure to your answer, which tackles the question directly and relevantly.

1.1 Implications

Obviously, the first thing anyone is going to look for as they begin to read your essay is evidence that you have seen the point of the question; that you have been able to interpret its meaning and implications accurately. But our ability to unravel the implications of an essay question largely depends upon our ability to unravel the implications of the concepts contained in it. Examiners will want to see that you can do this with clarity, insight and sensitivity.

No matter what the subject, you will find concepts dominating the implications of essay questions:

- Discuss the management of health **needs** within a population group in the Primary Care setting. (Nursing and Applied Clinical Studies, Canterbury Christ Church University)
- In the light of a number of recent high profile complaints about invasion of **privacy**, critically assess whether the press should continue to be self-regulating. (Journalism, University of Newcastle, Australia)
- Is **democracy** always compatible with individual **freedom**? (Politics, University of York)
- Are concepts of **anomie** and **subculture** still of value in the explanation of **criminality**? (Sociology, University of Oxford)
- What are the assumptions of the **revealed preference approach** to life valuation? (Biology, Stanford University)

Every academic subject has its key concepts that shape the way it discusses the issues that dominate its deliberations. Some seem quite ordinary, while others are more technical. Whenever you tackle an essay that uses them, you will have to analyse them to unravel the meaning and implications of the essay question:

In **history**: we need to be aware of the implications of using concepts like revolution, revolt, coup d'état, class and class consciousness;
In **literature**: concepts like tragedy, comedy, irony and satire;
In **politics**: concepts like freedom, ideology, equality, power and authority;

In **law**: concepts like punishment, obligation and the difference between law and morality;
In **business**: the difference between bribes, commissions, gifts, incentives and tips;
In **nursing**: concepts, like abuse, care and dignity;
In **social work**: concepts like inequality, discrimination, race and racism.

Examiners will want to see how sensitively and subtly you can analyse these concepts and then let this direct your thinking about the subject. Markers at the University of London are told to award the highest marks (70–100 per cent) to,

> those students who 'note subtlety, complexity and possible disagreements, [which they] . . . will discuss', while only average marks (40–60 per cent) are to be awarded to the student who adopts a 'More relaxed application' of the question, and who 'follows [an] obvious line . . . [and] uncritically accepts the terms of the question'.

In chapter 5 I said what we are doing when we analyse a concept is to lift the bonnet to look at the engine beneath. There we find what drives and directs our thinking. Unless we do this, we have little control over our thinking. The moment we analyse the concept we see the pattern of ideas beneath, which we can use creatively to come to surprising ideas that others will not have thought about. Indeed, without this, our essays can seem pedestrian and predictable.

Principle
If you want examiners to take notice of your essays, to be impressed by their insights and originality, use your conceptual skills.

1.2 Structure

Lifting the bonnet in this way not only reveals all the subtle implications of questions from the ideas that make up the concept, but inevitably also the pattern into which these ideas are organised. This gives your essay a clear, logical and cohesive structure from the moment you analyse the concept. This is the key to any effective essay. It does two important things for your essay:

1. It gives examiners a map to follow

In order to follow your arguments without getting lost, examiners will want to see the structure – a map of the essay that they can follow step by step. To some students this seems unimportant, but for the reader it is essential. Without a map it can be difficult to follow the writer's arguments and, quite simply, to avoid getting lost. If examiners get lost, they cannot give you marks, no matter how persuasive your arguments. They are even warned that they should not go back to reread a section that they didn't understand the first time.

2. It establishes relevance

A structure is also essential in establishing the relevance of your arguments to the implications of the question. Again, if they cannot establish this, examiners cannot give you marks, no matter how interesting and original your arguments. So a clear road map, tied into the analysis of the question in the introduction, that establishes the route and the relevance of your approach, is essential if you want to avoid losing the examiner and, therefore, losing marks.

For instance. . .

If you were a politics undergraduate you might be set a question like the following:

'The ideology of Nazism was internally incoherent.' Discuss

Many students might not think it is worth analysing the concept of 'ideology', but not only is this likely to produce an interesting and original way of answering the question with an essay that is full of quite unexpected insights, but immediately the analysis is done you have a ready-made structure that is relevant and easy to follow.

You might find, after analysing the concept of ideology, that there are three dominant interpretations of the concept: Karl Mannheim's 'System of beliefs' as both 'particular' and 'total' ideologies; Lionel Trilling's interpretation as the 'Science of Ideas'; and Marx's interpretation as 'false consciousness'. Here you have the structure for your essay composed of three parts, each involving a discussion of Nazism in the light of these different interpretations of ideology.

As you analyse the concept for structure, you are looking to pin down two things:

1. *how* many parts there are to the question;
2. and *what* weight you will need to give to each part.

Indeed, in many exams, if you fail to do this, examiners will deduct marks: they will expect to see you show that you can analyse difficult key concepts and allow this to influence, if not determine, the structure of the essay.

2. Dissertations

However, it is in our dissertations, perhaps even more than in our essays, that learning to think conceptually really shows results. A dissertation is not just about *what* you think, but *how* you think. For many students at university this is the first occasion when they will have to come out from behind the ideas that they have borrowed from authorities and think for themselves. Here is your chance to show that you can be an original thinker, someone who has interesting ideas, who can generate insights that nobody has thought about before.

> It is not just about what you think, but how you think.

A window into your thinking – are you a smart thinker?

Above all, a dissertation gives examiners a window into our thinking. We are expected to show not just our ideas, but how and why we organised our research and adopted the methods that we did. A dissertation is our opportunity to show that we are smart thinkers. In particular, we are being assessed on how well we can use our metacognitive abilities – can we think about our thinking?

- Have we chosen the most effective research strategy that will generate reliable evidence?
- How are we going to validate our results: do we understand and can we justify the research methods we've chosen to validate our evidence?
- Have we thought through all our ideas clearly?
- Have we analysed the concepts clearly and imaginatively to reveal the most important underlying issues of the problem?
- Are there different avenues of research and insights that we can uncover by synthesising our ideas into a new, original synthesis?

All of this calls for smart thinking. You are not just setting out a simple catalogue of what you believe to be right answers, nor are you just laying down a thesis and defending it. You are being assessed on your metacognitive ability to think about your thinking: to be aware of the *process* of thought, not just the *product*. The main purpose of dissertations is not just to communicate the results of your research, but to show examiners that the methods underpinning your research have been chosen well and used skilfully.

Originality

Yet, perhaps the most obvious feature of any dissertation is that it is designed to give you the opportunity to produce a substantial piece of independent work, which reflects a wider range of your skills and abilities. It may sound odd, but it's designed as an opportunity to do some genuine thinking. As we have already said, many of the courses in higher education allow students to slip into the comfortable, undemanding role as mere recyclers of received opinions, while teachers opt for the corresponding and easier task of teaching students *what* to think, rather than *how* to think.

In sharp contrast, a dissertation puts *you* into the driving seat. You decide on the focus, direction and organisation of your work. You choose the questions for which you want answers or the hypothesis you want to test. Your work has to display originality. This can be

- in the subject you have chosen;
- in the methods you have used to gather and validate your evidence;
- or, of course, in your thinking – in the way you have analysed the key concepts, synthesised your ideas to open up new ways of approaching the topic and in the ideas you have generated.

All three depend heavily on our ability to think conceptually. By analysing the key concepts and synthesising our ideas we can reveal new and interesting approaches to a topic. In this way we are more able to escape from the routine ways in which we understand topics and approach problems.

Finding the most interesting problems to research

1. Analysing concepts

Many students are surprised to learn that analysing a key concept is not just essential in finding an original solution to a problem, but, equally important, in finding an original problem. Your research doesn't have to be ground-breaking. It may just be that in your analysis of the key concepts and problems you see things that others have failed to see or failed to pay enough attention to.

For instance. . .

Let's say you are a law or history undergraduate. As you set about trying to choose the subject of your dissertation your attention is drawn to a recent statement by the official counterterrorism watchdog that the British definition of terrorism is so broadly drawn in legislation that it could even encompass writers campaigning against vaccination on religious grounds. So loosely do we now apply the term that even the passive civil disobedience of road protesters and environmental activists have been described as 'terrorism'.

Intrigued by the absurdity of this situation you decide to analyse the concept to see if there might be an original problem or an original approach to a problem that you might adopt for your research. From your analysis of the concept you reveal the following core characteristics:

1 Terrorists routinely use violence or the threat of violence directed at ordinary people selected randomly.
2 Their aim is to deliver a message of fear and to destroy civilian morale, both of which they expect will bring pressure upon governments.

Not only does it seem to you that, according to this, there are many forms of protest deemed to be terrorism that shouldn't be, but others that should be, but generally are not. If these are the core characteristics, you wonder, shouldn't we also include examples of the state's use of terror, like the deliberate targeting of civilians during the Second World War by bombing German cities, like Dresden, the bombing of Hiroshima and Nagasaki, and the plans to annihilate tens of millions of ordinary people as part of the nuclear strategies of the Cold War?

If you are a law or history student, here you have an interesting project: to analyse the different ways in which the concept of terrorism has been used to justify these policies. If you are a philosophy student, you may want to explore the ethical arguments offered in support of such policies.

2. Synthesising ideas

The reason that conceptual thinking is such a powerful engine for generating ideas is that it allows us to think imaginatively about all the possibilities; not just about what is at present a fact, but about how things might or should be. In previous chapters we found that the most significant breakthroughs in our understanding have come about not because researchers had new or better data, but because of the quality of their thinking and the type of concepts they created. The answers they found only finally came as a result of being able to think outside the accepted concepts and methods of their disciplines.

We can do the same as we design our own research strategy for our dissertation. Once we have analysed the key concepts, revealing the patterns of ideas they represent, we can:

- Reformulate these ideas in new ways;

- Or simply place the emphasis differently within the concept.
- Alternatively, we can gather our ideas under an existing concept that is not usually associated with these ideas;
- Or import a concept from another discipline or subject to see things in a new and insightful way.
- Combine two or more concepts, merging their patterns of ideas to create a new way of looking at a problem. In this way we can generate all sorts of unexpected, interesting ideas and ways of freeing us from routine, predictable responses.

The surprising lesson we need to learn from this is that in most situations you don't need more or new ideas: just a different way of thinking about the ideas you do have. Look back at chapter 6 to see how you can use these strategies to reveal new possibilities for intriguing projects. Use the practical method that we learned there.

Synthesising ideas – a practical method

1 Connect
2 Insight
3 Hypothesis/idea
4 Test
5 Adapt

Organisation and structure

Equally important, as we saw with our essays, thinking conceptually about our project not only gives us fresh insights, different ways of looking at a problem, but a structure with manageable tasks and questions that organises the way we set about researching the problem.

Most research questions involve concepts, which we can easily take for granted, even though at the heart of them lie the really interesting issues, questions and insights. By analysing them, we not only bring structure to our work, but, more importantly, we give our research that essential layer of sub-problems and questions, which are really the interesting heart of the problem. It gives us the mechanism that will drive our research by spelling out clearly what these abstract terms mean, what their implications are and how we will recognise them in our research.

By analysing the key concepts:

1 We bring structure to our project.
2 We give our research that essential layer of sub-problems and questions.
3 This is the mechanism that will drive our research by spelling out:
   3.1 what these abstract terms mean;
   3.2 what their implications are;
   3.3 how we will recognise them in our research.

Making ideas your own – more fluent writing, more persuasive presentations

As you use and develop your conceptual abilities you will be surprised just how well you can pull ideas together from different sources under one concept and, as a result, see a problem in a completely new way, opening up new and interesting ways of approaching it. We said in an earlier chapter that the most distinguishing characteristic of intelligence is not what you know, but what you can do with it.

But the benefits of conceptual thinking to your academic work don't end there. Your presentations will be more interesting and persuasive, and your writing will be more insightful and convincing by virtue of having made the ideas your own.

> You will write and present your ideas more convincingly as a result of making the ideas your own.

As we process the ideas more completely by analysing and synthesising them, we test them against our own beliefs and ideas, and integrate them within the structures of our own thinking. We become 'deep-level processors' as opposed to 'surface-level processors', who accept ideas passively without analysing, structuring and evaluating them. Consequently, we are no longer just borrowing ideas wholesale from sources we have read, but using our own.

- Your conceptual abilities will allow you to see problems in a completely new way, opening up new and interesting ways of approaching them.
- Your presentations will be more interesting and persuasive.
- Your writing will be more insightful and convincing, because you will have made the ideas your own.

Unfortunately, when many students are asked to express themselves they are not expressing *their* ideas, but what they think their teachers think they ought to think. They appear to be struggling to express ideas which are not theirs in a language they do not command. In effect, they do not share the needs of a genuine thinker. Consequently, they are not involved in what they are writing and expressing at a deeper level by making the ideas their own.

Employability

All of these benefits that flow from being able to think conceptually are not lost on employers. In previous chapters we learned the importance of concepts in that they lift us above the specific, the concrete and the present so we can see the general, the universal and all the possibilities for the future in any situation. They give us the ability to go beyond the particulars of our world and extend our understanding in ways that would otherwise be impossible.

Adapting to a changing environment

This is essential for all organisations, commercial and non-commercial. They know that to survive in a rapidly changing environment they need to escape the System 1 thinking that tends to dominate their day-to-day thinking. They must be able to adapt and to do this they need people who have the ability to think conceptually: to lift themselves above the present and see what is strategically possible. In other words, they must be capable of System 2 thinking. Like all smart thinkers they must be capable of metacognition and counterintuitive thinking.

All organisations realise that they need people:

1　Who can escape their System 1 thinking
2　Who are able to adapt
3　Who have the ability to think conceptually
4　Who can lift themselves above the present and see what is strategically possible
5　Who are smart thinkers
6　Who can use their System 2 thinking

---

1. Businesses and organisations

It's common in business education to insist that to be successful all businesses must become learning organisations. They must be quick on their feet, able to adapt to the changing environment. To do this they must avoid getting trapped in the internal culture of the organisation: the belief that this is the way we have always done things, so we should continue to work this way.

When managers find themselves concentrating on the day-to-day running of any organisation, it's easy to get drawn into the assumption that tomorrow will be the same as today as today is the same as yesterday. Consequently, they train their staff for yesterday's work, preparing them for the past, rather than the future.

2. Professionals

The same is true of many professionals, who find themselves so consumed with their day-to-day work that they overlook the need to adapt to a changing environment, which is placing new, unexpected demands on their expertise. Whether they are a teacher, a doctor, a nurse or a lawyer, they all need the skills to think conceptually, so they can stand back from their concept of someone in their profession and ask 'What do I need to do differently to meet the changing needs of my students, patients and clients?'

What benefits does conceptual thinking offer employers?

The more successful organisations are aware of this problem. They realise that they need to appoint staff who can see what needs to be done in the future, rather than just repeat the past. For this they need people capable of conceptual thinking, who can rise above the day-to-day administration and think strategically.

As we have seen in the previous chapters, this means analysing the concepts we use to understand our environment and the problems we confront, so that we can see the patterns of ideas they represent. We can then synthesise these ideas into new concepts and use our imagination to see the range of possibilities that are open to us.

In practical terms:

In practical terms this means an employee who can:

1   Analyse concepts to see clearly the issues that have to be tackled in any problem.
2   Synthesise ideas from different sources to see problems from different perspectives.
3   Create new concepts, new ways of promoting the organisation and new ranges of products and services.
4   Think differently about a problem and generate new, unexpected solutions.
5   Create presentations that are clear, perceptive and persuasive.
6   Produce clear, well-written reports that analyse all the important issues raised by a problem thoughtfully and perceptively.
7   In business, people who can make the most of opportunities to increase market share, improve efficiency and maximise profits.
8   In professions, people who can think strategically to meet the changing needs of those they serve.

For instance. . .

If you were a manager without the skills to think conceptually and you were presented with a problem, you would probably accept it in the form in which it has been presented and produce the kind of solution that has always been produced.

But if you can think conceptually, you will analyse the problem, redraw it by synthesising more ideas, out of which you can redesign a new system. The conceptual thinker will step outside a problem and represent it differently. She will create a new concept out of ideas that she has gathered, or synthesise them under an existing one. In this way she can create new insights and interesting ways of presenting the problem.

As we said in chapter 4, from those in PR and advertising, who think up novel ways of promoting a product, to inventors and designers, who create new types of product or service, to professionals, designing new ways of meeting their clients' needs, all are attempting to design new concepts.

Psychometric tests

Employers around the world are increasingly aware of the importance of these skills in an environment that is changing rapidly. As I explained in the introduction, there is a clamour for employees who can use these skills. Yet the overwhelming evidence is that graduates that have them are difficult to find. Employers complain that they are inundated with unsatisfactory applicants, the majority of whom have good degrees, but cannot think.

To sift through these, most employers are now using psychometric tests. Among these it is no surprise that a large proportion assess graduates' conceptual thinking skills. Their aim is to find answers to the three questions at the beginning of this chapter:

1 Can you analyse and use concepts imaginatively?
2 Can you demonstrate that you are sensitive to all their hidden subtleties and implications?
3 Can you use them to open up new ways of thinking that will bring new insights and ways of approaching problems?

For instance. . .

In the last four chapters we have seen how they assess applicants using

1 **Verbal reasoning tests** to assess our ability to interpret and distinguish between complex concepts, and understand complex written arguments, which we examined in chapters 3, 4 and 5;
2 **Abstract reasoning tests**, which we examined in chapter 4, where we learned a method for creating new concepts and making connections between ideas;
3 **Insight problems**, which we examined in chapter 6, where we learned a five-step method for synthesising ideas and tackling this type of question.

In effect they are asking you to demonstrate that you can lift the bonnet of a concept and unravel the hidden pattern of ideas revealed beneath. From the many applications they receive they want to find those who can, in a self-reflective way, question our use of these quite ordinary words. They want to know that you are the type of person who accepts that these cannot be taken for granted; that there are implications to them that will otherwise remain concealed and shape our thinking, unless we think conceptually.

Summary

1 To write successful essays we must analyse the concepts in the question to reveal its implications and structure.
2 Conceptual thinking is the key to finding the most interesting and original problems to research for our dissertations.
3 It also reveals the essential layer of sub-problems and questions, which will drive our research by spelling out clearly what these abstract terms mean.
4 Employers realise that to adapt to a rapidly changing environment they need employees who can think conceptually.
5 To assess graduates' conceptual skills and sift through the applications they receive, employers use a range of psychometric tests.

Conclusion

There is little doubt that the skills and techniques you have learned in the last four chapters will improve your employability skills and give you the tools you need to cope well with a range of psychometric questions. They will also lead to significant improvements in your essays, dissertations and in your academic work in general.

But even more, they are liberating in a much deeper sense. They are the first stage in creating a genuine thinker, someone capable of smart thinking with all its liberating potential. With these skills you will see more, generate more insights and open up a world of exciting possibilities unrestricted by what has gone before and the way in which things have always been done.

Creative Thinking

We tend to think that creativity is a talent possessed by a select few lucky enough to inherit the right DNA, yet we are all capable of being creative. Recent research suggests that around 50,000 years ago human DNA underwent a significant mutation with the emergence of the 'migration gene'. Linked to adventurousness, curiosity and risk-taking, humans with this gene dispersed from Africa in search of new things.

Yet although creativity is so important for our health, happiness and personality growth, driving us to explore new ideas and new things, its influence declines by over 50 per cent between the ages of 20 and 60. Most of us are surprised to learn that we had more individuality at the age of 20 than we do at 60. Life does the reverse of what we tend to think it does: we travel *away* from original thought not *towards* it. Without the time to give expression to our inmost thoughts and ideas, year by year we become more anonymous, like everyone else.

In contrast, the lives of children are full of creativity and wonder. With no preconceptions, they are engaged in the creative process of building their own internal map of the external world. They have a mental life that is rich in ideas and insights, which they keep concealed from the adult world. As Ernest Dimnet describes them, 'they are as self-contained as cats and continuously attentive to the magical charm of what they see inwardly'.[1]

Sunsets, patches of colour, water, waves, all generate wonder and curiosity. They might stare at a stone or a shell for what seems ages wondering what it is like to be this old. Concepts like eternity and infinity, space and time, capture their imagination and curiosity. Their innocence, uncorrupted by the adult world, brings that boundless wonder, so perfectly captured by William Blake in *Auguries of Innocence*:

> *To see a World in a grain of sand,*
> *And a Heaven in a wild flower,*
> *Hold Infinity in the palm of your hand,*
> *And Eternity in an hour.*[2]

But then the spell is finally broken as parents clamour for a comfortable sense of conformity in their children, who turn away from their childish imagination and speculative ideas. They begin to imitate adults and act 'normally' according to adult norms. What child can resist behaviour that frees them from the fear that they might be regarded by adults as somehow 'odd'?

Education, too, plays a similar role by imposing other people's thoughts on us, rather than helping us get back to our own. As teachers we are more comfortable teaching students *what* to think than we are teaching them *how* to think. The child with flashes of ideas and inspiration is thought odd – a non-conformist. And once repressed it is harder for such inspiration to break through a second time.

What is creativity?

The climate of certainty teachers spend so much time creating in universities, reinforced by the fear of failure, do more than anything to kill our search for novelty, new ideas and creative insights. Afraid of making mistakes, we reproduce the answers we believe our teachers want us to produce. Rather than using and developing our creativity and higher cognitive skills, we resort to regressive learning behaviour, using our lower cognitive skills to recall the right answers, show evidence of understanding and demonstrate faultless memories.

Yet in contrast to this world of order and certainties, the real world is full of uncertainty, where decisions have to be made to create order out of chaos. Creativity inevitably involves uncertainty and choice. Individuals, communities, companies and organisations all operate in a state of flux most of the time. All of it requires creative thought and decision-making. In his book *Swim with the Sharks without Being Eaten Alive* the entrepreneur Harvey Mackay tells all employers:

> *If you discover one of your employees looking at the wall . . . instead of filling out a report, go over and congratulate him or her. They are probably doing the company a lot more good than anything else they could be doing. They're thinking. It's the hardest, most valuable task any person performs.*[3]

Indeed, the human mind thrives on uncertainty. Neuroscientists have discovered that when we deliberately create new habits we create parallel pathways, new connections, even entirely new brain cells that can shift our train of thought onto new, innovative tracks. In fact the more things we try, the more inherently creative we become.

But creativity is not mere self-indulgence, a sense of non-conformity blindly rejecting what has gone before. It involves creating ideas that are both informed and effective. In the arts this means producing something that can bring us aesthetic pleasure; in business it means new products, the reorganisation of a company that results in new opportunities and increased profits; in academic work it means new ideas, concepts and theories, new systems for understanding the world. In this stage we will learn simple methods and techniques to develop these skills. As a result, we will learn to scale the walls we have built to contain our ideas and limit our capacity to wonder.

What is a creative thinker?

In this chapter you will learn. . .

- The 10 key characteristics of all creative thinkers.
- The importance of these for liberating us from the confines of System 1 intuitive thinking.
- The two principles that mark the difference between logical and creative thinking.
- The importance of not being afraid to seem odd or out of step with those around you.
- The extent to which you already think like a creative thinker.

One reason we fail to teach creative thinking in schools and universities may be that up until now there has been no unifying theory and method. Without this it is difficult to know where to start. Despite the many different forms it takes, creative thinking involves two common elements:

1 **Certain personal characteristics**, like a willingness to suspend one's judgement and ask naïve questions, and the courage to think differently;
2 And **skills** that we can all develop as a result of learning certain techniques and methods.

In this chapter we will explore the personal characteristics that all creative thinkers share, while in the remaining chapters of this stage we will learn the techniques and methods through which we can develop our skills.

Personal characteristics

You might wonder why these are so important. The simple answer is that they are the key to liberating ourselves from the confines created by our System 1 thinking with all its overpowering, routine intuitions. As we develop each characteristic we build the means of breaking through the walls that imprison our thinking so that we can do the two things, which we saw in chapter 2 define smart thinking:

1 We can think counterintuitively;
2 And we can think about our thinking (metacognition).

All of us have had those creative moments in our lives when blinding shards of light have lit up an idea that we knew nobody else had thought of. At times like these we escape the walls of our confinement erected by our System 1 thinking. We are able to think creatively using our System 2 thinking.

In what follows you will see that there are 10 key characteristics that will guide your way to becoming a more creative thinker:

The 10 key characteristics

1 Declutter your mind
2 Designing solutions, not finding them
3 Naïve thinking
4 Good at finding problems
5 Look for causes, effects and possible solutions
6 Open to new ideas
7 Suspend your judgement
8 Determined and resourceful
9 The courage to think differently
10 Optimistic

1. Declutter your mind

Creative thinking is a continuous, unbroken process: our ideas are constantly evolving, suddenly appearing in a new form. The quality of our work, therefore, depends upon our metacognition: whether we can think about our thinking and catch our brightest ideas and sharpest insights as and when they occur. For this we need to declutter our minds.

This is, perhaps, the most important thing that creative thinkers do. To lure good thoughts out we need to clear a space for them. Unfortunately, for much of the time our mental space can be full of irrelevant preoccupations that prowl around and hijack our minds: conversations we rehearse over and over again to get them right; imagined slights and confrontations to which we think we must respond; memories of things we have enjoyed and anticipations of those to come that we play endlessly.

And then there is the sheer volume of noise and time we waste on mindless distraction, not least on the Internet. All of this makes it that much harder to stay in touch with ourselves, to be quiet and reflect on what's going on inside, to understand the way our ideas are developing. There is even now a company called **Breather** that offers spaces where you can 'get peace and quiet, on demand'. That there is money to be made from this shows that there is a real demand for a space to think.

For instance. . .

Research suggests that company executives do not spend more than 10 consecutive minutes alone in any working day. As Charles Handy concludes, 'They have not had the time to think, even if they know what to think about and where to start.'[1]

For many of us it takes a lifetime to realise that there is no room for serious thought in such a half-shut, cluttered mind. The thoughts may be there, full of insight and vision, but you can so easily pass through life without even knowing that they are there at all. To let good thoughts come through we must clear a space for them. There must be no irrelevant preoccupations prowling around, hijacking the mind.

- Creative thinking is a continuous, unbroken process.
- The quality of our work depends upon catching our brightest ideas as and when they occur.
- To let good thoughts come through we must clear a space for them.

2. Designing solutions, not finding them

In those education systems that define a teacher's role in terms of simply teaching right answers and certainties, we learn to assume that solutions to problems are *found*, rather than *designed*. They are out there just waiting to be discovered. All we have to do is think logically and critically to reveal them by chipping away those things obscuring them: the inconsistencies in our reasoning, irrelevant arguments and unsupported assumptions. And as we all think in the same linear way, taking the same logical steps from premises to conclusions, the influence of our thinking on the result is neutral. It's just a mere tool.

This model of thinking searches for error. We learn early in our education that the way to succeed and pass exams is to avoid error and exchange enough right answers for marks. Unfortunately, studies show that this encourages us to play it safe. We tend to be intimidated by the fear of failure, of getting it wrong, so we avoid risk and creativity. Instead of thinking for ourselves, we reproduce what we have been told by our authorities, even though it may make no sense to us. We tend to be poor decision-makers, preferring instead to seek out authority and follow its lead.

Solutions are found.	Solutions are designed.
Thinking is a neutral tool.	All thinking is unique.
Judged by our mistakes.	Judged by our successes.
We avoid mistakes.	Mistakes are important for success.
We avoid risk.	We embrace risk.
Don't think for ourselves.	Trust our own ideas.
Avoid creativity.	Creativity is at the heart of thinking.
Poor decision-makers.	Good decision-makers.

But in reality the solutions to problems are *designed*, rather than *found*. They are not out there waiting for us to reveal them through logical and critical reasoning. What's more, our thinking is not neutral in its influence: what we know is shaped by the act of knowing. Only in retrospect, as we look back on the event with a complete account of the connections we have made between ideas, does it seem logical.

What we know is shaped by the act of knowing.

For instance. . .

When John Nash the American mathematician and Nobel Prize-winner discovered embedding theorems in relation to manifolds, he did so long before he had worked out the proof. He always worked backwards: after thinking about a problem he would get an insight, a vision of the solution.[2]

Other mathematicians, like Henri Poincaré, Bernhard Riemann and Norbert Wiener, worked in the same way. But, perhaps, the most remarkable illustration of this visualising process comes from Stephen Hawking, the British cosmologist and theoretical physicist. One biographer observed that, even before the first signs of motor neurone disease, he had 'an astonishing ability to visualise solutions to complex problems, without calculation or experiment'. Later, when equations became difficult to write, he 'concentrated on the geometry of the universe, which he could picture in his mind'.[3]

But, perhaps, the characteristic that marks the clearest difference between the design model and the traditional model is that, rather than fearing failure, we're free to make mistakes as we design solutions to our problems. We're judged not by our failures, but by our successes. Indeed, failed ideas are important steps in the design of successful solutions. If you're not producing failed ideas, you're not getting anywhere.

Two key principles

Nevertheless, even those who have made important breakthroughs using the design model often fail to see the difference. In retrospect, they describe their thinking in terms of assured logical steps taken with a clear view in sight. Yet, in reality, theirs is a messier, often illogical, path to the truth. Many times their insights appear to be stabs in the dark, followed by false dawns and disappointments, until a sudden insight finally lights their way.

Therefore, as you set about using and developing your creative skills be guided by two key principles that mark the difference between the two models of thinking:

1 **We don't have to be right at each step.**
2 **There is no single way of getting to where you want to be.**

Your approach to a problem is likely to be just as effective as anyone else's: there is no single way of getting to the answer. And don't worry if you stumble and hit dead ends; if your attempts seem to go nowhere and you appear to have gone in the wrong direction. This happens to us all: it is all part of probing and clarifying the problem until you see a way of designing the solution. So be patient with yourself. You are in the process of learning how to design solutions, how to cope with uncertainty and how to manage risk confidently. Failure is not to be feared: it is a way of learning about the problem.

3. Naïve thinking

Similarly, allow yourself the confidence to return to the sort of naïve thinking you exhibited as a child, that taking-nothing-for-granted curiosity that so filled our young lives with wide-eyed wonder about everything. Remind yourself that none of the great thinkers, who have pushed back the frontiers of our understanding, have come from those likely to have their thinking dictated by convention, fashion and an eagerness to be like everyone else.

For instance. . .

The innovative heroes of our own age, people like Bill Gates, Richard Branson and Steve Jobs, exhibited exactly the same fearless acceptance that they are likely to be seen as odd, out on a limb, even weird.

As I pointed out in chapter 2, the Ancient Greek philosopher Socrates professed an ignorance of any subject he discussed. This pointed to two of the most important convictions that underscored his philosophical method:

1 that wisdom begins with the recognition of one's own ignorance
2 and the unexamined life is not worth living.

Reading Socrates' famous dialogues leaves you convinced of how important this is for training the mind's eye to see what needs to be seen, but is so often missed. As we have already discovered, Einstein too would ask the most naïve questions that nobody else thought worth asking. His scientific method appeared to depend not on measurements and physical experiments, but on vivid, childlike questions, which could be expressed in words and images, like 'What would it be like to fly alongside a beam of light?'

For instance. . .

It is like an artist who learns to look at familiar objects naïvely, without the usual preconceptions, until they seem strange and alien: until, that is, she begins actually to see them, instead of seeing them the way she has always seen them through conventional lens. A flower is not 'a flower', but a collection of shapes, patches of colour, shade and texture.

Likewise in our thinking, we need to really think about things; ask naïve questions, taking nothing for granted; rather than think as we normally think about them. Like the artist who focuses her senses to see what is actually there, rather than some preconceived notion of what it should look like, the first contact with a problem should leave us with the most vivid impression of what the problem actually is, rather than an idea of the way it is generally understood. As all good detectives know, the solution to many problems is hidden in plain view, which our conventional ideas obscure. So being naïve is the first step in solving them.

4. Good at finding problems

On the other side of the equation, we need to be good at finding problems. The most successful creative thinkers are good at seeing in any situation several interesting questions. A creative entrepreneur sees a problem when nobody else does, and then he is able to see several interesting questions that the problem raises, some of which are likely to yield promising business opportunities.

Nevertheless, these are not just flights of fancy, something dreamt up off the top of his head during an idle moment. They develop out of a thorough analysis of the situation. The sensitivity to problems is one thing, but it must build on a detailed, in-depth understanding.

And even then, once the idea has been developed, this is not the end of it. The idea itself can give rise to new ideas and new opportunities as it adapts to the social and cultural environment. It's worth reminding yourself that our ideas, even the best, are just inventions that can be improved upon.

> **For instance. . .**
>
> Scientific theories are merely invented by scientists to explain observations. As one scientist develops a theory others then see if they can find problems with it and improve upon it.

The same is true of the concepts we create: they are just inventions that we can improve upon. They evolve in response to events and changes in the cultural and social context in which they are used.

> **For instance. . .**
>
> Twenty-five years ago the concept of a telephone meant a heavy object that sat in a fixed spot in a room connected by a cable to a wall. Then it became a small, lightweight, plastic object that we carry in our pocket. From there it evolved into a camera, a texting device and a computer, which we can use to check our bank balance, watch videos, order our shopping and seek out answers to the most arcane questions.

The same goes for all ideas: they can be improved upon. They tend to become less efficient unless they adapt to changing circumstances, and the engine for this is the problems we can find and the solutions we design.

> **For instance. . .**
>
> We have all heard politicians insist on the importance of promoting economic growth as the key economic measure of progress. But you may be one of those people who have felt uncomfortable about this explanation each time you have heard it. At the back of your mind something is telling you that this is not entirely convincing.

So you look for the problem. By asking naïve questions you bring it to the surface: 'How can growth be the best measure, when the earth's resources are already being consumed faster than they can be replenished?' It takes the earth 15 months to regenerate what we use up in 12 months: we are harvesting trees faster than they can regrow; depleting fish stocks faster than they can restock; taking nutrients from the soil faster than they can replenish; and emitting CO_2 faster than nature can absorb it.

Now that you have found the problem you can design a solution. What would be a better measure of progress? Living within the earth's means? Reducing the levels of poverty and hunger? Reducing the threat of climate change? Or, perhaps, some measure of happiness?

For instance. . .

Since 1971 Bhutan has rejected GDP as the only way to measure progress. Instead, it measures progress through the formal principles of gross national happiness (GNH) and the spiritual, physical, social and environmental health of its citizens and natural environment.

5. Look for causes, effects and possible solutions

Once you have the problem, the next step is to look for the causes, effects and solutions. Creative thinkers are constantly asking these sorts of questions about everything they come across. Whenever you read an article, hear a story or find a problem, get into the habit of asking yourself these questions.

1. What is the cause?

The creators of some of the most influential ideas, products, businesses and websites have developed the habit of searching for answers to 'how' and 'why' questions, even when it may involve a subject they know little about.

For instance. . .

You might hear a story on the news about the so-called 'Celibacy syndrome', which reports that the number of single people in Japan has reached a record high; that a 2011 survey revealed that in the 18–34 age group 61 per cent of unmarried men and 34 per cent of unmarried women were not in a romantic relationship, a 10 per cent rise in five years.

Instead of passing this story by with just mild interest, ask yourself why this is and begin to speculate on the possible reasons. Have they lost their interpersonal skills, because they spend too much time on their computers in the virtual world? Is it true in your own country? At this point some people would see a business opportunity.

> ### For instance. . .
>
> Let's say you are interested in the problem of why prisons in almost every country tend to dehumanise prisoners, why it is such a degrading experience, leaving inmates even more alienated from society, when we hope that, among other things, they will come out of prisons less likely to pursue their criminal behaviour.

The first thing you do is analyse the problem to find the possible causes. In this case it seems there are three components:

1 the prisoners themselves, who are likely to be antisocial and aggressive and, therefore, might contribute to an atmosphere of hostility and latent violence;
2 the prison officers, a job which calls for those who have the disposition required to enforce a rigorous, uncompromising regime;
3 and the prison itself with its cold, impersonal, authoritarian structure.

2. What are the effects?

Then look for the effects of problems like this. If we are more alert to the possible causes, we should also be more alert to the effects. Creative thinkers read about new technology, new trends or new government policies and imagine what is likely to be the implications of them.

> ### For instance. . .
>
> Now that we have identified the problem of why prisons seem to be dehumanising and analysed the possible causes, we have to find evidence of the likely effects of each of these. If it were possible, we would run an experiment that would measure the impact of changing each one in turn.

3. What are the solutions?

Once you have done this you can begin to design solutions. One of the main reasons we find this so difficult is that we fail to clarify the problem, leaving the mind free to find patterns of ideas that send us off in the wrong direction. Over the years of its evolution the mind has learnt that it must be quick to recognise a pattern. Yet, important though this has been for our survival, it is a distraction for our thinking about complex problems.

All too often these patterns or structures are the nearest approximations; they are obvious and superficial. By contrast, creative thinkers work hard to reveal clearly the *deep* structure, rather than the *surface* structure. If we always want instant results, our minds will take the easy way out and think with their System 1 intuitions. It's always tempting to believe that we already know all we need to know about a problem, which we define in terms of its surface structure.

> **For instance. . .**
>
> When Galileo argued that the earth spins on its own axis and orbits the sun, this was counterintuitive. Opponents pointed to the superficial evidence that we can't feel the earth spinning and it looks as if the sun goes round the earth.

This leaves us with very limited prospects for discovering more. In contrast, after they have revealed the problem's deep structure, creative thinkers often see the answer immediately. As Louis Pasteur is reported to have said, 'Chance favours only the prepared mind'.[4]

6. Open to new ideas

As you read these descriptions of characteristics, you may come to the conclusion that, although each is distinct from the others, they seem to be describing the same thing. To a large extent you are right, because they all describe a state of mind, in which they are integrated seamlessly.

The willingness of creative thinkers to ask naïve questions is matched by their openness to new ideas. They don't just set out to defend a point of view. Like children, they take nothing for granted and ask questions that others are unwilling to ask. They are not so weighed down with prejudices and preconceptions, so they are less willing to conform to the prevailing view and are more open to different perspectives.

> **For instance. . .**
>
> This might explain why politicians tend not to make the most creative thinkers. They are members of a party that supports them because they conform to a certain ideology, a set of beliefs, convictions and values shared by all other party members that determine not just *what* they think, but *how* they think. They often seem to tackle problems with similar solutions with each generation making the same mistakes as the last.

In contrast, creative thinkers are more willing to think ideas that may be thought to be unthinkable, ideas that may be dismissed as ridiculous. It matters less to them that their ideas are considered odd and they appear to be out of step with others. Evidence shows that those who can extend their thinking beyond the point when they might normally dismiss them as ludicrous or unworkable produce a greater proportion of good ideas. As the English philosopher A.N. Whitehead once said, almost all really new ideas have a certain aspect of foolishness when we first produce them.

Those who can extend their thinking beyond the point when they are dismissed as ludicrous produce a greater proportion of good ideas.

7. Suspend your judgement

To extend our thinking in this way we must generate as many ideas as we can. And to do this we have to learn to suspend our judgement. It's often tempting to pass judgement on an idea and dismiss it, almost as soon as we think of it. Our System 1 thinking is quick to pass judgement. The moment we produce ideas our minds set off in search of established patterns and then instantly pass judgement. Yet, most complex problems need careful reflection and delayed judgement, not instant decisions modelled on established patterns.

If we can suspend our judgement and keep in play the most unlikely ideas, we are more likely to generate creative solutions. Indeed, evidence shows that our best ideas come later in this process, so the longer we can keep the ball in the air, the better our chances of being rewarded with the most surprising insights.

For instance. . .

After reading Hume's account of causation, the German philosopher Immanuel Kant describes how he was awoken from his deep 'dogmatic slumber' and experienced his 'Copernican Revolution'. Instead of immediately dismissing Hume's account, which conflicted with his own, he suspended his judgement. The result was his first significant work, *The Critique of Pure Reason*, one of the most influential works in the history of philosophy.

But there is another important reason for resisting the urge to pass judgement. Coming up with good ideas is a continuous, unbroken process. Ideas, good or bad, breed other ideas. When we think about a problem we may produce an idea that clearly wouldn't work, but it is very likely to produce other ideas out of which solutions are likely to come. They are seeds that will bear fruit.

Our minds process these ideas while we are preoccupied with other things, so that when we return we discover new shape and clarity to our thinking. Therefore, by suspending our judgement and playing devil's advocate, even developing ideas we may not think workable, we are fuelling this creative process:

- To generate as many ideas as we can we must suspend our judgement.
- Our best ideas come later in this process.
- Ideas, good and bad, breed other ideas.
- To develop our higher cognitive abilities we must use them; to use them we must suspend our judgement.

Equally important, like any ability, to develop our higher cognitive abilities to think conceptually and creatively we must use them. But to use them, we must have the opportunity to think and for this we must suspend our judgement: things must be up for grabs. Once we accept something as true, there is nothing more to discuss and, therefore, no opportunity to develop our abilities. No matter how unsettling, learn to hang a question over things you would otherwise take for granted.

Principle
Suspend your judgement – hang a question over things.

8. Determined and resourceful

All of this underscores the importance of keeping constantly in front of your mind one object, one thought or problem, and letting it take over your mind, engrossing it. This means working without a net: without the comforting support of a book or other people's ideas. Solutions may come suddenly, but they are long preparing through a process of careful, sustained work.

It's the sort of active reflection that involves thinking attentively about the same thing many times over. This is not mere repetition; rather it indicates the presence in the mind of one object that takes it over until the mind and all its subconscious activity brings it to fruition in a solution.

For instance. . .

As we saw in chapter 2, when asked how he went about his work Einstein answered, 'I think and think, for months, for years, ninety-nine times the conclusion is false. The hundredth time I am right'.[5] And when Sir Isaac Newton was asked how he discovered the law of gravitation he answered, 'By thinking about it all the time'.[6] He explained, 'I keep the subject constantly in mind before me and wait 'til the first dawnings open slowly, by little and little, into a full and clear light.'[7]

Like Einstein and Newton we need to learn the value of allowing ourselves to become obsessed by an idea, so that it never gives us rest. To find the answer to a complex problem we may need to keep it in our minds for days or weeks on end.

Creative thinkers are simply more determined and resourceful; they have marked tenacity and perseverance. Newton, Einstein, Copernicus, Galileo, Kepler and Darwin; they all had similar obsessive natures. Creative thinkers are unwilling to give up on a problem. They are determined to finish what they have started. They will clear their mental desks and concentrate obsessively on just the one problem, thinking about it all the time.

For instance. . .

One of the best examples of such a determined, obsessive mind doggedly committed to finding an answer was revealed in 1995. The English mathematician Andrew Wiles spent over eight years in near-total secrecy working on a proof for Fermat's Last Theorem, one of the most famous theorems in the history of mathematics. This was first conjectured by Pierre de Fermat in 1637, which then stood for 358 years unproven, despite the work of countless mathematicians.

Confiding only in his wife, Andrew Wiles worked alone for hours every day on a theorem that many thought was impossible to prove. Finally, in 1995, he published the proof. Later he described what he needed to do to find it:

> Leading up to that kind of new idea there has to be a long period of tremendous focus on the problem without any distraction. You have to really think about nothing but that problem – just concentrate on it. Then you stop. Afterwards there seems to be a kind of period of relaxation during which the subconscious appears to take over and it's during that time that some new insight comes.[8]

It is not the speed of thought that matters, but your persistence; that thorough, painstaking determination to get to the bottom of a problem by understanding everything about it. The English philosopher John Stuart Mill attributed everything that he had achieved to this one characteristic:

> that of never accepting half-solutions of difficulties as complete; never abandoning a puzzle, but again and again returning to it until it was cleared up; never allowing obscure corners of a subject to remain unexplored because they did not appear important; never thinking that I perfectly understood any part of a subject until I understood the whole.[9]

There are many similar accounts that tell the same story. It is not the fast System 1 thinking that reveals solutions to the most difficult problems or the brightest insights, but the dogged, determined System 2 thinking that never gives up. One of John Nash's colleagues said of him, 'As he saw the problem get harder and harder, he applied himself more, and more and more . . . he didn't give up even when the problem turned out to be much harder than expected. He put more and more of himself into it.' Another described his 'ferocious, fantastic tenacity'.[10]

9. The courage to think differently

Perhaps the most distinctive feature of all creative thinkers is that they all seem odd in their various ways, out of step with those around them, eccentric, even weird. Yet, undeterred, they are determined to live their life their own way. It was the same for John Nash, Bill Gates and Steve Jobs: they were seen as eccentrics, culturally at odds with things going on around them. Indeed, in On Liberty (1859) John Stuart Mill, himself one of the most eccentric and gifted men of his age, praises the importance of eccentricity in all societies for generating new ideas that challenge the comfortable conventions of each age.

Equally significant, the fear of seeming odd doesn't eclipse their willingness to think differently. Creative thinkers are less inclined to search for the approval of others; they look within themselves for that. Indeed, they realise that being culturally at odds with those around them can often be a very creative situation.

And there is an intriguing explanation for this. Usually we assume that personality influences creativity: if you have a particular personality, you are likely to be creative. But the reverse is likely to be true: the experience of producing novel ideas and having them accepted or rejected seems likely to increase your self-confidence, your willingness to deviate from the norm, your openness to new ideas and naïve questions.

> **The experience of being creative is likely to increase your self-confidence, your willingness to deviate from the norm and your courage to think differently.**

Several studies have revealed that when individuals are encouraged to be more creative they become more confident in dealing with novelty, more playful, more prepared to criticise their own work. Judged by their family and friends, they appear to be more independent, goal-orientated, more determined and willing to make decisions.

For instance. . .

In one study, which compared amateur or semi-professional jazz musicians with a control group of laboratory technicians, the musicians showed more spontaneity; they were more able to generate ideas; they could draw upon a greater breadth of associations between ideas and were more willing to take risks. It seems the emphasis on spontaneity and individual expression in playing jazz, along with the expression of emotions, use of fantasy and lack of inhibition frees their latent creativity.[11]

10. Optimistic

Given all of this, it is not surprising to learn that, even though they may go through periods of self-doubt, creative thinkers have an abiding optimism that they will succeed. To keep this single-minded determination going, while you are at odds with the society in which you live, you have to be able to maintain your confidence that you will eventually find a solution.

But there's more to optimism that just keeping your spirits up, important though this is. Someone who is optimistic can visualise the goal more clearly, like a runner who can visualise the race he wants to run or a high jumper the jump she wants to make. In contrast, a pessimist's visualisation is clouded by the obstacles he sees in the way. It is more difficult for him to see the goal as clearly, so his subconscious drives are not directed at the final goal with the same precision and effectiveness.

> **Someone who is optimistic can visualise the goal more clearly and focus her thinking with more precision.**

1. Pessimists – fear of failure

There is also an important motivational element to optimism. Pessimists tend to be driven by the fear of failure. As a result, they are more cautious: they play it safe; they are reluctant to rely on their own judgement and achieve much less.

2. Optimists – hope for success

In contrast, optimists tend to be driven by the hope for success. As a result, they are more positive and have the confidence to rely upon their own judgements and decisions. Indeed, research shows that optimists generally do better in life, live longer and fulfil more of their ambitions.

> **For instance. . .**
>
> The Mayo Clinic conducted research on more than 1,100 patients over 30 years and discovered that optimists live 19 per cent longer than pessimists. Optimists were less likely to suffer depression and helplessness and were less fatalistic about their health chances. The researchers concluded that a positive mindset helps the mind and body work better and helps us achieve much more.

To some extent this is common sense. If you are driven by the fear of failure, your life is constrained by forces over which you have little influence. You will succeed or fail not by your own reckoning, but by forces and events beyond your control. You become fatalistic as you wait for the next setback around the corner. We are taught to accept this form of motivation at an early age from the tests and examinations we undergo in schools and universities. But we can shake off its influence by integrating these 10 key characteristics within our own pattern of work.

> **Try this. . .**
>
> As a starting point, assess the extent to which you think like a creative thinker by completing the following questionnaire.

Questionnaire – Do I think like a creative thinker?

On a scale of 5, how much do you agree with the following statements?

1 Strongly disagree
2 Disagree
3 Neither disagree nor agree
4 Agree
5 Strongly agree

1 I like to be sure that I have fully completed one stage, before I go on to the next.
2 I always work better if I'm certain that the way I'm working is correct.
3 I don't waste time asking silly, obvious questions.
4 I seem to spend a lot of time worrying about what other people think of me.
5 I don't like working with people who always seem to be uncertain about things.
6 After a while, if I can't figure something out, I move on to something else.
7 I'm often surprised that other people see problems that I don't.
8 I lose concentration; I easily get distracted.
9 I don't see the point of producing masses of ideas, most of which are not going to work anyway.
10 When I evaluate information, I place more importance on the source than on the content.
11 I think you have to have a strong sense of what's realistic, rather than expect things to turn out right all the time.

12 I prefer to work in a team, than on my own.

13 I have to be sure that everything is in its place, neat and tidy.

14 I worry a lot about whether I'm going to make the grade.

15 Some problems just don't interest me as they do other people.

Total: out of 75 = ...

Although not scientific, this will give you a rough guide to where you are in terms of becoming a creative thinker. If you scored below 35, you will already possess some of the key characteristics you need to become a creative thinker. If you scored 36 to 60 your potential as a creative thinker is probably being held back by two or three assumptions which have become an unexamined part of the way you work. If you scored between 61 and 75 you might have told yourself many times that you are simply not creative. Yet you will be surprised by just how creative your can be, if you work on each of these 10 characteristics.

Summary

1 To let good ideas come through we must create a space for them.

2 To solve problems we don't have to be right at every step and there is no single way of getting there.

3 Creative thinkers can suspend their judgements and entertain ideas that may seem unthinkable and ridiculous.

4 They are also determined and resourceful, even obsessive about problems.

5 The experience of being creative is likely to increase your self-confidence and your courage to think differently.

What's next?

The one thing we need to learn from this and other chapters in this stage is that we are all capable of being creative. It's not that we lack imagination or even that we just have less of it. Studies have shown that creativity is not something that is programmed into the DNA of a few gifted people, nor is it determined by our IQ. Indeed, it doesn't even depend upon having certain unique abilities, but on those virtually all of us have. The problem is that we *behave* less imaginatively: we rarely use these abilities, probably because we are never taught or encouraged to do so.

Research has revealed that most of us behave less imaginatively, because we fear the reaction our unconventional ideas might provoke. So we opt for safety and suppress our ideas, and, in time, this becomes a habit. To change this, first we need to develop different characteristics, a creative state of mind, which will give us a better chance of succeeding at creative challenges. Then we can learn simple routine methods we can work through each time we are presented with a problem. This is what we will be doing in the rest of this stage. In the next chapter we will learn simple methods to generate our own original ideas.

How to generate your own ideas

In this chapter you will learn. . .

- How familiarity with a subject can trap our thinking in orthodox patterns and expectations.
- How we can escape these shackles by learning a structured, questioning approach.
- Of the enormous potential of this strategy.
- How to generate ideas by seeing problems from different perspectives and levels.
- How to tackle inductive reasoning psychometric tests.

In the last chapter we found that creative ideas develop out of a thorough analysis of a situation. They are built on a detailed, in-depth understanding, which reveals clearly the *deep* structure, rather than just the *surface* structure. A striking example is Einstein's study of the theories of the electrodynamics of moving bodies. From this he realised that these theories failed to explain certain observations and he began work on what became the special theory of relativity, which he presented in his 1905 paper 'On the Electrodynamics of Moving Bodies'.

However, familiarity with a field, with its concepts, categories and solutions, can result in an inability to see novel solutions. Our thinking gets trapped in orthodox patterns and expectations. Einstein's paper provides an interesting contrast to this, in that he mentions only five scientists and makes no reference to any other publication. Unlike Einstein, most of us get used to thinking in accepted ways. We build mental barriers, which obstruct the creative process. They limit our abilities to make connections and see beyond our unexamined assumptions and explanations.

For instance. . .

During the inter-war period a German chemist was looking for what we would now describe as an antibiotic. Every evening before he left his laboratory he would set out bacteria in Petri dishes so they could grow during the night ready for him to work on them the next day. But day after day he noticed that many of the bacteria were dead with mould spores on them. He concluded that the spores came from the mould growing in the corners of the laboratory. Therefore he had it thoroughly cleaned and decontaminated, so he could carry on his work.

> Unfortunately he was unable to find a chemical substance that was successful in killing the bacteria. Yet, if he had been able to free himself from the orthodox explanations and expectations of his profession, he might have realised that the mould spores that killed the bacteria might have been a source of the very antibiotic he was looking for. He might then have won the Nobel Prize that later went to Sir Alexander Fleming, who discovered penicillin from similar mould that had destroyed his own cultures of bacteria.[1]

Similar stories could be told about our own lives. Studying a subject at university involves learning to think like those who teach, research and write about it. This involves learning the concepts, the sort of evidence that is used and the types of explanation that are accepted within the subject.

In the same way, an important part of any professional training involves developing an understanding of how people think in that profession. To be a lawyer we must learn to think like a lawyer as we must learn to think like a doctor, teacher, architect, auditor or police officer, if we want to enter any of these professions. We learn certain organised strategies and principles, which seem to define thinking in these professions.

- Studying a subject at university involves learning to think like those who teach it.
- Training for a profession involves learning to think like members of that profession.

In *The Structure of Scientific Revolutions*, T.S. Kuhn describes the same process of immersion within the dominant paradigm that rules a science. This powerful theory sets the basis upon which research is to be conducted, defining its broad assumptions: its goals, the problems to be worked on and the methods to be employed. As Kuhn explains, it answers the sort of fundamental questions that a scientific community depends upon and takes for granted, questions like:

> *What are the fundamental entities of which the universe is composed? How do these interact with each other and with the senses? What questions may legitimately be asked about such entities and what techniques employed in seeking solutions?*[2]

As a result, new ideas and original solutions are rare. Indeed Kuhn argues that

> *cumulative acquisition of novelty is not only rare in fact but improbable in principle . . . Unanticipated novelty, the new discovery, can emerge only to the extent that his (the scientist) anticipations about nature and his instruments prove wrong.*[3]

Indeed, it seems these barriers to creative thinking go beyond the scientist and the scientific community: they have been institutionalised. The essence of novelty is that it is previously unknown; therefore, it is impossible to say in advance what will be successful and what will not. To avoid this problem funding agencies almost seem to demand that research applications specify in advance what will be discovered, thereby guaranteeing that no novelty will be produced. It is significant that Darwin funded his own research, while Einstein's four ground-breaking 1905 papers were written while he was working at the Patent Office in Bern outside universities, none of whom would offer him a post.

Escaping the shackles

So how do we escape these shackles that so restrict the way we think? One answer, as we saw in the last chapter, is to develop the characteristics that will help us think like a creative thinker. There are two underlying approaches to thinking:

1   One welcomes the new and different. Those who adopt this approach are motivated by incompleteness, disharmony and uncertainty. A large number of studies show that a preference for a high level of complexity and asymmetry are reliable indicators of creativity; they stimulate behaviour to solve problems.
2   The other one rejects novelty and seeks to retain the status quo. It shows itself in a preference for neatness, harmony and closure.

Questioning: a structured approach

The other means of escape is to develop the skills you need to think creatively. In business we hear a lot about the importance of 'thinking outside the box', 'blue-sky thinking' and similar clichés, but we learn very little about how exactly we might go about this: how we can look at a problem differently and assemble the ideas we need to find a new and effective way of tackling it.

When anybody tells you to generate your own ideas, they mostly end up just giving you vague, unhelpful advice. They might tell you to, 'Think for yourself' or 'Ask yourself questions', which doesn't tell you exactly what you should do. You might be advised just to lower or remove altogether your inhibitions, as if there is a huge torrent of ideas just waiting to cascade before you, if only you could overcome your fears about appearing to be foolish by saying things that seem naïve.

And yet there is a simple, organised, systematic way in which we can all do this. Indeed, some of us already do it without knowing it. We begin by asking ourselves certain routine trigger questions, through which we assemble ideas we may not otherwise have thought of, but which get us thinking about a different way of solving the problem.

For instance. . .

Most of us who have struggled unsuccessfully to start our car know exactly what we mean by this sort of organised thinking. Well-meaning neighbours and passers-by gather around giving you advice as you vainly try to get the car started. Then the mechanic arrives and you know at once that you're in the presence of a thinking, intelligent brain. He quietly goes over the engine asking questions, testing and eliminating hypotheses until he arrives at the solution. It's clear he is using an ordered series of questions as he gathers information and eliminates one hypothesis after another.

The power of questions

This simple step can generate a wealth of novel ideas that provide the key to solving the most difficult problem. In *The Art of Clear Thinking*[4] Rudolf Flesch reminds us of the extraordinary power of a popular 1950s TV game to negotiate, through a series of questions, the vast territory of possible answers to a problem and come up with the answer we're looking for.

The programme, known as *Twenty Questions* or *Animal, Vegetable, or Mineral*, would set four panellists a problem. To find the answer they would be given between them 20 questions, which could only be answered by yes or no. In most cases, in a surprisingly short time, the answer would be found by a series of well-crafted questions. Why is this so extraordinary? Well, as Flesch reminds us, asked by a perfect player these 20 questions would cover a range of 1,048,576 possible solutions. In other words, in the space of five minutes, the time taken to ask and answer 20 questions, you can narrow it down to one answer in a million.

> Using a set of routine questions you can find that one-in-a-million original idea.

Moreover, this is not just the stuff of TV games. Prior to the computer age, police sketch artists would use the 'Identikit' system to help witnesses put together a likeness of a suspect. The face would be divided up into, say, 10 building blocks: the hairline, forehead, eyes, nose and so on down to the chin. Each would be represented on transparent strips with a variety of options to choose from. Let's say there were 10 hairlines, 10 foreheads, 10 eyes and so on, amounting to a total of 100 transparent slips. Using this it would be possible to create 10 billion different faces, out of which the witness could produce a very close likeness of the suspect quickly. So here you have a problem with 10 billion possible solutions, yet using this simple system, composed of a routine set of questions, it is possible to arrive at a solution in no time at all.

For instance. . .

Let's say you have recently learned that there are plans to build a wind farm near the village in which you live. You need to assemble your ideas and come to a decision whether you support the project, whether you oppose it, or whether you think it should only go ahead after certain changes have been made to the proposal.

To do this you need to generate freely as many ideas as you can, without, at this stage, stopping to critically evaluate them. The first step is to compile a list of questions that you can then work through systematically exploring all the ideas and issues they raise – something like the following:

1 What is the estimated cost?
2 How will it be paid for?
3 Who will own it?
4 What are the likely benefits?
5 How will the local community benefit?
6 How is the decision reached?
7 Who is consulted?

  8 What factors are taken into account?
  9 What does the local community think?
  10 What are the alternatives?

Of course, as you work through the questions others will occur to you, which you could also pursue.

Routine questions

Interestingly, this is what we all do to some extent, consciously or unconsciously. But those who set about it more deliberately are more likely to generate novel ideas. So, the first thing we must do is look carefully at the series of trigger questions we can routinely ask ourselves: a list we can work through systematically.

For instance. . .

If you were a police officer investigating a suspicious death, you might find yourself working through an alphabetical list of routine questions. Each one would remind you to gather evidence on a particular feature of the person who has been found dead.

  1 Age
  2 Build
  3 Clothes
  4 Distinguishing marks
  5 Ethnic origin
  6 Face
  7 Glasses
  8 Hair
  9 Items he or she had with them[5]

Similarly, each subject you study at university will have the same routine list of the most relevant questions to ask of each topic you study. If you are studying history, a well-designed course would teach you not just the facts of history, but how to think like a historian. So the sort of routine questions you would learn to ask might include:

  1 What was the cause of the event?
  2 What was his motive?
  3 Is there sufficient evidence to justify that explanation?
  4 What were the effects?
   4.1 How large?
   4.2 How significant?
   4.3 Who was most affected: individuals, groups, social classes?
   4.4 What type of effects: economic, social, political, intellectual?
  5 Who was involved: social classes, individuals, groups (religious, professional, military)?

If you are studying literature, you no doubt ask questions about the possible influences on a writer's work, comparisons with other writers and questions on plots, atmosphere and background, common themes, characters, style, dialogue, pace, suspense, humour, tragedy, and so on. The point is that for every subject and profession there is a routine set of trigger questions that we use to generate and marshal our ideas – things we routinely look for.

Compiling a trigger list

Most creative thinkers are constantly refining and adapting these questions, adding new ones they might hear elsewhere. Those whom we describe as geniuses, who solve problems by seeing something no one else can see, come to their solutions in exactly this way. They ask questions nobody else asks. They approach the problem from a different direction with different classifications.

> Genius: someone who asks questions nobody else asks.

In chapter 6 we saw the way in which William James and Carl Jung invented new categories and asked novel questions using concepts like 'tough-minded and tender-minded' and 'introverts and extroverts' respectively to open up new ways of looking at problems and new ways of explaining all sorts of behaviour. We also saw how the researchers at Cornell University opened up new avenues of research by asking unexpected questions about the attitudes of hotel guests.

> ### Try this. . .
>
> List the 10 most useful questions that you could use routinely in your own subject or profession to generate novel ideas of your own that will help you solve a problem.

Then, as you use it every day, be alert to every new question and classification you think might be useful or you hear others use, and add them to your list. Collect them like an avid stamp collector collects new and rare stamps. They are the generators of your most inventive ideas, those that nobody else is likely to have.

So what sort of questions should you expect to find on your trigger list? Although the following are not specific to any particular subject or profession, you will probably find some of your questions take a similar form.

1 What do we mean by X?
2 Why did that happen?
3 What is the connection between A and B?
4 How do we know that?
5 What evidence have we got for that claim? Is it reliable?
6 If that's the case, what follows?

7   How is it that A is the case when B is or is not the case? Is there an inconsistency?
8   What other examples are there for this sort of thing happening? Are there grounds here for a general rule?
9   What is the history, the background, to this?
10   Is it something quite unique, or has it developed out of something else?

As you work with your own trigger list, it helps to keep in mind four useful rules:

Trigger list – four rules

1   Generate as many questions as possible.
2   Make them as clear and specific as you can.
3   Collect new, interesting questions and add them to your list.
4   Pursue them as far as they will go.

Try this. . .

Many parents place intense pressure on their children from an early age to do well in competitive sports. They can be found on touchlines watching their children play football, abusing referees and coaches, and shouting at their children. There is a heavy weight of expectation on children, who may be desperate not to let their parents down. All authorities agree that this is not good for the child or for competitive sports in general. What can be done?

Devise a list of 10 questions that you think need to be asked in order to generate the ideas you need to design a solution to this problem.

Answer

Of course, there is no one answer to this. You are bound to have different questions than I have, many of them a lot more perceptive than mine. Some of mine, you'll see, lead onto other sub-questions that go into more detail or cover aspects that might not be covered by my original question.

1   Why do parents place so much importance on winning these matches? Is this sort of amateur sport becoming more competitive at all levels, if so what are the reasons?
2   What effect does it have on the child of the parent, who is shouting?
3   Does this discourage other parents from letting their children take part in organised football?
4   Does it discourage officials and those who might volunteer to become officials?
5   What impact does it have on other children playing in the match?
6   What do other parents watching the match think about this?
7   Is this type of behaviour becoming more common in all areas of life? If it is, why is this the case? What are the general causes for it?
8   Does this sort of behaviour occur at all sorts of football matches, including friendly matches in which there is no trophy or championship title at stake?

9 Does this sort of behaviour occur when the officiating is particularly poor, or does it occur more generally?

10 Are the comments directed at both the children and the officials equally, or does one receive more abuse than the other?

Try this. . .

Once you have devised your list take each of your questions in turn and answer it as fully as you can, taking brief notes. Use a mind map or pattern notes of your own design, whichever helps you record your ideas as fast as you generate them. Note your ideas in single words or short phrases.

If an idea comes to you out of sequence concerning another issue, note it. The mind works much faster than you can write, so the secret is to keep up with it and not allow your note-taking to put a brake on it. You want to catch every idea and insight your mind throws up, every connection it makes with other ideas. Don't tell yourself that you will list the idea or connection later, when you have a moment. The rich insights that the mind throws up rarely come again, so don't waste them.

You may come across concepts that you use to describe the issues. At this point ask yourself whether it might be useful to analyse the concept, so you can reveal its hidden implications. Almost always this is a very worthwhile thing to do, developing your pattern of ideas into a complex structure that allows you to catch even more subtle ideas.

The rich insights that the mind throws up rarely come again, so don't waste them.

As you can see by now, the reason this works is that we routinely remind ourselves to ask questions that we might otherwise forget or assume are irrelevant. As we work on one problem after another our minds register those ideas that helped solve problems and those that didn't. They then adapt by creating preferences for those that seem to work with shortcuts to them. This then becomes a self-fulfilling process: the more we use them the more we train our minds to believe that these are the best ideas and strategies to solve our problems, and the more we believe this the more we use them.

Of course, our minds then begin to filter information that doesn't neatly fit into these, discarding it as irrelevant. As a result, we are completely unaware that it exists, along with the possible solutions it might suggest. We go about our work probing the problem with our familiar strategies and get nowhere. To escape from this we need to remind ourselves that there are other ideas out there that could provide a solution. And this is what the trigger questions do. By routinely asking them we are reminding ourselves of the wealth of ideas and strategies for solving problems that lie beyond our familiar responses.

- Our minds register those ideas that helped solve problems and those that didn't.
- They adapt by creating preferences for those that seem to work with shortcuts to them.
- This is a self-fulfilling process: the more we use them the more we believe these are the only strategies to solve our problems.

- We filter information so that we are unaware of the existence of other ideas.
- Routine trigger questions remind us that there is a wealth of ideas beyond our familiar responses.

Exploring different perspectives on different levels

1. Perspectives

But that's not all there is to it. As we've said, creative thinkers take one further step: they invent new questions to open up perspectives others have not seen. And there is a simple method we can learn to do this that will get us thinking outside our own limited perspective.

For instance. . .

In the Cornell research it was counterintuitive to believe there are actually such people as 'dissatisfied stayers' and 'satisfied switchers', who would do something against their interests. Not until we change perspectives are we likely even to be aware of counterintuitive ideas.

Unfortunately, our routine patterns of thought and behaviour leave us blinkered to these other perspectives, which may yield ideas and insights that hold the key to a solution. This can have a serious impact on our performance in our academic work and in our profession.

For instance. . .

A teacher who can no longer see how difficult it is for his students to understand a topic in the way he presents it is unlikely to get the best out of them. A business person who goes into negotiations with a customer unable to put herself in the other side's position is going to find it difficult to get the business.

For instance. . .

Edward de Bono argues that when western business people first started doing business with Japanese companies they were confused about what was going on in their negotiations. To the Japanese executives the information and values that were expressed were put forward not as the basis for argument, but as inputs, which gradually came together to form an outcome or decision.

The western business executives were confused by this because they deal in arguments and propositions first and these determine what's relevant to discuss. They complained that at a meeting the Japanese executives would seem to hold back and make no proposals at all. But the Japanese were not holding back; they simply didn't have a position or an idea at that stage; these emerged only later.

The ability to empathise with others by placing yourself in their position and vicariously experiencing their feelings, anxieties, hopes and fears is an important part of some subjects and professions. In most humanities and social sciences the ability to enter the lives of others and predict what would be a reasonable assumption or behaviour from their point of view is the first step in crafting a convincing explanation. Indeed, more generally, the empathy we display, for example in our addiction to reading novels, is important for the moral health of society: it produces people who are more curious about the experience of others.

Similarly, in some professions, like nursing and social work, learning to change perspectives in this way so you can see more clearly the situation from your client's or patient's perspective is an important part of the job. In business education modern stakeholder analysis involves thinking about a problem or situation by placing yourself imaginatively in the position of each stakeholder who affects or is affected by the decision you make: employees, customers, suppliers and shareholders. Failure to do this can lead to poor decisions.

Try this. . .

Football parents

Now that we have brainstormed the 10 questions we listed, we must think about the problem from the perspective of all of those that affect and are affected by it. So compile a list of those perspectives you think ought to be included.

This will include not just those directly affected, like a parent who is shouting from the sidelines and his child who is playing, but those who are indirectly affected too, like parents and children who may be thinking of joining a team. Our aim is to brainstorm the problem from each of these perspectives, adding these ideas to the structure of notes we compiled from answering our trigger questions.

Answer

1 Shouting parents
2 Their children on the pitch
3 Other parents of children on the pitch
4 Their children
5 Spectators
6 Officials
7 Those considering whether or not to volunteer as an official
8 Coaches
9 Those thinking of volunteering as a coach
10 Children and parents who may be thinking of joining a team

---

Try this. . .

Now, taking each perspective in turn, list the different ways in which they affected, or were affected by, the problem. Start with one perspective and brainstorm your ideas, then move to another. Work in the same way as you did with the trigger questions, using a mind map or pattern notes. Noting your ideas in single words or short phrases will help you catch them all.

Once you have completed this, you will have two structures: one containing your ideas generated in response to your trigger questions and the other representing each perspective. At this point you need to marry the two. With some problems the issues raised by your trigger questions will be the main focus, so you will need to feed in the perspectives that are relevant to these. With other problems, particularly moral problems, it will be the people who are involved, so you will have to feed into this structure the relevant ideas you have generated from your trigger questions.

2. Levels

Now you have in front of you a complex network of interrelated ideas and insights that you probably never dreamt of when you set out to address this problem. Yet, there is still one further step to take: to think about this problem from these different perspectives or issues, whichever is your main focus, but on different levels. If you regularly get good marks in your academic work, you probably already do this to some extent, but, perhaps, not in a structured way with a set of tasks to work through systematically. This will release you from the bonds of orthodox thinking, allowing you to see things that others will certainly miss.

Yet the value of this extends beyond your academic work to your employability skills. Traditionally, professionals, like doctors and accountants, worked in one-to-one relationships with their clients, engaged in relatively simple activities, and this shaped our concept of professional skills and responsibilities. But today we live in much more integrated societies where professionals, like doctors, play an important role in a complex pattern of interrelations. Their influence is felt on different levels:

1 The individual level (biological, psychological, moral, intellectual);
2 The physical level (material needs, transport, climate, food and shelter, and the environment);
3 The social level (cultural, political, economic).

For instance. . .

In chapter 5 we discussed how the role of a local doctor has changed. Today she is not just responsible for her patients individually, but for the prevention of illness generally in the community by promoting healthier lifestyles, even influencing planning decisions that might adversely affect the environment in which her patients live. She is, therefore, publicly accountable for the values she promotes, which have a significant impact in redesigning our communities. Her responsibility is not just for her individual patients, but for the whole community.

The effects of our decisions are felt not just on the individual level as they affect particular self-interests, but on the values and well-being of society and the physical conditions of life in our communities.

For instance. . .

A decision to invest in a new manufacturing plant not only improves the lives of individuals by creating jobs, but has an impact on the local community by increasing the demand on local shops and businesses. The local council might need to invest in new schools and roads to relieve traffic congestion. The environment might be affected as local residents suffer noise and air pollution. Wider still, it may have an impact on the national economy and even climate change.

However, despite the apparent complexity of this, no matter what your business or profession or what subject you are studying at university, it is not difficult to think in this way routinely. Once you have answered all your trigger questions and explored them from different perspectives, think about each one on the different levels:

Levels	
Physical	1. Material needs 2. Transport 3. Climate, etc.
Individual	1. Biological 2. Psychological 3. Moral 4. Intellectual
Social	1. Cultural 2. Political 3. Economic

Try this. . .

Why do parents place so much importance on winning these matches?

Earlier we compiled a list of questions to work through systematically. For this exercise, let's take just one of these questions; why do parents place so much importance on winning these matches? After brainstorming this as one of our trigger questions and then generating ideas from the perspective of the parent shouting from the sideline, now we need to explore what we have on the three levels to see what additional insights this generates.

Answer

1. Physical:

1.1 Material:

1.1.1 Parents may have read stories of other children being taken on by professional football clubs, so the prospect of their child making it to the professional level increases the intensity of their involvement.

1.1.2 In an era when top professionals earn more in a week than parents can earn in a decade the dreams of such material wealth can be overwhelming.

2. Individual:

2.1 Psychological:

2.1.1 Some parents might be unused to allowing their children to make their own decisions, so they shout instructions from the sidelines. Yet decision-making is a key part of the game and essential to growing up, bringing with it self-esteem.

2.1.2 For some parents, who suffer from a build-up of latent aggression and frustration in other areas of their lives, this may be their only opportunity to release this.

2.1.3 For many parents their children's achievements at football are an important element of their own self-esteem. They are living their lives through their children, who, they hope, will achieve what they were unable to achieve.

2.2 Intellectual:

2.2.1 From watching matches on TV it is easy to assume that you know as much about the game and coaching as the professionals.

2.3 Moral:

2.3.1 Parents are conscious of the heavy responsibility they have to push their children as much as possible to get the most out of their talent and ensure that they don't waste it.

3. Social:

3.1 Cultural:

3.1.1 By promoting materialism and consumerism the commercial media has had the effect of legitimising wealth and the accumulation of possessions as the only criterion of success. So, with competitive sport at all levels it is no longer just about having fun, but, above all, about winning.

3.1.2 The extensive TV coverage of football seems to have convinced many parents that football is the most viable means for their children to get on in the world and be comfortably well off.

3.2 Economic:

3.2.1 It can be expensive in terms of both time and money transporting children to venues far from home, so it is easy for parents to feel frustrated if they believe their children are not trying or not working at their game as much as they should.

A powerful ideas generator

Of course, not all of these levels will be relevant for each perspective and for each problem, but a routine that gets us to explore them before we reject an idea makes it less likely that we will miss important counterintuitive ideas.

As you can see from this, here you have a very powerful ideas generator at your fingertips. In this exercise we have taken just one question from our 10 and just one perspective. For each of your 10 trigger questions you have different perspectives. Then for each of these you have three different levels, each of which is subdivided further. So from a comparatively simple set of questions you can generate not just hundreds, but thousands of ideas.

Psychometric problems

Our ability to generate ideas in this way is usually assessed by inductive reasoning problems. These come in different forms, but they all assess our ability to draw reliable inferences. In the following version you are given conclusions that are the result of a completed process of reasoning. In other words, you start at the end of the process we have examined in this chapter and work backwards to find the question or questions that were not asked when the ideas were generated.

> **For instance. . .**
>
> Recent research reveals that those who receive private medical care are in better health than those who don't. It's clear from this that the best way of ensuring a healthier society is to increase our investment in private hospitals and clinics, while encouraging greater numbers to take out medical insurance.

Answer

This argument suggests that there may be a causal relationship between private medical care and healthier people. But the question that hasn't been asked is what other causes there might be that would be the cause of both things: in this case the socio-economic status of those who can afford private medical care. This may be the underlying cause of the other two in that those who are better off benefit from a healthier lifestyle, including not just better medical care, but a healthier diet, membership of fitness clubs, better working conditions and so on.

> **Try this. . .**
>
> **What question or questions would you need to ask before you were able to safely draw the following conclusions?**
>
> 1 Citing official data from different parts of the country showing that men are responsible for twice as many fatal car accidents as women, a reporter concluded that women drivers are twice as safe as men.

2 You are an attorney defending a man who has been charged with shoplifting. The prosecution's case largely rests on a photograph alleged to show him caught in the act.

3 Last year's crime statistics for two boroughs in London show that in one reported rapes increased by over 20 per cent, whereas in the other they remained broadly the same. The press are describing this as an example of crime running out of control in the first borough.

4 A pilot attributed the successful completion of a hazardous mission to the mascot he was carrying.

Summary

1 No matter what our subject or profession, we all become trapped by the accepted ways of thinking within it.

2 By using trigger questions we can release an avalanche of ideas that would not otherwise have occurred to us.

3 By exploring these ideas from different perspectives we can think outside our limited framework to ask counterintuitive questions we would have dismissed as unthinkable.

4 Thinking about these ideas on different levels allows us to see the complex pattern of interrelations between our ideas.

5 This method gives us a very powerful ideas generator we can use routinely to generate thousands of ideas.

What's next?

We began this chapter by focusing on the problem that familiarity with a field often restricts our ability to see novel solutions. Our thinking gets trapped in orthodox patterns and expectations. To escape this we need a style of thinking that is quite different from logical and critical thinking: one that is open, divergent and far less controlled by its own internal laws. In this chapter we have learned how to think divergently using trigger questions, perspectives and levels.

What we end up with is a set of ideas that are much more open, offering us more choices than we are used to. Now we need to structure these ideas in the most effective way. We need to see how they combine and interrelate; how some reinforce each other, while others are irrelevant to the overall issue we need to think about. In the next chapter we will organise these ideas into a structure to reveal their interconnections. Then, in the chapters that follow, we will work with this structure to design the best solution.

Companion website

You will find similar examples of the sort of psychometric problems shown in this chapter on the companion website. www.he.palgrave.com/smart-thinking

How to structure your ideas

In this chapter you will learn. . .

- That representing our ideas in structures is indispensable for solving problems and revealing new meaning.
- How important this is for releasing us from the shackles of dominant ideas.
- The importance of causal analysis for the reflective thinking and practical knowledge of professionals.
- A simple practical method for revealing the causal relations that structure our ideas.
- The sort of psychometric problems that are set to assess the skills we use in causal analysis.

Uncertainty is the crucible of creativity: it is where it all begins. The human mind thrives on it, because it entails choice, the first step in creativity. In contrast, we are taught certainties: fixed habits, order and answers that purport to be right. At this point creativity ends, because it is denied the possibility of choice.

In fact, of course, we live in a world of uncertainties. Out of this we create order. We make connections between ideas, creating structures through which we can make sense of the world. These are our internal representations of the external world, which we store in our memories and use to predict what will happen if we do certain things. They help us interpret the world, to see it as a systematic and largely understandable system. Just imagine the unpredictability of life without them.

For instance. . .

In 1953, at the age of 27, Henry Molaison underwent an operation to cure his epilepsy. Two holes were drilled in the front of his skull and the front half of his hippocampus and most of his amygdala were sucked out. Sadly, the procedure went badly wrong, leaving Henry with no ability to store or retrieve new experiences. He lived the remaining 55 years of his life, until his death in 2008, in the permanent present. Suzanne Corkin, now professor of neuroscience at MIT, spent 46 years working with Henry. They spent many days in each other's company. But for Henry each day was the first time they had met.

Representing our ideas

Losing the ability to structure and retain experiences robbed Henry of much of his ability to interpret and make sense of the world. The more we can represent our ideas in structures, the more meaning we create and the more our imaginations are fired to go further. Indeed, good representation is indispensable to solving problems and understanding more. As Herbert Simon maintains, 'Solving a problem simply means representing it so as to make the solution transparent'.[1]

For instance. . .

The famous American theoretical physicist Richard Feynman observed that different representations of the same physical law can evoke different mental images and trigger new discoveries as a result. Newton was able to discover the law of gravitation because he had previously found a new way of representing the problem – the differential calculus – which others didn't have.[2]

As this makes clear, the way we represent ideas is not just passive. It makes different properties of the same information more accessible. Just try multiplying or dividing using roman numerals.

Try this. . .

Multiply XI by XXXIV. It is very difficult. But now use Arabic numerals (11 by 34) and you can see just how much simpler it is. This probably accounts for how much further advanced the development of mathematics was in early Arabic cultures.

Dominant ideas

Representing our ideas differently can also release us from the shackles of familiar, dominant ideas, which can, as we discovered in the last chapter, leave us blind even to the most obvious solutions. The German chemist who thoroughly cleaned his laboratory of the mould that was killing his bacteria was blind to the obvious truth that this mould was the source of the very antibiotic that he was looking for. Indeed, this is a very common experience.

For instance. . .

Edward de Bono gives us the example of a man who was tired of letting his cat in and out, so he hit upon the idea of making a hole in the door to allow the cat to come and go as it pleased without bothering him. But then he acquired a kitten. As soon as it arrived he cut a second, smaller hole in the door.[3]

The one way of dispelling the power of dominant ideas like this is to generate our own ideas and then structure them to make the dominant idea more obvious. The way we represent ideas makes different properties of the same information more accessible, so the idea that is blocking our progress becomes much clearer.

How do we structure our ideas?

Our aim is to reveal the scaffolding of our thinking, the hierarchy into which our ideas are organised. Using this we can generate different meaning, through which we can find new ideas and new ways of solving problems. We can work with it by testing and adapting it; we can see it from a different perspective, reinterpreting it by concentrating on different parts.

To unravel the deeper meaning in our ideas, we must reveal the connections between them and map out their interrelations. The two most effective ways of doing this are by analysing the conceptual and causal relations between them.

Structuring ideas

1 Conceptual relations
2 Causal relations

---

1. Conceptual relations

In Stage 1 we learned of the immense power of concepts to generate meaning by structuring our ideas. They are our most effective means of interpreting our world, reducing the confusion of life and giving us the capacity to shape our environment. They give us the ability to go beyond the particulars of our world and extend our understanding in ways that would otherwise be impossible. We group all those things that share particular characteristics under one concept, so that each time we use it we bring our understanding gained from the past to bear on the present and to shape the future.

By analysing concepts we can reveal, at the heart of them, the ideas and the structure of their interrelations. Normally when we use a concept we allow one or more of these ideas to dominate our thinking, generating meaning from one particular perspective. But by analysing it, as we did in chapter 5, we are able to see the underlying structure and the alternative ways in which we can interpret and use it.

By starting from a different point with a different idea we can open up new ways of solving problems. In an earlier chapter we saw how Einstein worked to show how we can unlock the latent energy trapped in matter. We can do likewise when we analyse concepts, releasing the meaning lying trapped in their structures.

2. Causal relations

The other method of mapping out the structure of our ideas is to search for the causal relations between them. We all use this method in our academic work and in our professional lives.

> **For instance. . .**
>
> You may be the manager of an organisation that is failing to achieve its efficiency targets, so you want to know why, what is the cause? Similarly, you may want to know what was the cause of the French Revolution, why the levels of unemployment are rising when interest rates are low, or why children in certain ethnic groups do better than others at mathematics.

To answer these questions we need to generate our ideas and then structure them by doing a causal analysis. Then we can look for something that has changed in the environment: in the relations between individuals, within an organisation, or wider still in society and the economy. This will also tell us whether we are looking for a single cause or a pattern of causes.

> **For instance. . .**
>
> An estate agent might experience a sudden fall in the number of enquiries he is getting. Properties that were being sold within a few weeks of going on the market might now be taking months to sell. The first thing he must do, therefore, is map out the factors in the market that influence buyers' decisions.
>
> He may discover a single local cause. There may be lay-offs in a few local businesses. Hearing about them one by one, he may have underestimated the total number. Or he may see a pattern of causes all reinforcing each other: an increase in interest rates may have been compounded by a rise in food and utilities costs and by tighter regulations on mortgages.

Once he has mapped out the causal pattern he will be in a much better position to design an effective solution. He will certainly be less likely to fall back on a pattern of behaviour that has worked in the past, but may no longer indicate the most effective response in these changing circumstances.

Complex decision-making of this kind calls for a different type of thinking than routine pattern compliance. It involves analysing the pattern and evaluating the relations between the ideas it represents. In this way we identify and eliminate false and misleading inferences and assumptions. Then we can use the pattern to find a solution to the problem.

- We all use causal analysis to structure our ideas.
- We need to structure ideas to see whether the problem is the result of a single cause or a pattern of causes.
- We can then more easily avoid the temptation of falling back on a familiar pattern of behaviour, which is no longer effective.
- In this way we can also avoid false or misleading inferences and assumptions.

Revealing and adapting our causal patterns – a practical method

There are simple steps we can take to identify the pattern of causal relations in any problem situation, similar to those we learned in chapter 4.

Revealing and adapting our causal relations

1 Lay out a complete account
2 Revealing the hierarchy
3 Testing and eliminating
4 Convergences and divergences
5 Hypotheses

1. Lay out a complete account

The first thing to do is lay out as complete an account as you can of the key ideas as you see them. In the last chapter we did this by brainstorming our ideas in response to our trigger questions and then from the different perspectives of those involved and on different levels.

Often we take it for granted that we are aware of everything, so we see no point in doing this. Consequently, we not only miss obvious things, but fail to register possible solutions and questions we need to ask. Setting our ideas down, as we did in the last chapter, often reveals for the first time interpretations that we have never considered. Things simply jump out at us because they are no longer obscured by the veil of our routine thinking.

2. Revealing the hierarchy

Along with the ideas, you will, of course, also begin to map out the relations between them. In the last chapter we did this in the form of a mind map or pattern notes. Your structure will reveal itself as a hierarchy with some ideas playing a more important role than others.

1 Some will be deductions from more fundamental beliefs.
2 Others will perform a supporting role as evidence or illustration.
3 The same will be true of your preferences, interests and values: some you may regard as non-overridable and beyond compromise.

3. Testing and eliminating

Once we have mapped out the relations between our ideas we need to test them to make sure they are all consistent. You are likely to find that some of them conflict.

1 When beliefs conflict it indicates that our understanding of the situation is inconsistent and we need to review it.
2 When preferences and values conflict it means that we must consider again the relative importance we attach to them. To hold one value as non-overridable might

mean that we will have to be prepared to compromise on another. Similarly, it may become clear that we can no longer satisfy two conflicting preferences and interests.

Testing the relations between our ideas and eliminating some things in this way makes the structure clearer and simpler. As a result, it is easier to see the decisions we need to take. We begin to see not just how our ideas are organised, but ways in which we can adapt the structure to find different solutions to the problem we're trying to solve.

4. Convergences and divergences

Some of the problems we have to solve involve moral issues: how to maximise the preferences, interests, needs and values of those involved. Others involve causal explanations: why did something happen; what was the cause?

Try this. . .

In 1847, at the renowned General Hospital in Vienna, the largest teaching hospital in Europe, Ignaz Semmelweis, a 28-year-old assistant professor, was facing the most serious challenge of his life. Within the hospital, deaths among women in labour from puerperal, or childbed fever had reached unprecedented levels and nobody had any idea how to cure or control it. After women had given birth, inflammation would develop all over the abdomen, so leaches would be applied. Later, when high fever developed, they would resort to bloodletting. Finally, when the patient turned delirious, leather belts would be applied to restrain her.

Conventional wisdom maintained that the fever was the result of two possible causes: external and internal. The external cause was a prevailing miasma that hung over the hospital. This explained the high death rate in the hospital compared with those who had their labour at home. The internal cause was the accumulation of milk in the body, instead of being discharged through the breast or uterus, resulting in milk peritonitis.

But neither explanation fitted the facts. Women who were not pregnant also developed the fever. One of Semmelweis' patients, who came in to have a tumour removed from the neck of her womb, developed the fever and died. And in the doctors' division of the hospital five times as many women died from it as in the midwives' division. It was impossible to see how a miasma settling over the whole hospital could have such a different effect on the two divisions.

If you were in Semmelweis' position knowing the facts that he did and without the benefits of hindsight, where would you start and how would you get from the facts to a hypothesis that will explain them? Remember, you know very little about microbiology or bacterial medicine. So anything could be relevant.

1 What facts would you look for?
2 What sort of pattern would you impose on those facts? Facts on their own don't suggest theories, so we have to process them, creating a structure that will explain and solve the problem.

Professional investigators start by searching for convergences and divergences in what they know to see if they can identify a pattern from which they might be able to form a hypothesis, which they can then test. A detective investigating a criminal case will look for commonalities in the evidence that link ideas. Semmelweis did the same.

4.1 Convergences

However, first we need to be sure about what we mean by convergences. They come in different forms:

1 Reinforcing – the strongest is found when two events occur, both suggesting one cause. They may provide evidence that supports a particular interpretation.
2 Complementary – we are also likely to find examples of two things that are complementary: one cannot be present without the other. You may find that if A is to be true, there must also be B.
3 Supplementary – although weaker, still useful are those things that converge by virtue of being supplementary to a more significant idea: they might support or illustrate it.

Convergences

1 Reinforcing
2 Complementary
3 Supplementary

4.2 Divergences

As for divergences, these are often easier to find. They can also be used rather differently from the way we use convergences. Like convergences, they can be the source of hypotheses, but they are perhaps more often used to test the hypotheses that we formulate from convergences. They are useful in narrowing down the possibilities.

Try this. . .

Now that you have the information that Semmelweis had, think about how you will create connections between your ideas to build a structure that would allow you to formulate hypotheses that you could test.

Answer

Divergences

In this case the best place to start is with the divergences we can identify. If you analyse the situation carefully, you will see that there are three that are worth looking at:

1 Between the treatment patients received at home and in the hospital;
2 Between the doctors' and the midwives' divisions;
3 And those within the doctors' division itself.

Between the treatment patients received at home and in the hospital

As we know, the incidence of the fever in the hospital was very high, whereas in the home it was rare. Most women knew this and would do all they could to avoid having to enter the hospital. If they had no choice, they would leave their arrival as late as possible. They would wait until their labour started in the streets or in the cab that brought them and then go in to have their babies delivered. This way they would reduce their risk: those who had already started their labour when they went into the hospital hardly ever developed the fever.

Between the doctors' and the midwives' divisions

Semmelweis reasoned that, as those women who were brought into the midwives' division were not subject to the same risks as those in the doctors' division, it couldn't be the miasma, as all the patients, irrespective of the division in which they were treated, were equally subject to that. So he concentrated on the differences between the two divisions to identify those factors that he thought might be the cause.

Starting with the dissimilarities between the ways in which each division was run, he formed hypotheses based on each one and tested them one after the other.

1   The diet was different, so Semmelweis ensured that all patients received the same meals.
2   The position in which the women gave birth was different: in the midwives' division they delivered in the lateral position, whereas in the doctors' division it was in the dorsal position. In future all women were to give birth in the lateral position.
3   In the doctors' division a priest and a bell-ringer would walk through, but not in the midwives' division. So, Semmelweis made them go around the doctors' division.
4   However, the one difference he could do nothing about was that in the doctors' division the students examined the women, but not in the midwives' division. This suggested a possible cause: the students were thought to be clumsier than the nurses.

Unfortunately, there was no decline in the high rate of deaths from the fever in the doctors' division as a result of all these changes.

Within the doctors' division itself

With none of these changes yielding anything, he turned his attention to those differences he could find within the doctors' division. Here he found four that looked interesting:

1   Those women who had a long labour seemed more prone to the fever than those who had a short labour.
2   The number of women who developed the fever was higher in some periods than in others. It had been higher since Professor Klein had taken over the running of the teaching hospital than it had been under his predecessor, Professor Boer.
3   The same was true of those times when Semmelweis was working at the hospital and those when he wasn't. At one point he was dismissed from his post and the number of deaths declined. When he was reinstated the number rose again.
4   The same was true of the foreign students. Professor Klein hated foreigners and barred the students from the ward. This was followed by a fall in the number of deaths.

Divergences
Hospital/home
1. High incidence in hospital/low at home. 2. Low among those starting labour in the street.
Doctors/midwives
1. Diet 2. Delivery position 3. Priest and bell-ringer 4. Students' examinations
Within the doctors' division
1. Long v short labour 2. Boer's time v Klein's 3. Periods of Semmelweis working v dismissed 4. Period when the students were barred

Convergences

As for the convergences these were more a matter of interpretation. When you look at the facts so far assembled you may see more than one. But perhaps the most obvious is that many of the facts seem to converge on the impact of the examinations of the women and in particular the students' examinations. Here it is possible to identify five facts that converge on this:

1　It was the doctors' division, where examinations were done regularly as part of the teaching function of the hospital, which had the high incidence of deaths from the fever.
2　A woman would be more likely to develop the fever the longer she was in labour; and the longer she was in labour the more opportunity there would be to examine her.
3　The women appeared to go down with the fever in the order in which they were examined.
4　Semmelweis and the students did most of the examinations and when they were both absent the incidence of deaths fell.
5　When Professor Klein took over from Professor Boer the number of deaths increased. Professor Klein taught students using actual patients, whereas his predecessor used a wooden model.

Convergences
1. Doctors' division – high incidence 2. Long labour therefore more examinations 3. Developed in order of examination 4. Semmelweis and students did most examinations 5. Klein taught using actual patients v Boer didn't

On the next page you can see the structure that we have been able to create from this process of identifying convergences and divergences.

Convergences/Divergences

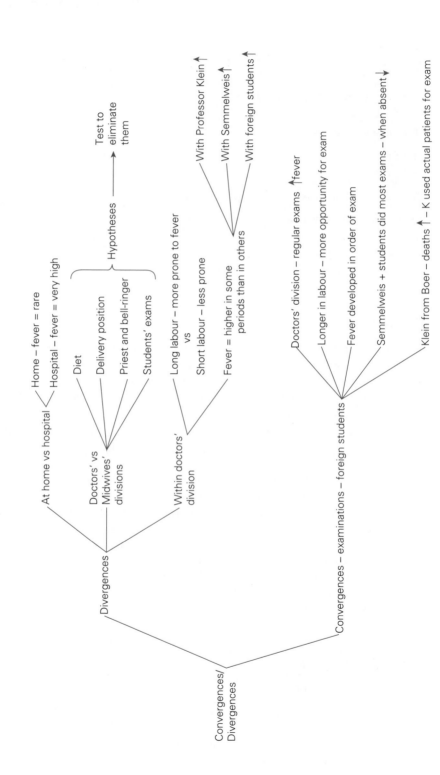

Convergences/
Divergences

Divergences

At home vs hospital ⎰ Home – fever = rare
⎱ Hospital – fever = very high

Doctors' vs
Midwives'
divisions
⎰ Diet
⎰ Delivery position
⎱ Priest and bell-ringer
⎱ Students' exams ⎱ Hypotheses → Test to eliminate them

Within doctors'
division
⎰ Long labour – more prone to fever
⎱ vs
⎱ Short labour – less prone

Fever = higher in some
periods than in others

Convergences – examinations – foreign students
⎰ With Professor Klein ↑
⎰ With Semmelweis ↑
⎱ With foreign students ↑

Doctors' division – regular exams ↑fever
Longer in labour – more opportunity for exam
Fever developed in order of exam
Semmelweis + students did most exams – when absent ↓
Klein from Boer – deaths ↑ – K used actual patients for exam

5. Hypotheses

The process of finding a workable hypothesis that explains why something has happened involves three stages:

1 Formation
2 Testing
3 Adapting

Each of these may take place rapidly. A hypothesis may be formed, tested, adapted and finally discarded, if it doesn't work, in a matter of minutes. Indeed this rapid sequential framing and evaluation of hypotheses is not unlike the work of scientists as they do their early probing before they settle on a theory. Although much of his work was characterised by careful, patient collection of data, rather than being theory directed, Darwin still confessed that he could not resist forming a hypothesis on every subject.

Try this. . .

Having seen all the convergences and divergences, what hypotheses can you generate to explain the high incidence of puerperal fever in the doctors' division compared to the midwives' division? After you have generated one, test it and then adapt it to see if you can produce a workable hypothesis.

Answer

In what follows you can see the way in which Semmelweis probably reasoned, until he found the right answer. This was triggered by a tragic accident, which highlights the relevance of Louis Pasteur's famous insight: 'chance favours only the prepared mind.'[4]

We can interpret these facts in various ways. If it hadn't been for the cases in which women who were not pregnant developed the fever, it might have been reasonable to assume this was a problem associated with labour and childbirth. After all, the women who went through the longest labour seemed to be most susceptible.

However, Semmelweis noticed that the different mortality levels in the two divisions seemed to be complemented by the fact that the women contracted the fever in the order they were examined by the doctors.

Hypothesis: This, then, seems to narrow it down to the examinations as somehow the cause. Those women who arrived too late to be examined seemed to be less at risk, while those who went through a long labour and were examined frequently, were more at risk.

Test: But then this doesn't explain why the fever was less of a problem in the midwives' division, where women would be examined just as often.

Adapt: So, perhaps it was the experience of being examined by men that was somehow the cause?

Test: But then again women who gave birth at home and were examined by male doctors usually had no problem.

Adapt: This suggests that it is something to do with being examined by men in the hospital, which seems to be consistent with the facts that when Semmelweis and the students were not there to examine the women, and during the time of Professor Boer, when they were not examined for teaching purposes, the numbers dying from the fever fell.

Yet, although this takes us closer to the cause, we still have some way to go to find a working hypothesis that would give us a solution. For Semmelweis a tragic accident was to point the way, when his close friend and colleague, Jakob Kolletschka, suffered a puncture wound to his finger from a student's scalpel, while performing an autopsy. Soon after, he died from cadaveric poisoning and Semmelweis realised that this probably came about as a result of a minute particle of putrid organic matter passing into the blood stream.

Hypothesis: This suggested that the doctors and students were infecting patients in the same way by passing cadaveric material into their bloodstream when they were examined each morning by students, who had come straight from the dissecting room, where they had been performing autopsies on those who had died the previous day.

Similarly, it explained why the death rate fell when Semmelweis lost his post and why it did under Professor Boer. Semmelweis was determined to find the cause so he spent more time in the dissecting room little knowing that he himself was an agent of the disease. As for Boer, he did no dissections and, as we've seen, taught on a wooden model rather than by examining the women. It also offers an explanation of why the death rate should decline when the foreign students were barred from the ward: they tended to be more conscientious than the others and examined more often.

Test: To test his theory Semmelweis ordered the students to wash their hands in a solution of chloride of lime before each examination. Within a month deaths had dropped from 12 per cent to 3 per cent, falling below 2 per cent the following month.

On the next page you can find the structure of ideas that we were able to create as a result of this process of hypothesising, testing and adapting.

Hypotheses

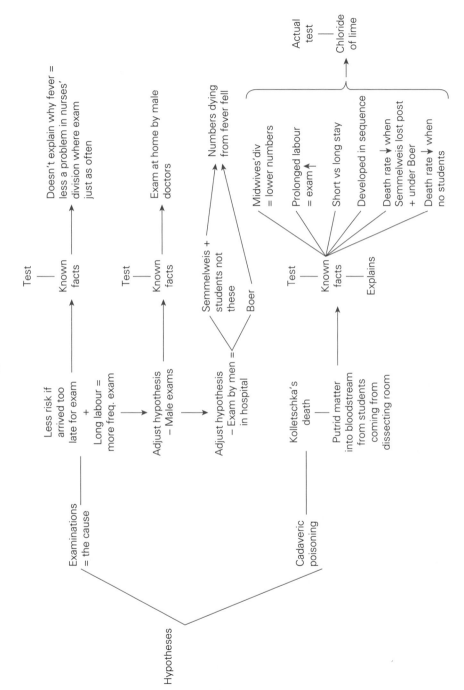

Practising your skills

As you can see, this is an effective method of bridging the gap between the facts and solutions, one that we can easily learn to use routinely. First, like all professional investigators, we reveal the structure into which the ideas we have generated are organised by searching for convergences and divergences. Then we create hypotheses that we can test and adapt until we find the answer. In this way we sever our reliance upon intuitive stabs in the dark. Now, use the following exercise to refine and practise your skills.

> **Try this. . .**
>
> Some years ago in Quebec City in a short period 50 cases of illness occurred all with the same symptoms: nausea, shortness of breath, a cough, stomach pains, loss of weight and a marked blue-grey colouration. This all suggested severe vitamin deficiency, but there were too many cases in too short a time for this to be the explanation. What's more, the post-mortem results on the 20 who had died revealed severe damage to the heart muscle and the liver. Both features were inconsistent with vitamin deficiency.[5]
>
> Although you are probably not medically trained, in general terms what sort of questions would you ask to gather the information you think might be useful?

Now trace the route that the Quebec health inspectors took as they went about their work gathering and analysing information, finding convergences from which they could develop hypotheses and then testing them on divergences, until they found the solution.

Convergences and divergences

1. Convergences

Having mapped out the structure of everything they knew about the case, the health inspectors started to search it for convergences, a commonality between all the sufferers, which might indicate a possible cause. Eventually they found it: all 50 were prodigious beer drinkers, and they habitually drank one particular Canadian brand. So it seemed obvious that it was in some way connected with this beer, which was brewed in both Quebec and Montreal.

2. Divergences – testing hypotheses

First hypothesis – the beer was the cause

This convergence gave them a tentative hypothesis: the cause of the illness was the beer. All of those involved had symptoms that could be accounted for by the consumption of this particular beer. The next stage was to test this hypothesis by looking for a divergence that would falsify it. They soon found it: those who drank the beer brewed in Montreal shared none of the symptoms.

Second hypothesis – it was the brewing process that was the cause

So it now appeared there must be a significant difference in the brewing process at the two plants. And so it proved: the Quebec brewery had added a cobalt compound in order to improve the head of the beer, but the Montreal brewery hadn't. What's more, the compound had been added only a month before the appearance of the first victims and as soon as the brewery stopped using it, no more victims appeared.

Third hypothesis – it was the cobalt compound that was the cause

So another hypothesis appeared: that it was cobalt compound that had caused the illness. This was substantiated a short time later when 64 beer drinkers in Omaha manifested the same combination of symptoms and it was discovered that a local brewery was using the same cobalt compound. When it stopped using it, no more cases appeared.

Nevertheless, the inspectors were still cautious, because the amount of cobalt in the beer was not sufficient to kill a normal person. That it killed so many (30 in Omaha in addition to the 20 in Quebec) seemed to be due to the victims' heavy drinking that had reduced their resistance to the chemical.

As you can see, in this case, as in so many, the solution came from identifying the important convergences and divergences:

Convergences

1. All the victims drank large quantities of beer.
2. All drank one particular brand.
3. Only drinkers of beer were affected.

Divergences

1. While drinkers in Quebec were affected, those in Montreal were not.
2. Moderate drinkers were not affected.

Psychometric problems

To test these skills employers use the same sort of psychometric test as in the last chapter, which assesses our inductive reasoning skills. But there they were used to assess our ability to draw reliable inferences by getting us to work backwards to find the question or questions that were not asked when the ideas were generated.

In this chapter we have learned a method for structuring our ideas so that we can draw hypotheses and then test and adapt them. To test these skills we are given statements made on the basis of a passage. We must choose the one statement that can be safely inferred from statements made in the passage and the connections made between ideas. This mirrors what we did in drawing hypotheses in the cases above. Any inference that goes beyond the information in the passage will be wrong, because it assumes more than the passage gives us.

For instance. . .

Gertrude Stein is credited with labelling the post-First World War generation as the 'lost generation'. Over time, the phrase came to refer in part to the generation of writers who came to literary maturity after the war. Literary scholars have noticed a trend among these writers. The end of the First World War brought about a change in literary consciousness and a definite movement towards modernism in literature, often notable for throwing off the restraints of tradition and conveying an overall sense of emptiness and indifference. Modernism in literature had been developing prior to the war, but was not yet firmly established. Another scholar has also noted an unexpected trend: post-First World War authors produced more fantasy literature than any other generation in history.

   Which of the following may be inferred from the statements made in the passage above?

A.   Post-First World War literature is among the bleakest and most apathetic in all of literary history.
B.   All post-First World War authors rejected the traditions of the past to embrace non-traditional forms of literature.
C.   Literature became the primary outlet of frustrated veterans who experienced the horrors of the First World War.
D.   Relatively few soldiers survived the First World War, and those who did were greatly altered by the experience.
E.   The experiences of the First World War prompted many authors to turn to literary forms that were not as common before the war.[6]

Answer

E. The passage discusses the rise of modern literature and of fantasy literature after the First World War. It also explains that both forms of literature were in existence before the war, although not pervasive. This suggests that the war itself contributed to these forms of literature in which the 'lost generation' chose to write. Answer E best explains this.

   Similar inductive reasoning problems ask you to choose from a list of statements one that most strengthens the conclusions drawn from the passage.

Try this. . .

Studies have shown that men aged 18–27 who have owned a pet for at least two years before marrying are 35 per cent less likely to divorce. Researchers conclude that caring for a pet prepares men for long-term, healthy relationships in marriage.

   Which of the following, if true, most strengthens the conclusion that men who have owned pets are prepared for healthy marriages?

A.   Studies have shown that pet ownership drastically reduces daily stress levels.
B.   Many successful marriages are based on emotional investment in a common interest, such as a pet.

C. Many men who have been married for 25 years or more continue to own pets.
D. Men who have not owned pets for at least two years before marrying are more likely to divorce.
E. Men whose wives owned a pet for at least two years are equally as unlikely to divorce.

You will find the answer on the companion website.

Summary

1 Representing and structuring our ideas differently reveals new meaning in our ideas.

2 To structure our ideas we must map out their connections by analysing their conceptual and causal relations.

3 In causal analysis we search for convergences and divergences to find hypotheses we can test.

4 Using this method we can use our patterns of ideas to help us understand the situation and decide what to do.

5 Using this simple 5-step method we can bridge the gap between facts and solutions.

What next?

We began this chapter by emphasising how important representing and structuring our ideas differently is to revealing new meaning in our ideas. In this way we can find original solutions to problems that might otherwise seem insoluble. Of course, if structuring our ideas in this way doesn't produce a hypothesis that solves the problem, we can always do as we normally do and compare this structure with those which have worked in the past. However, in a rapidly changing, complex world this is not always a reliable option. If it fails, we must either adapt our structure, which we will learn to do in chapter 12, or search for a new way of interpreting our structure, which we will learn to do in the next chapter.

Companion website

You will find similar examples of the sort of psychometric problems shown in this chapter on the companion website. www.he.palgrave.com/smart-thinking

Designing solutions to problems 1: Using analogies

In this chapter you will learn. . .

- That analogies give us new ways of interpreting our structure of ideas.
- That applying an analogy to an unrelated problem allows us to shake off the shackles of routine System 1 thinking.
- That analogies have been the vehicle for important breakthroughs in the history of thought.
- How to find effective analogies.
- How to distinguish between reliable and unreliable analogies.

In chapter 2 we learned that smart thinking has two core elements: metacognition and counterintuitive thinking. The latter involves challenging our normal responses, thinking the unthinkable, generating ideas and making connections between them that we would not otherwise make.

In Stage 1 we discussed the different ways we can do this by creating and analysing concepts, and synthesising ideas. To the same end, in the last two chapters we have learned to generate and structure our ideas; to represent them in different ways, so that we can reveal new ideas and unexpected meaning. This gives us a surprisingly effective way of seeing things differently, new insights and novel ways of solving problems that might have seemed insoluble. In fact it has brought about some of the most significant breakthroughs in our understanding in all fields.

For instance. . .

All the doctors and nurses at the General Hospital in Vienna knew what Semmelweis knew. They all had the same information as he did. But he alone was able to structure his ideas differently, to create a new representation of them, from which he was able to design a solution.

His refusal to accept the conventional wisdom of his day and his ability to think differently was to be the inspiration for the work of Louis Pasteur and the great advances in bacteriology that were to come. Without his courage the development of this field, considered by many to be the greatest single advance in the history of medicine, might never have occurred.

Searching for new ways of interpreting our structure

But now, say our new structure of ideas fails to produce a solution, what then? Well, we have three options:

1 Compare this structure with those which have worked in the past;
2 Adapt our structure;
3 Search for a new way of interpreting our structure.

As we said at the end of the last chapter, in a rapidly changing, complex world the first option is less and less reliable. As for the second, in the next chapter we will look at the various ways we can adapt our structure to design a solution, but before that, in this chapter, we will learn to search for new ways of interpreting our structure, some related to quite different situations.

Analogies

The most common source of these are analogies. Although they are related to quite different problems and different subjects, analogies present structures of ideas that are similar to ours, which we can use to interpret our structure to give us inferences that will solve the problem we're working on. They give us a sufficiently stable structure that we have used before in different circumstances, which is reliable enough for us to conclude that given one event another will follow with high probability. We might conclude from the fact that A, B and C all have characteristics x and y, and A and B in addition have characteristic z, that C too will probably have characteristic z.

> **For instance. . .**
>
> In his general theory of relativity (1915) Einstein argued that gravity was not a force as Newton had maintained in his universal law of gravitation, but the consequence of the distortion of space and time ('space-time'). All objects distort the fabric of space-time; the bigger the object the bigger the effect. This may seem difficult to comprehend; even more difficult if you are Einstein having to come up with the idea in the first place. But then use an analogy and, not only does this give us a way of interpreting our structure of ideas, but it yields inferences that can be tested.
>
> Imagine a bowling ball on a trampoline. What you see is the fabric of the trampoline being distorted by the weight of the bowling ball. Now if you were to roll a marble around the bowling ball it would be drawn towards the ball. With this we can now argue that in the same way the planets and stars warp space-time. In our solar system the Sun distorts space-time and the planets follow the distortion, like the marble around the bowling ball. The reason they never fall into the Sun is because of the speed at which they are travelling.

From an early age, in the form of parables, we learn the power of analogies to explain the most complex ethical problems. Understanding the parable helps us learn how to interpret a structure of ideas and the important ethical message it teaches.

Similarly, much of the scientific progress over the last 350 years has developed out of the use of simple analogies. They have provided models and pictures out of which scientific theories have been constructed, fuelling research and extending our understanding of the world.

> **For instance. . .**
>
> Molecules, atoms and electrons were thought to behave like small, solid balls, like billiard balls, that we can touch, see and observe in motion. Light has been thought of as acting like a wave travelling through an elastic medium. Both analogies have guided scientists in their experiments and in the interpretation of their results in an intelligible way.

Smart thinking and counterintuitive thought

Our ability to identify and use analogies in this way has been the source of many of those moments of blinding insight in the history of thought, when individuals have been able to see the answer to problems that have long held up their progress. Analogies can open up new, fertile avenues of investigation that transform the way we think and explore our world.

To do this we need to develop that fearless habit of mind which allows us to think about ideas and make comparisons that to anyone else might appear absurd and unthinkable. But courage alone is not enough. We also need to develop the skills and habits to think counterintuitively. In chapter 2 we said this involves two things:

1 The ability to detach ourselves from routine patterns of thought and apply seemingly unrelated mental frameworks to the problem.
2 The ability to forget about what we might wish or expect to be the case and focus our attention just on the situation as we have laid it out in our structure of ideas. Unburdened by normal expectations, we are freer to think about the nature of the structure we have created and the similarities it might have with previously unrelated structures, into which all the pieces might fit.

As you can see, both of these entail shaking off the shackles of routine System 1 thinking and getting back to the naïve thinking that filled our childhood with such wonder. Indeed as children we were particularly adept at this. Developmental psychologists have frequently noted that young children develop the ability to think analogically on their own without any help from parents or teachers. It seems that the mind just works this way. Indeed the cognitive scientist Douglas Hofstadter has described it as 'the core of cognition'.[1]

The effectiveness of analogies

When we think analogically we use our ability to distinguish the structure of our ideas from the background and then compare it with unrelated, yet similar, structures. In this way we are able to see things differently. It often produces the most surprising rewards.

Insight and moments of genuine originality can occur in response to a fact that means nothing to others.

For instance. . .

Early in his work Darwin assumed that stability in species was the norm and variety the exception. But this seemed to be at odds with the immense, bewildering variety of species that he saw all around him. If stability were the norm, why was it that species appeared to go on generating even more variety? The competition for survival should restrict this: the more competitive an environment, the more likely it was that a few successful species would dominate. But, now, how was he to explain this?

He found the answer in the analogy of industrial progress that he had seen developing in nineteenth-century Britain. It was clear that fierce competition in overcrowded markets favoured those who could use and adapt their skills to fill niches. The individuals who thrived in these circumstances were those that seized new opportunities and filled niches as they opened. When he looked at crowded markets he saw they were full of all manner of people with different skills, each working next to each other, but not in direct competition.

Nature, he realised, was no different. The same pressure of competition forced species to adapt to fill unoccupied niches. And the greater the functional diversity of species the more an area could support. Indeed, nature was even more efficient at this than industry. Natural selection increased the 'division of labour' among animals who were caught in competitive situations, resulting in the immense variation in species. [2]

So, whenever we try to explain something the most natural thing to do is search for a close analogy. We assume that because things resemble each other in some respects they will continue to resemble each other in a further respect and this gives us our inference. The key to understanding the implications of our structure lies in the way we understand something familiar. By using what we know we can already rely on, analogies give us an invaluable way of extending our knowledge.

For instance. . .

Today, in their more developed forms as models, analogies lie not only at the heart of scientific thinking, but also play a central role in political and business planning. Computer models of the economy, the market or a company's likely performance are little more than very elaborate analogies. Their explanatory power can be quite remarkable. The best can often suggest similarities not envisaged in the original design, which turn out to explain phenomena that has long puzzled researchers.

The effectiveness of this and analogies in general is that they give us a situation that we can handle much more effectively. Whether it is a concrete situation converted into an abstract model or an abstract situation converted into a concrete analogy, either way this conversion gives us the power to change the variables and see the results more clearly. The restrictions placed on our thinking by the original situation are not carried over into the analogy, so we can change things more easily. We can then carry over what we have learned from the analogy into the actual situation and in this way generate new ideas and ways of approaching the problem.

- To make sense of isolated facts and ideas we must create a structure through conceptual and causal analysis.
- Then analogies give us an effective way of interpreting this structure.
- They often produce the most surprising insights, moments of genuine originality.
- By using what we know we can already rely on, they help us extend our knowledge.
- They give us the power to change variables and see the results more clearly.

Try this. . .

To illustrate just how effective analogies can be in throwing new light on a problem consider the following famous example created by the psychologist Karl Duncker:[3]

> Imagine you were a doctor faced with a patient who has an inoperable stomach tumour. You have at your disposal rays that can destroy human tissue when directed with sufficient intensity. At the lower intensity the rays are harmless to healthy tissue, but they do not affect the tumour either. How can you use these rays to destroy the tumour without destroying the surrounding healthy tissue?

Clearly this is a very difficult problem to solve. But say you come across the following story. Does it help?

> A physicist needs to use a laser to fix the filament of a light bulb, but the intensity of the laser that is needed would shatter the fragile glass bulb that surrounds it. So she surrounds the bulb with lasers and sets them on low intensity, such that they converge at the same time on the filament with the combined intensity that's needed to fix the filament.

You probably saw the similarity between the two problems as soon as you read it and in your mind devised a similar solution for the X-ray problem: surround the patient with X-ray machines so that each delivers a low dose of radiation converging on the tumour at the same time. But now say you had come across the following story instead of the light-bulb story. Could you have seen the similarities between it and the X-ray story?

> A fortress surrounded by a moat is connected to land by numerous narrow bridges. An attacking army successfully captures the fortress by sending only a few soldiers across each bridge, converging upon it simultaneously.

In fact, if they have no analogy to work with, only 10 per cent of people solve the X-ray problem using the convergence solution. When they are shown the fortress story first, the success rate increases to 30 per cent. But when they are shown the light-bulb story first, the success rate improves dramatically to 70 per cent.[4] This demonstrates just how effective a good analogy can be.

Finding analogies

Analogies are events or objects that are 'isomorphic': that is, they have structures in common. So finding them involves mapping out the structure of one and then searching for similar structures that will correspond with it. It calls for a selective imagination to identify previously unrelated structures into which all the pieces fit.

Some of the most effective involve the most unlikely comparisons between two things. These can often produce the most surprising rewards. And, indeed, the insights they generate can occur in response to a fact that means nothing to others.

Although this is an art rather than a simple step-by-step process, the following three questions will help you find them:

Three simple questions:

1   Is there a parallel?
2   Does the pattern fit?
3   Would it solve the problem?

1. Is there a parallel?

Obviously the first question we need to ask is whether the two objects or events we are comparing have similar structures. This search for parallel structures, involves simple pattern recognition. It is a fairly common form of reasoning in many subjects and professions.

For instance. . .

In many legal systems one of the most distinctive elements of legal reasoning is the use of precedents. Yet it is just an instance of the larger process of reasoning by analogy.

Comparisons are made between an undecided case and a similar case that has already been decided. Lawyers will apply decisions made in a previous case to one currently under consideration, if they think sufficient similarities exist between the two. Lawyers and judges are constantly involved in making these sorts of comparisons and distinctions between different patterns of ideas, facts and concepts.

But to do this well we have to prepare our minds thoroughly, immersing ourselves in the ideas. The analogies are there for all of us to see, if we can only prepare ourselves to see them. The problem is the mind is not naturally creative; it can only see what we have prepared it to see. Nevertheless, the experience of scientists, like Darwin and Einstein, shows that once you have immersed yourself in the ideas and prepared yourself to see them, the analogies will come. Then, it is just a question of analysing their structures and choosing the best fit.

2. Does the pattern fit?

To answer this question we have to concentrate on two things: the quantity and quality of the similarities. Obviously, if one structure is similar to another in many different ways we feel more confident about the conclusions we draw. But the quality of the similarities is important too: we have to ensure that the analogy establishes credible connections in our experience.

> Concentrate on two things: quantity and quality of similarities

2.1 Quantity

When we search for such connections we are identifying a sufficiently stable pattern in our previous experience, which we think is reliable enough for us to conclude that given one event the other will follow with high probability. The larger the number of As that have been Cs and the fewer As that have not been Cs, the likelier it is that all As will be Cs, and therefore that the next A will be a C.

2.2 Quality

In contrast, the quality of the connection might seem more difficult to pin down. What we are looking for is a credible connection. As we will see later in this chapter, this underlines the important difference between a correlation and a causal connection.

> **For instance. . .**
>
> If we found a correlation between violent crime and the sales of violent films on DVD, we might begin to think there is good chance of a causal connection between the two. But if we found a correlation between the sales of chewing gum and violent crime, we are unlikely to see any real significance in this.

Accidental generalisations

This is what is known as an 'accidental generalisation': there may be many instances of one thing occurring with another, but is this just an accident, a coincidence, or is there likely to be a causal connection between the two?

> **For instance. . .**
>
> We might find that all the cars in a carpark are Fords, but this doesn't mean we can conclude, therefore, that the next car to enter the carpark will also be a Ford. It is only an accidental generalisation. As the philosopher William Kneale famously argued, from the premise that all the men in the next room are playing poker we cannot conclude that, if the Archbishop of Canterbury were in the next room, then he would be playing poker too.

Although in this context it would be tautologous, you could say that there must be something analogous between the two events. In other words, it is not just sufficient to find two structures that are similar in important ways; we must also believe that the connection this suggests will actually produce the result that we are trying to explain.

For instance. . .

Let's say we find that incidents of car accidents are perfectly correlated with two factors:

1 drivers having tattoos;
2 a new braking system.

Unless you have other evidence that allows you to correlate drivers with tattoos to other behaviour that is likely to be the cause, such as drivers with tattoos are more likely to drive under the influence of alcohol or drugs, or that a chemical in the tattoo ink impairs judgement, you are more likely to choose 2 as the cause.

This shows the importance of our prior beliefs in determining what we will accept as a reliable analogy. And, of course, this can lead to biases in our reasoning: we are unlikely to accept an analogy, if we refuse to believe the theory it endorses or find its consequences objectionable.

For instance. . .

Despite overwhelming evidence, the majority of Americans refuse to accept the theory of evolution. According to the 2009 Gallop Poll only four out of 10 accept the theory.[5]

Indeed, ironically, there may be an evolutionary explanation for this. In survival terms it has always been better to err on the side of caution and think conservatively in accordance with accepted beliefs and rules of behaviour that have secured the survival of previous generations. It is better to flee in response to a certain pattern of colour and movement that suggests a predator, than question these beliefs and stay put. You may make a mistake, but you are still alive.

3. Would it solve the problem?

Once we have established that the resemblance between the two structures is more than superficial, we have to ask a third question: would it change our interpretation of the problem, suggesting an alternative way of approaching it? Often when this occurs – when the pattern fits the situation – something clicks; suddenly everything makes sense. It is one of those significant moments in the process of genuine thought.

Afterwards, it appears that the key to the problem was a hidden clue that we just didn't see or didn't take notice of because it seemed quite irrelevant. But in fact it wasn't irrelevant at all. It was just that we were using a different pattern to interpret the ideas. Change the pattern and it becomes relevant.

Identifying unreliable analogies

Unfortunately, not all analogies can be relied upon to organise our ideas into patterns from which we can draw relevant and reliable inferences that will help us solve a problem. The best create causal connections, which give us sound explanations. But we can easily be tempted to adopt an analogy simply for its ability to give us a powerful and persuasive explanation, when there are in fact no relevant and reliable connections to be made.

Vague associations are often the source of error and oversimplification. Many superstitions, myths and rituals began this way and survive because we lack the will to critically evaluate them. Seeing a black cat, we are told, is lucky, presumably because someone, at sometime, saw a black cat and subsequently had good luck. Politicians are always eager to exploit our gullibility by using a graphic analogy on which to hang their argument, even though with a little probing it is not difficult to see that it will bear very little weight.

For instance. . .

When they hold up a bag of purchases in one hand representing how little the pound or dollar will buy now compared with the bag in the other hand representing what could be bought when they were in power, you know that a great deal is missing from the argument.

Why is each item more expensive? Is it the result of reductions in supply or increased production costs, rather than inflation that could be associated with the government? And does the comparison take into account the *real* value of a family's income, not just the *money* value, which could mean that, though the pound or dollar buys less, the average family still has the same or a better standard of living?

The point is not only are analogies effective in creating a vehicle through which we can devise solutions to difficult problems, they are remarkably persuasive too, helping us clarify, simplify and make more vivid a complex idea. In this lies their capacity to mislead. It's worth reminding ourselves that analogies are only a guide: although we use them to *suggest* a conclusion, they are incapable of *establishing* one.

We can only safely argue from one set of characteristics to another when there is a causal connection.

As we discovered earlier in our discussion of accidental generalisations, we still need to test them against the evidence to find the causal connection. We can only safely argue from the possession of one set of characteristics to another when there is a causal connection between them and not just a vivid similarity.

To distinguish between reliable and unreliable analogies it helps if you carefully work through the following checks:

1 the nature of the connection between the analogy and the explanation;
2 the number of similarities involved;
3 the reliability of the relation between the analogy and the conclusion derived from it.

1. Connection

First, concentrate on the sort of connection that it makes. Does it allow us to establish a causal connection with the event we want to explain, or is it just a vivid way of presenting an idea? Earlier we found that on the surface an analogy can be convincing, but the more you probe it the more you realise that it only allows us to establish that there is a *correlation* between two things, not a *causal connection*. In many cases, as in the case of the shopping bags, you will immediately see that the comparison is oversimplified: it leaves too much out to establish a reliable connection.

> ### For instance. . .
>
> Over the last few years there seems to have been an increase in the number of volcanoes, so scientists have been wondering whether there might be 'seasons' in volcanic activity. The four seasons, as we know, are caused by the Earth's axis of rotation tilting towards and away from the sun. But there is another similar change, which might affect the Earth volcanically. Due to factors such as the gravitational pull of the sun and moon, the speed at which the Earth rotates constantly changes. As a result, the length of the day varies from year to year, albeit by just a few milliseconds.
>
> The evidence shows that between 1830 and 2013 relatively large changes in rotation rate were followed by an increase in the number of volcanic eruptions. The question is, are these merely correlations or can we argue that the changes in rotation caused these large eruptions and there really are 'seasons' in volcanic activity?

The second thing we need to ask ourselves about the connection that the analogy makes is when does it break down? They all have a tendency to at some point, even the most reliable, and a good thinker is always looking for the point at which this breakdown occurs. The history of science is littered with analogies that provided the platform for years of research, only for them to break down, forcing researchers to find some other way of explaining their results.

> ### For instance. . .
>
> Newton used the analogy of billiard balls to explain the behaviour of light as particles. Although useful, it reached a point when it became clear that light behaves in ways the analogy could not help us explain. Along with other electromagnetic radiation, it behaves like a wave motion when being propagated and like particles when interacting with matter. So, a conflicting theory appeared, modelled on a different analogy of light as waves travelling through an elastic medium.

2. Numbers

As for numbers, this is more obvious. Up to a point the number of examples we can find that share the same features as the analogy the more confidence we are likely to have in it. The same is true of the number and variety of characteristics shared by the analogy and the actual situation. Are they similar over a range of different characteristics or does the similarity just involve the same type of characteristic? Problems emerge when we place too much weight on an analogy that is similar in only a limited range of characteristics; we tend to ignore the differences and push the similarities beyond what is reasonable.

For instance. . .

The financial crash in 2008 was due to banks making ever more risky mortgage loans in a booming property market. Unfortunately, when this collapsed so did banks, like Lehman Brothers, while others were left teetering on the edge. However, governments decided that these banks were too big to fail, so they bailed them out with taxpayers' money. Understandably, in many quarters this was deeply unpopular, so in the USA the Federal Reserve Chief, Ben Bernanke, appeared on TV to justify his decision, using an analogy.

He explained, say you have an irresponsible neighbour who insists on smoking in bed and sets his house alight. Should you allow him to face the consequences or should you call the fire brigade? What if your house and those in the neighbourhood were all made out of wood? We all agree, he argued, that in these circumstances we should first concentrate on putting the fire out. After that we can see what went wrong and address the issue by rewriting the fire code and putting in place fail safe procedures for anything like this in the future.[6]

You can see why such an analogy would work with the average TV viewer: we all understand the devastation that fires can bring about. The failure of banks would be equally devastating, endangering our money and the possibility of borrowing in the future. But there were many who were not convinced. Indeed, if you Google 'Bernanke burning analogy' you will get over 160,000 hits. At the top of the list is one by Professor Michael Hudson posted on the Centre for Research on Globalization website. He asks, 'What's false about this analogy?'

For starters, banking houses are not in the same neighborhood where most people live. They're the castle on the hill, lording it over the town below. They can burn down and leave the hilltop to revert 'back to nature' rather than having the whole town gaze up at a temple of money that keeps them in debt.

More to the point is the false analogy with US policy. In effect, the Treasury and Fed are not 'putting out a fire'. They're taking over houses that have not burned down, throwing out their homeowners and occupants, and turning the property over to the culprits who 'burned down their own house'. The government is not playing the role of fireman.

'Putting out the fire' would be writing off the debts of the economy – the debts that are 'burning it down'.[7]

As you can see, the analogy only holds for a limited range of similarities and ignores important differences. Now try one yourself.

> **Try this. . .**
>
> In the 1980s, in an effort to persuade us that cuts in government expenditure were unavoidable, some governments seized upon what seemed like a useful analogy telling us that 'The economy is like a household budget' and we were simply spending beyond our means and getting into debt. Can you see any reason why this may be regarded as unreliable?

Answer

One important difference is that what you spend in a household budget doesn't usually generate more income and jobs in the household, whereas in the national economy such investment not only can improve productivity, but can have significant multiplier effects, lifting economic activity, increasing revenue from direct and indirect taxes and reducing welfare costs by taking more people into jobs.

3. Relation to the conclusion

Lastly, we have to be sure that the conclusion drawn from the analogy is of the right strength and takes into account all the significant similarities and differences between the analogy and the situation it helps to explain. Once we have noted these we must decide how significant they are and whether we've overlooked other conditions, which need to be considered to make the analogy safe.

Usually, the greater the number of differences, the weaker is the conclusion. In some cases you will find the most effective of all criticisms is whether you are able to use the very same analogy to argue the opposite case.

> **For instance. . .**
>
> A newspaper account of a speaker at a conference reported, 'He told the Conference last week that football hooliganism was exacerbated by press coverage. This was rather like blaming the Meteorological Office for bad weather.'

It may indeed be true that in many cases newspaper reports had no influence on the activities of football hooligans, but the analogy the report uses differs in such significant and obvious ways as to make the conclusion quite untenable. As you can see, the key difference which weakens the conclusion is that the weather cannot be influenced in its behaviour as football hooligans can by reading press reports of them and their behaviour.

Analogies – evaluation

1 The connection:
   1.1 Does the analogy establish a causal connection or is it just a vivid way of presenting an idea?
   1.2 When does the analogy break down?

2 Numbers:
   2.1 How often, in how many cases, does this similarity hold?
   2.2 How many characteristics are thought to be similar?
   2.3 Are they similar over a range of characteristics or just the same type?

3 Relation to the conclusion
   3.1 Is the conclusion drawn from the analogy the right strength?
   3.2 Can I identify any significant differences between the analogy and the situation it helps to explain?
   3.3 Can I turn it back on itself to argue the opposite?

Try this. . .

Read the following arguments and assess the analogies on which they are based by working your way through the three issues outlined above. You can find the answers on the companion website: www.he.palgrave.com/smart-thinking

1. Recently, an American politician defending nuclear power argued, 'We don't abandon highway systems because bridges and overpasses collapse during earthquakes.'

2. 'Some basic facts about memory are clear. Your short-term memory is like the RAM on a computer: it records the information in front of you right now. Some of what you experience seems to evaporate – like words that go missing when you turn off your computer without hitting SAVE. But other short-term memories go through a molecular process called consolidation: they're downloaded onto the hard drive. These long-term memories, filled with past loves and losses and fears, stay dormant until you call them up.'[8]

3. During the Watergate hearings in the 1970s, the second-in-command at the White House, John Ehrlichman, used two analogies to explain why he thought it was appropriate to burgle the offices of the psychiatrist who was treating Daniel Ellsberg, the Pentagon consultant who released the Pentagon Papers to the press. Clearly they were after something they could use to discredit, or even blackmail, him.
   Ehrlichman said the situation was like the following: suppose you heard that there was in a safe deposit box in a bank vault in Washington, DC a map showing the location of an atomic bomb due to go off the following day in the middle of

the city. Breaking into the vault would be like breaking into the psychiatrist's office. It was the only reasonable thing to do.

One of the senators on the investigating committee then suggested that in such circumstances it would have been more appropriate to phone the bank president, ask for the keys and explain why you needed them. In response, Ehrlichman argued that they had, in fact, attempted the equivalent: they had tried to bribe a nurse in the psychiatrist's office to give them the file.[9]

4. 'The only proof capable of being given that an object is visible, is that people actually see it. The only proof that a sound is audible, is that people hear it: . . . In like manner, I apprehend, the sole evidence it is possible to produce that anything is desirable, is that people do actually desire it.'[10]

Summary

1 One of the most effective ways of stimulating counterintuitive thinking is to compare our structure of ideas with an analogy.

2 In this way we can shake off the shackles of System 1 thinking and generate real insight.

3 Analogies can be surprisingly effective in suggesting solutions to problems that seem insoluble.

4 We can only safely argue from one set of characteristics to another when there is a causal connection.

5 Analogies can be remarkably persuasive, helping us clarify, simplify and make more vivid a complex idea.

What next?

In this chapter we have seen just how effective it is to be able to see things differently by distinguishing the structure from the background and then compare it with unrelated structures. This has produced moments of genuine originality and real insight that have radically changed the way we see the world, so much so that in retrospect the solution appears simple, even obvious.

Smart thinkers can do this: they can detach their minds from habitual routine patterns of thought and apply those which seem to have no relevance, except, of course, that they have a similar structure. However, there will be times when we cannot find similar structures, so we will need to adapt our structure. In the next chapter we will learn four simple, yet powerful, ways of doing this.

Designing solutions to problems 2: Adapting your structures

In this chapter you will learn. . .

- About the negative effect that our previous experience has on our ability to solve new problems.
- About the importance of asymmetries to creative thinking.
- The importance of seeing problems differently to escape the inertia of established ideas.
- Four simple, yet powerful, strategies to produce different ways of interpreting our structures of ideas.
- How to use these strategies to tackle insight or lateral thinking problems in psychometric tests.

In 1942 the Gestalt psychologist Abraham Luchins conducted his famous water jar experiment. He asked subjects to solve a series of problems that involved measuring a certain volume of water using jars. After solving the first few problems with the same solution, subjects continued to use this to solve later problems even though a simpler one existed. This became known as the *Einstellung effect*, which highlights the negative effect that our previous experience has on our ability to solve new problems.

This cognitive trap makes it difficult for us to behave in ways other than those in which we have already behaved. And it affects the trained expert and untrained novice alike. It also takes different forms. In the *confirmation bias* we have the tendency to interpret new evidence as confirmation of our existing beliefs and theories. In the *framing effect* the way a problem is described influences how we solve it.

> **Definition**
> The *Einstellung effect*: our previous experience restricts our ability to solve new problems.

All of this makes insight a very rare thing. It shows just how important it is to develop methods of being able to see a problem in a different way. Our minds organise the ideas we generate, creating patterns of connections, which then direct and restrict what we can think. Now that we have learned methods that will help us reveal this structure and all the ideas it contains, we must learn to step back from it, release ourselves from the confines that it places on our thinking and start to adapt it, reinterpret it and think about it differently.

For instance. . .

The stonemasons and architects who built the huge, awe-inspiring gothic churches and cathedrals throughout Europe in the thirteenth, fourteenth and fifteenth centuries worked with patterns of behaviour, standard operating procedures, handed down over hundreds of years from one generation to another. On the face of it they seemed the most conservative of workers, bound by traditional patterns of behaviour, which constrained how they used their every skill.

Yet their boundless imagination produced these breathtaking buildings. They challenged what was thought to be possible by building ever higher, more daring, innovative structures. Abandoning their routine patterns of behaviour, they created flying buttresses, taking weight off the walls to open them up with large, beautiful stained-glass windows. The colour and light flooding through transformed the dark, forbidding interior and with it the vision of worshippers. As the great shards of light streaked across them, it seemed to them that the geometry of each intersecting beam testified to the majesty and order of God's creation.

In the work of these medieval stonemasons and architects we can see all the problems faced by modern decision-makers. In the same way, we will learn to work with our structure of ideas, adapting it to meet the demands of change, rather than just repeat the lessons of the past.

Asymmetries

All forms of creativity arise from developing asymmetries between the structures we use to understand the world; unusual contrasts between them, created by being able to see things differently from a different perspective or interpretation.

For instance. . .

In the last chapter we said that all the doctors and nurses at the General Hospital in Vienna knew what Semmelweis knew. They all had the same information as he did. Yet he alone was able to structure his ideas differently and see a new way of designing a solution.

Einstein, too, knew no more than anybody else. He did no experiments nor gather any new information before he created the theory of relativity. He just adapted the same structure of ideas to see it differently.

Think!

Just think how many new ideas there are out there in information that has already been gathered just waiting to be rearranged and reinterpreted by someone who can think differently.

In this chapter we will learn to use simple strategies to step outside the structures that we normally use, so that we can more easily see different ways of solving problems. As you solve them using these strategies you will, in retrospect, be surprised that you hadn't seen these answers before, but this comes from having created a different perspective from which to see them, where all the answers now seem so obvious. In the process you will learn more about the potential of your creative imagination and the exciting possibilities open to you as you begin to develop your skills to use these strategies.

Working with the structure

Thinking differently about our structure of ideas involves adapting it and seeing it from different perspectives. You can learn to do this quite simply by using the following four strategies. Indeed, all creative work is grounded in the solid foundations of such routine work. By using them we can place ourselves in the position of being able to think outside the norm, revealing what might otherwise have seemed an inspired way of approaching the problem.

Working with the structure

1 Change the structure.
2 Approach it from a different direction.
3 Start from a different point.
4 Create a new structure.

Changing the structure involves reorganising the elements and their relationships. By contrast, the second and third strategies involve accepting the structure as it is, but looking at it differently. We either approach it from a different direction, looking at it from different points of view, or we start from a different point. The fourth strategy is perhaps the most radical. This involves creating a new structure, either by combining other structures, or by changing the basic concepts in terms of which the situation is described and interpreted.

Strategy 1: Change the structure

This is what we might describe as a bottom-up strategy: starting with the ideas we've gathered, we restructure them. The fact that the solution comes through changing the structure as a whole and not just one or two parts explains why it always appears like a sudden insight with the answer revealed as a complete whole.

For instance. . .

In *The Structure of Scientific Revolutions* Thomas Kuhn explains scientific progress using the same terms. The sudden shift between one incompatible paradigm and another comes in the form of a complete revolution; it is not a gradual process.

The problem, of course, is the inertia we've already described: the *Einstellung effect*. As Edward de Bono argues, once we have begun to dig a hole we are reluctant to sacrifice the time and effort we have invested and start another instead. It's easier to go on digging than wonder what else to do. And our education reinforces this. It is designed to make us appreciate the holes that have been dug; to follow in the footsteps of experts, who understand the present holes better than anyone else. Its role is communicative, not creative: it is to make us more aware of the available knowledge that seems to be useful.

To overcome the influence of this we have to learn how to manipulate and change our normal patterns of expectations using simple methods to change the structure so that we can see things from new and more effective perspectives. We can do this in three ways:

Changing the structure

1 Split it up.
2 Rearrange it.
3 Reinterpret it.

1. Split it up

The simplest method is to split up the structure into two or more parts. In many cases this can reduce a bewilderingly difficult problem into two simple problems, whose solution is plain to see. Either we discover that each one can be solved by the application of a structure we have used before, or by a parallel structure, an analogy. Failing that, once it's split up we can then use one of the other methods and rearrange or reinterpret the problem to come to a solution that way.

For instance. . .

As we saw in chapter 3, the compilers of crossword puzzles often have this strategy in mind when they set their clues. To find the answer to the clue 'Frequently decimal (5)' the compiler expects you to split it in two with both parts leading to the answer 'Often'. (The number in brackets indicates the number of letters in the answer.)

2. Rearrange it

Again the simplest example of this is to be found in crossword puzzles. Some answers are found by just rearranging the letters of the clue.

For instance. . .

The clue 'Fibber and return rail fair (4)' is solved by taking the word 'rail' and reversing the order of the letters to make 'liar'.

In the same way, we can rearrange our structure of ideas. We might have a structure that we have created through causal analysis, so we have to think about how we can rearrange it.

> **Try this. . .**
>
> You are a teacher in charge of improving the academic skills of the sixth form. You want to know why it is that, despite putting on study skills courses, too many students still struggle to take good notes, read texts efficiently and write good essays.

The way you understand the situation can be represented in the following causal analysis:

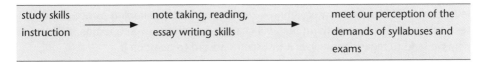

| study skills instruction | → | note taking, reading, essay writing skills | → | meet our perception of the demands of syllabuses and exams |

Up until now you have thought that study skills courses will shape the way students use their skills to meet the demands of syllabuses and exams. In order to think differently about the problem you need to rearrange this structure. So you do the following:

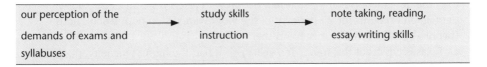

| our perception of the demands of exams and syllabuses | → | study skills instruction | → | note taking, reading, essay writing skills |

Rearranging this by thinking about the influence of our perception of the demands of exams and syllabuses gives us an alternative explanation:

> *It may be that, despite all the instruction in study skills, the way teachers shape students' perception of the demands of syllabuses and modes of assessment, like essays and exams, results in students still taking notes, reading and writing in the same way, exhibiting exactly the same problems.*

If students believe that learning is largely about knowing things and exams test how many 'right' answers they can recall and trade for marks, despite taking study skills courses, they are likely to continue to read word for word and take verbatim, unstructured notes, fearing that if they leave anything out they might be missing a right answer. If this is the case, the solution lies not in planning more and better study skills courses, but in reshaping students' perception of learning tasks, like exams and essays.

What's important in this method is identifying a factor that can be moved or changed. Try looking at each factor as something that will change the situation.

For instance. . .

Semmelweis adopted just this method when he changed in turn each thing in the situation to see if it had any effect. Looking at the ideas in the structure he had created, he changed the position in which the women gave birth, their diet in the doctors' division, and the route of the priest and his bell-ringer to see if each one changed the situation.

3. Reinterpret it

The other thing we can do is reinterpret the structure, changing its meaning. As we've seen, the way we make sense of it can lead us in the wrong direction. So, without even changing the structure, we can sometimes find the solution by just looking at it naïvely, without any preconceptions, as someone who has never seen it before.

> Reinterpret something that seems obviously true; something that will change everything.

In most cases this means reinterpreting a key assumption: questioning something that seems obviously true; something that will change everything if you question it. This is why we tend to regard it as naïve: it just seems absurd to question it.

For instance. . .

Most people standing for election in the US know that to get elected they must talk tough on crime. As a result, the prison population has been growing 13 times faster than the general population, so that a nation with just 5 per cent of the global population accounts for 25 per cent of the worldwide prison population and is spending $70 billion a year keeping them there.

Texas is typical of this trend. Ten years ago it had the highest incarceration rate in the world with one in 20 adults in prison, on probation or on parole. It trebled in 20 years, while other states with slower rates of growth saw faster falls in crime. Meanwhile one in three inmates was back in prison within three years. Worse still for the average taxpayer, the state was running the biggest deficit in state history and just couldn't afford to build the new prisons that were needed.

This was the problem that the Republican Jerry Madden faced when he was appointed chairman of the house corrections committee, responsible for criminal justice, jail and parole.

How would you tackle this problem? The answer was to reinterpret the structure of ideas that had justified this rate of incarceration; to question something that seems obviously true; something that will change everything.

The assumption that everyone seemed to share, politicians and judges alike, was that everybody had had the same education and upbringing as they had, so if they broke the law, they did so out of unfettered free will. Once they had re-examined this assumption and looked at the background of inmates, they began to get a measure of the needs of inmates and how to deal with them. One judge admitted, 'The people we are dealing with are not like you and me. I found this a shock. I grew up in a house with married parents, both of whom had college degrees. I thought this was normal, but now I know it isn't.'

At the heart of the reforms of the justice system in Texas is the alien idea to many on the right: to understand more and condemn less. As a result, funds have been diverted into sophisticated rehabilitation programmes to reduce recidivism, into probation, parole and specialist services for addicts, the mentally ill, women and veterans. And it has worked with even violent crime falling at more than twice the national average, at the same time cutting costs and prison populations.[1]

Try this. . .

Find the answer to the following crossword clue in the same way, by reinterpreting the structure:

   H, I, J, K, L, M, N, O (5)

Answer

To find the answer we have to read the letters differently from the obvious way as a sequence of letters from the alphabet. Reinterpreting them gives us 'H to O', easily converted into 'H_2O' and the solution: 'water'.

Strategy 2: Approach it from a different direction

With some problems, without changing the structure, we can solve them by just approaching them from a different direction, from a different point of view. In Conan Doyle's story *The Problem of Thor Bridge* Sherlock Holmes describes one aspect of his theory of detection when he says, 'When once your point of view is changed, the very thing which was so damning becomes a clue to the truth.'[2] This strategy seems to be routine with some thinkers. Whenever a problem arises they devise a method of approaching it in a different way from others. Donald Newman, a mathematician who knew John Nash at MIT, said this of him:

> *everyone else would climb a peak by looking for a path somewhere on the mountain. Nash would climb another mountain altogether and from that distant peak would shine a searchlight back onto the first peak.*[3]

The most common strategy is to reverse the order of things: to turn it upside down, inside out or back to front.

Approach it from a different direction

1   Turn it upside down.
2   Inside out.
3   Back to front.

---

1. Turn it upside down

Becoming a smart thinker means learning to detach ourselves from our routine patterns of thought and forget about ourselves and what we would most prefer to be the case. One of the best examples of this is the challenge of turning something upside down to approach it from a different direction. This involves reversing the *relations between ideas*; changing the way we think about things so that we think in quite a different way.

For instance. . .

In order to produce cheaper and better public services local and central government have traditionally resorted to pumping out public information based on theories about how things could work more efficiently. If they want to improve refuse collection, a local council might introduce a new system of recycling and then send out information to every household to get them to change their behaviour in line with the new system. This is a top-down process common to most organisations with hierarchical structures of managers at the top, determining the policy, and those further down falling into line.

But over recent years, with the popularisation of behavioural economics, this relationship has been reversed and a bottom-up strategy tried instead. Some councils have used the 'value modes' approach to analyse the different motivations and values of the local populace to understand better the sort of triggers, interventions and incentives that are likely to be the most effective in changing people's behaviour.

The problem has been that sending out the same message to all in a 'one-size-fits-all' approach hasn't worked, so harnessing the collaboration of different groups with different values could be more effective in delivering cheaper, more efficient services. In the value mode analysis done in Coventry and Croydon the population was classified into three types:

1 Settlers – those who value stability and belonging and are risk averse;
2 Prospectors – who are keen on gathering the outward signs of success;
3 Pioneers – the post-materialists, who tend to be driven by ethical concerns.

Using this knowledge, councils can more effectively mobilise the collaboration of residents in their attempts to improve public services.

For instance. . .

In their provision of school transport for children with special educational needs, Coventry city council tried to harness the influence of pioneers, who were willing to transport their own children. Their example was instrumental in persuading the other groups to follow suit. The predictions suggested this could save up to 15 per cent and improve residents' sense of independence.[4]

---

2. Inside out

With this method, rather than reverse the *relations between ideas*, we reverse our *intuitive assumptions*, turning them inside out. In effect, we approach the problem from a different direction by deliberately thinking the opposite to see what we can find.

> **For instance. . .**
>
> The most important medical discovery of the eighteenth century came about in just this way. Like others before him, Edward Jenner had asked himself why it was that people got smallpox. It wasn't until he turned this problem inside out by reversing his assumptions that he was able to develop a cure in the form of a vaccine, which largely eradicated it. Instead of focusing his attention on why people got smallpox, he asked why it was that milkmaids apparently did not. From here it was a short step to discovering that harmless cowpox gave them protection.

The challenge of this method lies in resisting the influence of what we already believe. If we believe that a certain approach is the right one, it is difficult to reverse this assumption and abandon our beliefs. The influence of cognitive traps, like the *Einstellung effect* and the *confirmation bias*, makes it difficult to be smart thinkers and detach ourselves from our routine patterns of thought and what we would most prefer to be the case.

> **For instance. . .**
>
> The American psychologist Stanton Samenow worked for many years with the criminally insane. As a classical Freudian therapist, his work was grounded in the belief that he could influence their behaviour, reforming many of them, so that they could lead normal lives. But after years of work he realised that he was not having the success he expected.

Given this problem, what would you do? Samenow decided to turn the problem inside out. Hitherto he had believed that *he* was the one exerting the influence, but, he wondered, what if I reverse this assumption: what if it's the other way around. He came to the conclusion that the inmates were not sick, but were just brilliant manipulators of the legal and psychiatric systems. Their mental life was a rich dreamscape of depredations and, rather than reform under classical therapy, they learned to fool their Freudian therapist, playing the psychiatric game by mouthing insights.

Having reversed his assumption, he changed his strategy. He began by holding the criminal completely accountable for his offences. There are no excuses, no hard-luck stories. At the heart of the treatment is the premise that they are free to choose between good and evil. Gradually the therapist teaches the criminal how to change his behaviour by learning how to deter criminal thinking. He learns how to make certain reasons more prominent than others: how to think of something else when he sees a women and thinks of rape. In short, Samenow explains that it calls for criminals to acquire the sort of moral values that enables civilisations to survive.

3. Back to front

When we use the third method, rather than reverse the *relations between ideas* or our *intuitive assumptions* as we did with the first two methods, we reverse the *order of things*;

we turn things back to front. Copernicus argued that the earth moved around the sun, rather than the sun around the earth. Einstein argued that it wasn't that the planets moved in a curved motion through space, but that space itself was curved.

For instance. . .

Imagine you are a mathematics teacher and you want to improve your students' understanding of the way they reason in maths. At present they just do the calculations, but they aren't developing an understanding of the intellectual processes that they use to get the answer. You want them to realise that producing the right answer is not the most important aim. If they can develop their understanding of the processes involved, it will give them the confidence and freedom to be more creative.

So you have to find some way of getting them to reflect upon how they go about tackling problems. You could ask them to explain in class what they do, which would help, but you realise this would have little depth to it.

You then think about getting them to write about how they reason in mathematics. However, our normal pattern of expectations tells us that to write clearly we must first think clearly, so that doesn't seem to help.

Clear thinking results in ⟶ clear writing

But then you wonder what would happen if we turned this order of things back to front: perhaps our normal expectations are wrong; perhaps clear writing makes for clear thinking.

Clear writing results in ⟶ clear thinking

Now you have an altogether different and interesting solution. You could get them to write journals, which they would then submit for marking along with other written explanations of how they solve the mathematical problems they are set.

You even realise that by getting them to think through their ideas with greater clarity and care, writing could play a more important role not just in mathematics, but across the curriculum. By writing about how they come by their ideas and solve problems, students could begin to understand more about the processes of how they think in other subjects, like the natural sciences.

All three of these different ways of approaching a problem involve reversing different things:

1 Turn upside down – reversing the relation between ideas
2 Inside out – reverse our intuitive assumptions
3 Back to front – reverse the order of things

Strategy 3: Start from a different point

In contrast, this strategy works by starting at a different point. We focus our attention onto different parts of the structure and start from there. We might start at the end, rather than the beginning, but wherever we start, our aim is not to take the ideas for granted, but see them from a different perspective.

The easiest way of doing this for most of us is to start with the key concepts around which our topic is organised. As we've seen, by analysing a concept we are able to reveal the structure of ideas at the heart of it, which helps us organise our thinking. One or more of these ideas are likely to dictate the way we generally use the concept. So, by analysing it and revealing the structure of ideas we are able to see clearly those we usually ignore, which give us different points from which to start. They throw different light on the problem and present interesting angles from which to approach it.

For instance. . .

You might be the promoter of a new production of a well-known tragedy. But all the ideas you have come up with so far to promote it seem to be rather predictable. You want something that is new; that will give a fresh insight into the play. So you go back to the concept of 'tragedy' and analyse it carefully. Here you find an alternative interpretation of it as something that is self-defeating in that, without meaning to, we destroy the very thing we value most. Now you have a unique angle on the play and a fresh, innovative way of promoting it.

But if the key concepts of your topic don't offer you a way of starting from a different point, try something that might seem disarmingly simple: step back from your topic and approach it from the more general standpoint of someone who is not technically involved in your subject or profession. In chapter 6 we saw how Niels Bohr in an exam at the University of Copenhagen invented different ways of using a barometer to measure the height of a building by just thinking in this naïve way. To adopt the same approach, get used to asking questions that might seem too simple or obvious to ask.

For instance. . .

As we have seen, one reason for the stunning success of Einstein's four ground-breaking papers in 1905 was his habit of starting his work with naïve, simple, almost childlike questions. What would it be like to fly alongside a beam of light? If you flew at the same speed as the light beam, would it, for instance, appear to stand still? What happens to passengers in an elevator when it falls into emptiness?

When he was asked by a reporter why, as a man in his twenties, he should have been concerned by such childlike questions, he explained that he was a late developer. Unlike other people, he only got around to asking them as an adult. And, at his age, unlike a child, he wasn't prepared to be fobbed off with a simple, dismissive answer.

Sometimes a problem is only a problem because it is looked at in a certain way. Change the way in which you look at it and there is no longer a problem. By just shifting the emphasis from one part to another the solution becomes so clear that you wonder why you haven't seen it before.

For instance. . .

An equation in mathematics is nothing more than two ways of describing something. Having two ways of expressing the same thing either side of the equals sign, gives you a different way of looking at something and the ability to manipulate things and find the answer.

Strategy 4: Create a new structure

However, if none of these changes work, you may find the solution comes from creating a new structure. In contrast to the others, this is a top-down strategy, in which a new theory is put in place of the ruling one. There are two ways of doing this.

Creating a new structure

1 Combine structures
2 Change the basic concepts

---

1. Combine structures

Perhaps the most effective way of doing this is to import a theory or another way of interpreting things from another discipline, another profession or just from everyday life. Synthesising structures in this way can open up entirely new ways of approaching problems.

For instance. . .

As we saw in a previous chapter, with the rise of totalitarian leaders in the 1930s and 1940s and their mesmeric influence on crowds, some historians began to wonder how significant the crowd and a leader's capacity to manipulate collective sentiment had been in previous periods with leaders, like Napoleon. So they combined different structures by borrowing from political science the theory of totalitarianism and re-evaluating their own historical understanding in the light of this. As a result they were able to open up new lines of investigation with surprising results.

It's worth reminding yourself as you search for a solution that creative thinking often means disregarding our own cultural conventions, those that govern the way we study a subject or the way an organisation or profession works. There may be in your subject or profession an accepted way of approaching a problem, but don't let this trap your thinking.

> **Creative thinking often means disregarding our own cultural conventions.**

It starts with the realisation that there is no particular virtue in doing things the way they've always been done. Organisations that allow for this are likely to be the most successful, particularly if they have weak cultures and strong ethics. In other words, they allow for the creativity of employees by freeing them from unnecessary conventions as to how the organisation has always worked, while at the same time generating their trust that they can give of their creative best and be assured that they will be treated well by getting the rewards they deserve. It is sometimes said that this explains the success and creative energy of many Silicon Valley technology firms, like Apple, Google and Yahoo.

2. Change the basic concepts

Alternatively, think again about changing the basic concepts in which your problem is described. As we have already found, a concept represents the structure through which we understand a situation. Each one is a system of learned responses which we automatically apply to organise data and make sense of our experience.

But they also influence our behaviour: they represent a readiness to respond in a particular way quite independently of our intentions. A word or phrase can set off a train of thought which results in behaviour which we regard as normal, but leaves us unable to solve a problem, unless we analyse and change the concept.

For instance. . .

In a previous chapter we examined the problem of parents on the touchline shouting at officials, coaches and particularly at their children. One solution might be to change the basic concept of competitive football for children of this age. If this were changed, making it a non-contact sport, this would remove tackling as a major source of controversy on the sideline with parents abusing referees for missing what they regard as a foul, while children are encouraged to 'get stuck in'.

Instead, football could adopt the same approach as touch rugby. As soon as players are touched they would lose the ball. This would shift the emphasis onto developing other key skills of the game; ball control, dribbling, picking out a good pass and executing it quickly and accurately. Children's football would no longer be the-kick-and-run type of game dominated by the big kids, who can kick the ball long and then chase after it faster than the others. Instead, the skills necessary to play possession football would be more important. The diminutive, gifted midfielder with good passing skills would then play a larger role.

Of course, this may not be the solution to the problem, but it's worth reminding yourself that, although your first idea may not work perfectly, it is a vital step in the process of finding an effective solution. The lesson to learn is not to take the concept for granted. See it from a different perspective, even though this perspective may at first seem absurd; what comes afterwards may not be. So, reinterpret the concept, concentrate on other parts of its meaning and let these dominate your search for a solution to see where it takes you.

On the next two pages you can see the pattern notes developed by using each of these four strategies to tackle the problem of parental behaviour at children's football matches.

Solutions 1

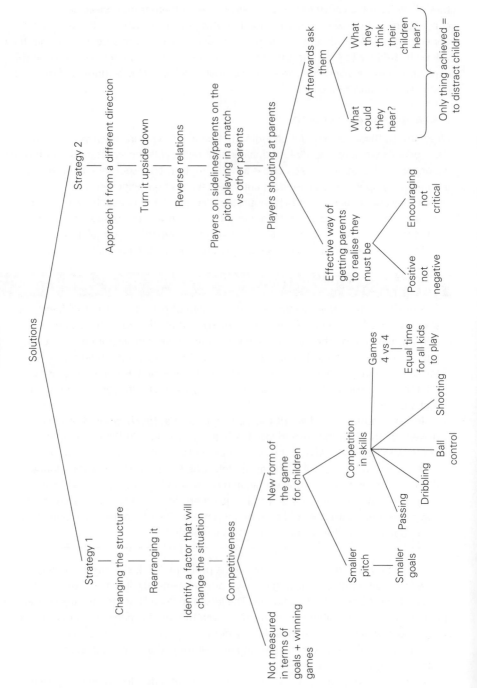

Solutions 2

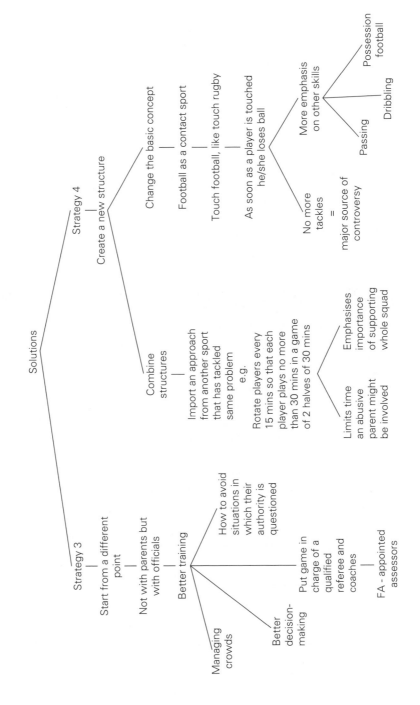

Solutions

Strategy 3

Strategy 4

Create a new structure

Start from a different point

Not with parents but with officials

Better training

How to avoid situations in which their authority is questioned

Managing crowds

Better decision-making

Put game in charge of a qualified referee and coaches

FA - appointed assessors

Combine structures

Import an approach from another sport that has tackled same problem e.g.

Rotate players every 15 mins so that each player plays no more than 30 mins in a game of 2 halves of 30 mins

Limits time an abusive parent might be involved

Emphasises importance of supporting whole squad

Change the basic concept

Football as a contact sport

Touch football, like touch rugby

As soon as a player is touched he/she loses ball

No more tackles
=
major source of controversy

More emphasis on other skills

Passing

Dribbling

Possession football

Psychometric tests – insight problems

We began this chapter by discussing the importance of asymmetries, the unusual differences and contrasts, which are often the source of the most surprising insights and are created by changing the way we normally think about things.

They can also be the source of solutions to insight or lateral thinking problems in psychometric tests. This type of problem comes in three forms: spatial, verbal and mathematical. But they are all tackled in the same way. As I explained in chapter 6 (pages 106–7), the key is to look at them differently, so we can see alternative interpretations of the problem beyond our normal expectations.

1. Representation

It all starts with good representation. In chapter 6 we learned the importance of laying out all the information as clearly as possible, making connections between ideas to create a structure.

2. Asymmetries

Then we search for asymmetries: contrasts, different ways of looking at it that will point to the answer.

For instance. . .

During a recent census, a man told the census taker that he had three children. The census taker said that he needed to know their ages, and the man replied that the product of their ages was 36. The census taker, slightly miffed, said he needed to know each of their ages. The man said, 'Well the sum of their ages is the same as my house number.' The census taker looked at the house number and complained, 'I still can't tell their ages.' The man said, 'Oh, that's right, the oldest one taught the younger ones to play chess.' The census taker promptly wrote down the ages of the three children. How did he know, and what were the ages?[5]

The answer depends on how well we can represent the problem mathematically. The important step is to represent clearly all the numbers that multiply to 36, along with their sum:

D1	D2	D3	SUM
1	1	36	38
1	2	18	21
1	3	12	16
1	4	9	14
1	6	6	13
2	2	9	13
2	3	6	11
3	3	4	10

Then, we need to search for different ways of looking at it that will point to the answer. The key to this case is the sum of their ages, which must be 13, otherwise the census taker would have known their individual ages as soon as he had been told that the sum matched the number of the house. This gives us two to choose from. But since the oldest daughter taught the younger ones to play chess, the ages must be 2, 2 and 9, because if it were 1, 6 and 6 there would not be two youngest.

Try this. . .

Here's an example of a spatial insight problem. At the start of the Second World War the *Brighter Blackout Book*[6] was published to entertain people during the blackouts with games, puzzles, stories, short plays, crosswords and so on. One of the puzzles asks you to create a swastika using just four playing cards.

Answer

Again, the secret is to search for different ways of looking at it. In this case, it is to use the cards not to make the swastika, but the white spaces left by the swastika. Try it yourself.

Try this. . .

Using the four strategies we have learned in this chapter, try the following questions. You will find the answers on the companion website.

1   To answer the following well-known problem you will find it helpful to use the second strategy – approach it from a different direction.

Two trains are on the same track 100 km apart heading towards one another, each at a speed of 50 km/h. A fly, starting out at the front of one train, flies towards the other at a speed of 75 km/h. Upon reaching the other train, the fly turns around and continues towards the first train. How many kilometres does the fly travel before getting squashed in the collision of the two trains?

2   Barbara is half as old as Clive was when Clive was five years older than Barbara is now. How old is Barbara now?

(Represent the problem as an algebraic equation. Then you will have two contrasting representations of the same thing on either side of the equals sign. This will give you asymmetries: two ways of looking at the same thing that you can begin to manipulate and adapt to find the answer.)

3   Take a pencil and connect the following nine circles with only four lines without retracing a line or removing your pencil from the paper.

O O O

O O O

O O O

4 Helen and Susan were born on the same day of the same month of the same year to the same mother and same father, yet they are not twins. How is this possible?

Summary

1 Our thinking is easily trapped by the inertia of previous experience.

2 All forms of creativity arise from the asymmetries between the structures of our ideas.

3 There are four simple strategies we can use to generate these.

4 Using these we can find solutions to the insight or lateral thinking type of psychometric problem.

5 The key to solving insight problems is clear representation and finding asymmetries.

What's next?

As we have seen, creativity arises from the asymmetry we create by looking differently at the structures of ideas we use to understand the world. By adapting our structures, as we have in this chapter, so that we can see things differently, we can produce genuine insights. They may not appear immediately. We may need to leave them to incubate in the subconscious, but with persistence they will come. As a result, we will have a number of possible solutions to choose from. In the next stage we will learn to evaluate these, assess risk and make a rational decision on the best one.

Companion website

You will find similar examples of the sort of psychometric problems shown in this chapter on the companion website. www.he.palgrave.com/smart-thinking

Creative Thinking

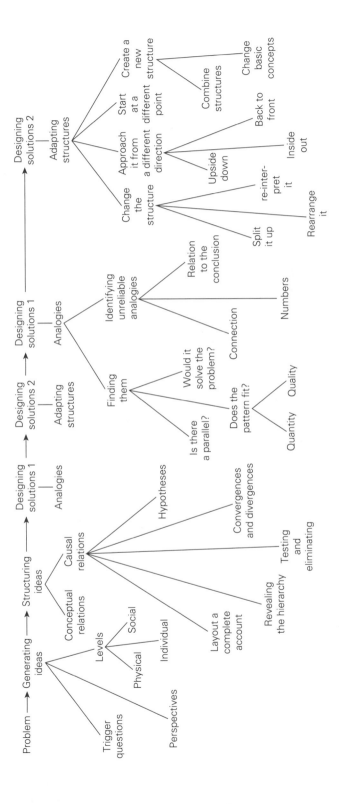

How will this improve my grades and employability?

In this chapter you will learn. . .

- How to inject your own thinking into your essays by brainstorming your ideas using your trigger questions.
- How to make sure your presentations are consistently argued, relevant and persuasive.
- That by using your creative thinking skills you can find problems for your dissertation that are interesting and original.
- That employers worldwide are eager to employ graduates with the creative thinking skills we have learned in the last five chapters.
- That these skills are the key to tackling the three most common psychometric problems.

The best teaching is full of transformative experiences. A student who has, up until now, been quiet and unresponsive at the back of the class, suddenly bursts into full bloom with interesting ideas that he or she develops with confidence and courage. The most dramatic of these transformations occur once the teacher has convinced students that they have important and valuable ideas of their own: a genuine contribution to make to their own learning.

At this point genuine creative thinking starts. They show all the signs of a smart thinker. They are obsessed by ideas and eager to share them. They are tenacious and resourceful. They have the courage and confidence to ask the most disarming, naïve questions full of insights that throw the most surprising light on the most complex problems.

Academic work

Unfortunately, too many of us go through education without ever experiencing this. We are led to believe that education is largely a process of recycling authoritative opinion, which leaves us convinced that ours is an imitative role demanding little of us or our abilities. We are left on the periphery of genuine learning experiences. We don't share the concerns of a real thinker:

We don't see the need to make ideas genuinely our own.

We don't see the need to consult our own ideas, so when we launch into a piece of work we don't know what we think or the sort of questions we want answers to as we read our sources. Consequently, we don't graft these ideas onto our own beliefs and values to make them genuinely our own, which leaves us struggling to use them with any confidence.

Our work lacks relevance

Without the clarity of our own insights to guide us through the material we struggle to distinguish between ideas that are relevant and those that are not. As a result, in seminars our explanations are unpersuasive and in our essays irrelevant and distracting ideas cloud the issues and confuse the reader.

We have no basis from which to critically evaluate what we read

Our critical skills are stunted in the same way. If we don't take into account what *we* think and believe, we have no point from which we can begin to critically evaluate what we read and hear in seminars. By failing to make clear what we think and the questions we want our authors to answer, we either don't ask any questions of the author at all or those questions we do ask are unclear. And if we fail to ask clear questions, we fail to get clear answers.

The question, then, is how do we free ourselves from the confines of our undeveloped abilities? The answer is simple: we must learn to think creatively and to accept that we do have a genuine and valuable contribution to make. As we begin to generate our own ideas and design solutions to problems, we will begin to realise just how original and valuable these are.

1. Essays

The impact this can have on our academic work is immediately obvious in our essays. As soon as we have unravelled the implications of the question by analysing the key concepts, we need to brainstorm our own ideas using our trigger questions from different perspectives and on different levels as we did in chapter 9. The importance of this lies in staking your claim as early as possible by emptying out your mind and your ideas without the aid of books or other sources. By doing this you are asking two questions:

1 What do I know about the question – what are my beliefs and ideas?
2 What do I need to know and find out from my sources? We have to ask clear questions to get clear answers that are relevant to the implications of the question that we have already revealed.

This reveals the overwhelming significance of creative thinking to our academic work. Not only does it give us that realisation that we have a real contribution to make, that our ideas have a unique value, but by giving us the skills to generate these ideas we arm ourselves with the ideas we need to negotiate with our sources and process their ideas without becoming enslaved by them. If we fail to arm ourselves in this way with our *own* ideas and what *we* know about the topic, two things will almost certainly happen:

1. The authors we read for our research will dictate to us

Without our own ideas to protect us, it will be difficult, at times impossible, for us to resist the pull of their ideas and the persuasiveness of their arguments. As a result, we'll find ourselves accepting the case they develop and the judgements they make without evaluating them sufficiently, even copying large sections of the text into our own notes.

2. And, equally serious, we will find it difficult to avoid including a great mass of material that is quite irrelevant to our purposes

We end up including them in a long, discursive, shapeless essay, in which the examiner frequently feels lost in a mass of irrelevant material.

2. Seminars

The same improvements show up in our work in seminars, both in our presentations and in our contributions to discussion. As we are clearer about what we think ourselves, we will be clearer about the relevance of the arguments that are presented by other students and about our criticisms of them. Moreover, as the ideas we have uncovered in our research are now more genuinely our own, having been grafted onto our own network of beliefs and ideas, we will be able to present our arguments not only with more conviction, but more consistently and persuasively.

- The clearer we are about what *we* think, the clearer we are about the basis of our criticism and the relevance of arguments.
- Having grafted the arguments onto our own network of beliefs, we argue more consistently and persuasively.

3. Dissertations

However, the impact of our creative thinking skills on our academic work goes beyond our ability to generate our own ideas in a systematic and thorough way. Now that we know how to structure our ideas and then find answers to problems, either by searching for analogies or by adapting our structures using the four methods we learned in chapter 12, we are better able to produce in our essays, dissertations and in seminars innovative solutions and ideas that are likely to surprise even ourselves.

Finding an original problem

Moreover, we are now likely to work with a lot more confidence, knowing the depth and range of imagination that we can bring to our work. Nowhere is this more important than in our dissertations, where we have to show that we are capable of suspending our judgement and playing devil's advocate to consider new or neglected answers to problems, rather than simply recycling those we have read in our texts.

We are likely to work with a lot more confidence, knowing the depth and range of imagination that we can bring to our work.

Finding the right problem to tackle in our dissertation presents us with exactly the same challenge as problem-solving, just in reverse. It involves the same skills and methods. Now that we know how to develop and use our creative thinking skills, we will find it much easier to generate a number of different problems that a topic might raise, from which we can choose the one that is most likely to produce an interesting and original piece of work.

For instance. . .

In chapter 9 we discussed a proposed wind farm project and how we could generate our own ideas through trigger questions to explore systematically all the ideas and issues they raise. This is exactly the method we would adopt if we were exploring this topic for issues that we might research for our dissertation.

First we would explore each trigger question from the perspective of all those who affect or are affected by the project. We would place ourselves in their positions and see the project from their perspectives: how do they feel about it; what changes are they likely to see to their lives; will they benefit or will they be disadvantaged? To do this we would look at each of them on different levels: physical, individual and social. Each one of the perspectives is likely to generate interesting ideas for a research project, but for this exercise let's just take one to explore on the three levels to demonstrate the wealth of ideas this generates.

For instance. . .

Local residents

1. Physical:

   1.1 Local residents may fear that it will damage the attractiveness of the local countryside.

   1.2 It may increase the number of vehicles in the local area, making it difficult for local residents to get around and perhaps making it more dangerous on the small local roads.

   1.3 On a broader level, there will be many residents who will agree that such a development is important in that it will contribute to the reduction in carbon emissions that are necessary to avoid catastrophic climate change and they might acknowledge that some community has got to have them.

2. Individual:

   2.1 Local residents may fear that the increase in traffic and the blight on the local countryside may affect the value of their property.

   2.2 They will want to know whether it will cut their energy bills or go straight into the national supply and have no effect on the cost of local electricity.

3. Social:

   3.1 Many residents will agree with the project in terms of it reducing the country's reliance on sources of imported energy that are likely to increase in price as supplies of non-renewable fuels diminish, while relying more on low carbon energy sources that will help the country meet its climate change targets.

3.2 They will want to know who will own the wind farm: the local community, central government or a private company? If it's the latter, are these foreign owned, over which local residents may have limited influence and who are likely to make decisions more in the interests of their shareholders than the local community?

3.3 How much influence can local residents exert? Who will ultimately make the decision: local or central government, both of which are likely to be composed of people who live some distance from the area and share few of the concerns of local residents?

Possible research projects

Already you can see that in many of these arguments there is the basis for interesting projects that would produce a fascinating dissertation, and this is just from one perspective!

For instance. . .

Example 1: Costs and benefits

You may be interested in how the adverse impact on the local community is to be addressed: what plans there are to ensure a fair distribution of costs and benefits. It would be unfair on the local community if they were to bear all the costs and not benefit anymore than any other consumer of electricity in the country. It would offend the principles of distributive justice. So, it might make an interesting project to look at how the local community will benefit, what compensation local residents are likely to receive, their opinion on this and whether they have alternative ideas.

Example 2: Locally owned renewable energy projects

It may be interesting to research some of these alternatives. What about locally owned renewable energy projects that ensure a greater flow of benefits to the local community over the longer term and greater local involvement? Are there examples of this and how successful have they been?

Example 3: Local influence over the decision-making process

Alternatively, you might want to examine the sort of influence that the local community can exert over the decision-making process. What plans do local residents have for organising themselves? Are there pressure groups that can lend them their resources and knowledge about the process? What about previous projects: how many went the way of local objections and how many favoured the big corporations? Is there any system of appeal, if so, how successful have appeals been?

As you can see, in this systematic way it is possible to generate a whole range of interesting ideas that you would not otherwise have realised were there, which could be developed into fascinating projects. And within each one you can see that there are three or four interesting sub-questions that will guide your research.

Employability

Today all organisations, businesses and professions face rapid change bringing with it challenges that they have never had to face before. Yet most graduates leaving university and applying for jobs are ill-equipped to meet these demands. Employers need people who can respond and adapt, using all of their cognitive skills and problem-solving abilities to meet the challenges. In essence, they need people with all the characteristics and skills of a smart thinker, like openness, flexibility, the ability to generate new ideas, to tolerate uncertainty and to solve problems.

However, this is not the whole of the problem. Organisations, too, find it difficult to adapt. In an earlier chapter we discussed the *Einstellung effect*, which highlights the negative effect that our previous experience has on our ability to think creatively and solve new problems. This cognitive trap makes it difficult for us to behave in ways other than those in which we have already behaved, which characterises many organisations and businesses. This makes insight a very rare thing and highlights just how important it is to develop methods of being able to see a problem in a different way.

For instance. . .

It has been estimated that 70 per cent of the cost of a product is determined by its design. Creative design, therefore, can lead to substantial savings, which explains why corporations in the USA are now budgeting billions of dollars for creativity training programmes.[1]

And, before we allow ourselves to believe that this has nothing to do with us, because it only affects those who are creative in the classic sense as artists and designers, we ought to remind ourselves that it affects all jobs.

For instance. . .

A salesperson in a hardware store may have a customer who is looking for something to do a particular job, but nothing the salesperson shows the customer fits the bill. Instead of shrugging his shoulders and responding with some annoyance to a difficult customer, a creative thinker will go back to the description the customer has given, ask more questions and create a new concept. If nothing on his shelves fits this concept, he will adapt it, until he finds a solution.

In this way not only does he get a satisfied customer, who then becomes an engine for generating good publicity for the company, but the company might find that, as a result, it now has a wider range of products to meet a larger demand or, perhaps, even that it is the only supplier in a niche market.

Characteristics

As this example illustrates, there are certain characteristics that all creative smart thinkers possess that are important to the success of all organisations. These develop out of the acceptance of the two key principles we discussed in chapter 8:

1 We don't have to be right at each step.
2 There is no single way of getting to where you want to be.

Creative thinkers are patient with themselves, because they realise that the process of designing solutions is full of false starts, dead ends and changes of direction. It requires someone who has the 10 characteristics that we examined in chapter 8.

The 10 key characteristics

1 Declutter your mind
2 Designing solutions, not finding them
3 Naïve thinking
4 Good at finding problems
5 Look for causes, effects and possible solutions
6 Open to new ideas
7 Suspend your judgement
8 Determined and resourceful
9 The courage to think differently
10 Optimistic

Skills

But, as we know, it is not just a question of possessing the right characteristics. We also need to develop the right skills and methods to release our creative abilities.

1. Generating ideas

In chapter 9 we learned to generate our own ideas using a simple, routine method of answering a comprehensive set of trigger questions to gather the information and ideas we need. For an employer this demonstrates not only that you have developed effective strategies to think creatively, but that you are also organised and thorough in your thinking. It demonstrates that you have the abilities and personal qualities to tackle problems competently without overlooking anything. In most jobs this is vital.

For instance. . .

If you are responsible for making a presentation to company executives on why they should adopt a particular product, you must be prepared for any question that might be fired at you. So, as you prepare, you must design a list of trigger questions that cover every conceivable question that might be asked, systematically covering every angle and every issue that might arise – something like the following:

1. What is the primary market for the product?
2. What is the size of this market?
3. Are there notable characteristics to this market?
4. What are the key characteristics of the typical consumer?
5. Are there important secondary markets?
6. How large are these?
7. What are the main competitors?
8. What key advantages does the product have over its competitors?
9. What are its key selling points?
10. When will the product be ready to go into production?

Success in a profession depends upon the same creative skills to generate your ideas in an organised and thorough way. If you are advising a client, a patient or a student, you have to know that you have generated as many ideas as you can that cover every angle so you can design the best solution, which you can recommend with complete confidence.

For instance. . .

If you were an investment manager thinking about whether to recommend that a client invests in a particular fund, your concern would be to get a clear idea of when demand will be greater than supply, causing a price spike: the maximum point of profit. If you are a skilled creative thinker, you will assemble the ideas and information you need by asking questions, like the following:

1. Will the price of commodities rise (oil, wheat, corn, industrial and precious metals, etc.)?
2. Are the factors that cause the price rises in place?
   2.1 Is there strong demand? Are the inventories high?
   2.2 How are the factors influencing supply? Are suppliers cutting production (OPEC, mining companies, farms)?
3. Are governments implementing policies that will affect supply or demand?
   3.1 Subsidies e.g. biofuels
   3.2 Low interest rates stimulating consumer purchases and investment to increase production
   3.3 Tariffs
4. Geography – where are commodities produced? Transport and the price of oil are underlying price components.
5. Are there significant changes in social and economic behaviour? e.g. changes in the nature of populations and consumption habits bringing about increased demand for certain products, e.g. cars, consumer goods, etc.
6. What are the movements in price?
   6.1 If prices are falling, investors will sell in the hope of buying back in at a lower rate in the future.

> **6.2** If prices are rising, they will buy in the hope that they can sell at a higher price in the future.
> **7** Are there significant currency fluctuations? Most commodities are priced in dollars, so the strength of the dollar affects demand.
> **8** What are the risks and rewards?
> **8.1** Is the increase in demand/price sustainable?
> **8.2** Is supply at full capacity?[2]

However, this represents more than just good organisational skills. Over the last five chapters we have learned how important it is for creative thinking to take one further step to ask questions on different levels and from the perspectives of all of those who affect and are affected by the problem we are analysing.

This not only generates new and surprising ideas, but helps us to develop the skills that are so important to many organisations and professions: the skills to think empathetically by placing ourselves in someone else's position and vicariously experience their thoughts and feelings. This method gets us to think outside our own limited perspective to ask questions we might otherwise dismiss as irrelevant and unthinkable.

2. Using analogies to find solutions

Once we have generated our own ideas in this way and created structures out of them, we have to find solutions, either by finding an analogy that points to a way forward or by adapting them. Both of these depend upon our ability to think counterintuitively, which involves two things:

1 The ability to detach ourselves from routine patterns of thought and apply seemingly unrelated mental frameworks to the problem.
2 The ability to forget about what we might wish or expect to be the case and focus our attention just on the situation as we have laid it out in our structure of ideas. Unburdened by normal expectations, we are freer to think about the nature of the structure we have created and the similarities it might have with previously unrelated structures, into which all the pieces might fit.

This addresses a critical problem that most organisations and professions are forced to confront. To survive in a rapidly changing environment they need to escape System 1 thinking that tends to dominate their day-to-day thinking. They must be able to think strategically and adapt.

To do this they need people capable of System 2 thinking. In other words, they must be capable of detaching themselves from routine patterns of thought and from what they might wish or expect to be the case, free themselves from normal expectations, ask naïve questions and apply unrelated structures to find solutions to problems that might otherwise defy solution.

> To escape the day-to-day thinking of System 1 thinking, organisations need people who can think strategically and use their System 2 thinking.

In this way we are able to see things differently. As we discovered in chapter 11, it can often produce the most surprising rewards. Insight and moments of genuine originality can occur in response to a fact that means nothing to others. Analogies can open up new, fertile avenues of investigation that transform the way we think and explore problems. By developing our ability to identify and use analogies in this way we can see answers that may well lead to new ways in which an organisation can develop or a professional can meet the needs of her clients.

3. Adapting structures to find solutions

If we cannot find an answer by using analogies, then we need to overcome the inertia of routine day-to-day thinking by using the four strategies we learned in chapter 12 to adapt our normal pattern of expectations:

1 Change the structure
2 Approach it from a different direction
3 Start at a different point
4 Create a new structure

By using these simple strategies we can place ourselves in the position of being able to think outside the norm, revealing what might otherwise have seemed an inspired way of approaching the problem. Often, having created a different perspective from which to see the problem, the answer then seems obvious. We saw in chapter 12 how organisations and professionals, working in what seemed to them the most sensible and effective way, found themselves in situations in which everything they did seemed to make matters worse.

For instance. . .

We found that in Texas the state government's corrections policy was based on assumptions that were shared by politicians and judges alike, but which resulted in the highest incarceration rate in the world, while one in three inmates was back in prison within three years. Worse still for the average taxpayer, the state was running the biggest deficit in state history and just couldn't afford to build the new prisons that were needed.

So, not only was this an ineffective system, it was also unsustainable. It wasn't until one judge decided to reinterpret the routine structure of ideas that had justified this rate of incarceration, that a solution was found.

It was assumed that everyone had had the same education and upbringing as the judges and politicians, so if they broke the law, they did so out of unfettered free will. Once they had challenged this assumption, the solution was obvious: try to understand more, condemn less and invest in rehabilitation. Not only did this work with even violent crime falling at more than twice the national average, but costs were cut and so too were prison populations.[3]

We saw similar examples of other professionals and organisations, which were able to escape the routine assumptions that had ruled their day-to-day work by adopting one of the four methods.

> **For instance. . .**
>
> We saw how the American psychologist Stanton Samenow, who worked with the criminally insane, turned his own routine assumptions inside out to find a solution to his problem. As a classical Freudian therapist, his work was grounded in the belief that he could influence inmates' behaviour, reforming many of them, so that they could lead normal lives. But after years of work he realised that he was not having the success he expected.
>
> He had believed that *he* was the one exerting the influence, but, he wondered, what if I reverse this assumption: what if it's the other way around. Having reversed his assumption, he changed his strategy. He began by holding the criminal completely accountable for his offences.

The problem is that all organisations, businesses and professionals face the challenge of adapting to meet the demands of rapid change, yet many are wedded to the way they have always worked and see no way of changing. As Edward de Bono argues, once we have begun to dig a hole we are reluctant to sacrifice the time and effort we have invested and start another instead. It's easier to go on digging than wonder what else to do. And our education reinforces this. It is designed to make us appreciate the holes that have been dug; to follow in the footsteps of experts, who understand the present holes better than anyone else.

- Once we have begun to dig a hole we are reluctant to sacrifice the time and effort we have invested and start another instead.
- Our education is designed to make us appreciate the holes that have been dug.

Psychometric tests

It is no surprise, therefore, that employers worldwide are eager to employ graduates who have the creative thinking skills that we have learned over the last five chapters. Without these they are more likely to fall back on routine patterns of behaviour and ideas that they may never have seriously challenged or evaluated. As a result, they will continue to tackle today's problems with yesterday's solutions.

Unfortunately, as we have seen, most employers are inundated with unsatisfactory applications from graduates who have good degrees, but cannot think. To select the best, three types of psychometric questions are normally used:

1. Inductive reasoning problems

These come in different forms, but they all assess our ability to draw reliable inferences. In chapter 9 we saw how to tackle those that assess our ability to generate ideas, while in chapter 10 we saw how to answer those that test our ability to structure our ideas, draw hypotheses from them and then test and adapt them.

2. Verbal reasoning tests

These too come in various forms. In chapter 11 we learned the skills to answer those that ask us to distinguish between safe and unsafe analogies by getting us to choose the closest synonym or antonym for a word.

3. Insight or lateral thinking problems

In chapter 12 we learned how to tackle insight problems. This type of problem comes in three forms: spatial, verbal and mathematical, although they are all tackled in the same way.

The widespread use of these tests demonstrates the urgency of the need for these skills. The Chartered Institute of Personnel and Development in its 2012 learning and development survey concluded that these 'higher level creative skills are key to our competitive future'.

But it also demonstrates the critical lack of creative thinking skills among graduate applicants. The World Bank concluded that education institutions must 'refocus the assessments, teaching-learning process, and curricula away from lower-order thinking skills, such as remembering and understanding, toward higher-order skills, such as analyzing and solving . . . problems, as well as creativity'.

Summary

1 By making it clear what *we* think by generating our own ideas we are less likely to be dictated to by our sources.

2 If we can graft the ideas we read onto our own network of beliefs, our arguments will be more consistent and persuasive.

3 Finding an interesting and original problem for our dissertation involves the same methods and skills we use in problem-solving.

4 To meet the challenge of adapting to change all organisations are searching for graduates who have the skills we have learned in the last five chapters.

5 But the urgent demand and the short supply mean that there are exciting possibilities for those who have developed these skills.

Conclusion

We began this chapter by talking about the transformative experiences that occur when you realise that you have something of your own of real value and importance to contribute. Genuine education starts at this liberating point. It's not a question of which textbooks you have read or the knowledge you can recall. The question is can you produce unique solutions to problems and insights that are genuinely yours?

It is this that will have the greatest impact on your academic work and on your employability. The skills you have learned over the last five chapters will improve your academic work: your essays, your dissertation and your presentations. As you make the ideas your own, your arguments will be more relevant, consistent and persuasive. Equally important, you will be able to demonstrate to employers that you have the creative skills they need to meet the demands of a changing environment.

Making Decisions

So far we have stressed the importance of suspending our judgement for fear of slamming the door on ideas before they are fully developed. We have learned to work with ideas that might at first seem ludicrous, knowing that studies have shown that those who force themselves to resist the temptation of dismissing them produce the greater proportion of good ideas.

But now we have reached the stage when we must commit ourselves. Coming to a judgement and making a decision is an integral part of smart thinking. It is at this point that we make these ideas our own by testing and integrating them within our own network of beliefs and understanding.

When we fail to do this, we make it more difficult for ourselves to use these ideas convincingly. We struggle to express them with any clarity and use them with confidence. In our essays, reports and dissertations we're likely to stumble from one unconvincing explanation to another as we struggle to express ideas which are not ours in a language we do not command.

Unfortunately we are not helped by education systems that encourage us to believe that for every decision there is an authority to lean upon. We don't have to make our own decisions, just rely on our authorities. As a result, we are content just to recycle the opinions of authorities, while our teachers settle for teaching us *what* to think, rather than *how* to think.

Uncertainty in the workplace

Yet, the real world is full of uncertainty, so we have to make our own decisions to create order out of chaos. However, learning to live without this ready-made certainty and make our own decisions is not something we have ever found easy.

Much of human history has been shaped by the need to find certainty in whatever form: faith in God, national allegiances, ideologies, inspiring individuals, who seem to have the answer to our deepest fears. It probably explains why the shelves of bookshops are crammed with texts on various forms of self-improvement, psychotherapy, meditation and modern-day religions, all of which appeal to a growing number of people in search of faiths that will bring them instant certainty.

With these to lean on we have no need to understand uncertainty, how to measure risk and how to come to a good decision based on it. Consequently, most people, regardless of their education or profession, struggle to assess risk and draw reliable inferences from it. Doctors often know the error rates of a clinical test and the base rate of a disease, but not how to infer from this the chances that a patient with a positive test has the disease. The courts, too, struggle in the same way, which leads to unjust convictions that have to be revised.

For instance...

In 1999 Sally Clark was found guilty of murdering her two infant children and given two life sentences. It was not until two other women had been convicted on the same basis that in January 2003 questions were asked about the figure given for the likelihood of two cot deaths occurring in one family.

At the original trial this had been calculated as one in 73 million, which was arrived at by squaring 1 in 8,500, the figure for the chance of one event occurring. But it was based on the assumption that the two events were independent of one another, when in fact several studies had shown that there is an increased frequency of cot deaths in families where one had already occurred. This should have been challenged by the defence, but it wasn't. Nobody seemed to understand the implications of the original assessment of the risk.

In this stage we will learn to cope with the void that has been filled in previous centuries by faith in God, nations and ideologies. We will learn what makes a good decision-maker, what makes a good decision, the steps we need to take to make them and how to assess risk and probability. In the process, we will learn the skills we need to make our own decisions in a world without certainty.

What makes a good decision-maker?

In this chapter you will learn. . .

- About what is meant by decision-making.
- The different types of decision-maker.
- What makes a good decision-maker.
- What makes a good decision.
- What's involved in decision analysis test (DAT) questions.

A radio producer in Washington, DC a few years ago, was awarded a promotion on the grounds that he was a 'good decision-maker'. Where most of us might have accepted it gratefully and said nothing, he wondered why, when so many of his decisions had not worked out well. The company, though, wasn't at all bothered by this. 'Being a good decision-maker means you're good at making decisions', one executive told him reassuringly. 'It doesn't mean you make good decisions.'[1]

In fact, of course, it does: it's not just a question of making decisions, but of making the right ones. We invest our savings in a mutual fund trusting that the fund manager is not just good at making decisions, but that he has a consistent record of making good ones. Yet, unfortunately, studies reveal that most of us are much poorer at it than we think.

What is decision-making?

To become better decision-makers we must first be clear about what decision-making is. The term is frequently used to describe a number of things: making a choice, expressing a preference, arriving at a judgement, indeed all those operations that bring a process to an end. In effect, it is a bridge between thinking and acting, even though no overt action might take place. In many cases it involves an internal process of choosing whether to accept ideas or values by testing and integrating them within our own network of beliefs and understanding.

But the process is the same whether it involves this or an overt action. It consists of seven steps. The first three represent the work we have already done in the first two stages of smart thinking: conceptual and creative thinking.

Making a good decision

1 Pin the problem down through conceptual thinking: creating concepts, analysing them and synthesising ideas;
2 Generate and structure our ideas;
3 Design solutions to the problem;
4 Evaluate how well each solution will meet their goals, preferences and values;
5 Assess risk: the probability of the success and effectiveness of each one;
6 Make a decision;
7 Reflecting on the decision.

It is essentially a process of converting inputs into outputs. The quality of our output depends upon the quality of our inputs. Working through the first two stages of smart thinking has ensured that we have the best inputs we can design. As we have seen, this depends upon not having a narrow vision, playing devil's advocate by generating a wealth of ideas from which we can design different solutions to problems. In this way we ensure that we consider as many approaches as we can, even those we find uncomfortable.

It is also a process of understanding the uncertainty and risks involved, so that we can reduce them as much as possible to allow for a reasonable choice to be made. Every decision involves risk, it is unavoidable. If you don't have uncertainty, you don't have a decision to make: you are merely left with an algorithm – a procedure or formula for solving a problem.

For instance. . .

In July 2011 David Cameron was criticised for being indecisive in the Coulson affair involving charges of phone tapping. So, the Culture Secretary, Jeremy Hunt, came to the Prime Minister's defence: 'As soon as the Prime Minister had all the facts', he said, 'he made a decision and acted decisively.'

Putting aside the apparent tautology, this misses the point: if he has all the facts, he is no longer making a decision; he's just working out a problem. The real challenge is when you don't have all the facts, when you have to make a decision in a situation that is uncertain and full of risk.

- Decision-making is the bridge between thinking and acting.
- It involves an internal process of deciding whether to accept ideas as well as an overt action.
- If there is no uncertainty, all we have is a procedure for solving a problem.

Types of decision-maker

Already you can see that there are different types of decision-maker. Indeed, you could say that there are broadly three types:

1 The decisive decision-maker

2 The indecisive decision-maker

3 The non-decision-maker

1. The decisive decision-maker

To describe someone as a 'decisive' decision-maker seems tautological, but for this type doubt in any form is an utterly alien experience. They arrive at their decision without a systematic analysis of the issues, relying entirely on System 1 thinking: their intuitions. In the 1960s the British psychologist John Cohen described them as having 'Dante's Disease'. In the *Convivio* (1307) Dante described them as suffering from 'this terrible malady', the victims of which are 'so presumptuous that they suppose themselves to know everything . . . everything is true that approves itself to them, and everything false that does not.'

For instance. . .

Politicians exhibit these characteristics more than most. Cohen describes them as being 'sublimely insensible to the possibility that they could ever be mistaken . . . unencumbered by that gift for suspending judgement which hampers the ordinary man'. They dare not admit political ignorance, because they are, by definition, well informed. To admit any shadow of doubt, they would be accepting the possibility that their opponents might conceivably be correct, and that must at all costs be ruled out.[2]

Of course it is natural to want to be confident in your own beliefs about complicated matters, particularly those we have to act upon. But we live in a culture that venerates decisive people, people of action, like the Washington radio producer; even though we know that anyone can make a decision. Over the last 30 years we have seen the popularisation of what we might describe as the 'Just do it!' culture. Not to come to an instant decision is to show weakness. To deliberate at all is to show that you don't know your own mind.

For instance. . .

A favourite riddle among managers at the Royal Bank of Scotland (RBS) before its collapse was the '5-Birds riddle'.

Question: Five birds are sitting on a log. Two decide to fly away. How many are left?

The answer three probably comes to mind. But the correct answer is, in fact, five. Two birds *decided* to fly away, but that doesn't mean they actually did. The managers were convinced that this endorsed one of the most important reasons for the company's success: its bias towards action.[3]

2. The indecisive decision-maker

In sharp contrast is the indecisive decision-maker, those who are so overwhelmed with information that they face decision paralysis. They simply cannot make up their minds; they are in a perpetual state of doubt. The problem is that too much choice can be demotivating.

> **For instance. . .**
>
> In a study conducted several years ago, shoppers who were offered free samples of six different jams were more likely to buy one than shoppers who were offered free samples of 24. This result seems irrational – surely you're more apt to find something you like from a range four times as large – but it can be replicated in a variety of contexts.

In these conditions information overload occurs. We have so much information that we can no longer manage or process it effectively, which handicaps our decision-making skills. As a result, we either use the information in an arbitrary, selective way to support a preconceived solution, or we make a hasty, careless decision.

> **Too much choice can be demotivating as we struggle to process all the information.**

However, there is one other explanation for this behaviour. All of the decisions we make are made in the context of other decisions. There is a stream of decisions that lead up to every decision we make. This not only makes future decisions possible, but also limits our freedom. As we make one decision we open a door, but we close another at the same time. People who struggle to make decisions might be said to feel the loss of this freedom and, therefore, are reluctant to decide.

3. The non-decision-maker

In contrast to the other two, the non-decision-maker doesn't recognise that there is a decision that needs to be made at all. This can be broken down into two types.

3.1 The purveyors of certainty

If you believe there are only certainties, you don't have a decision to make. You merely have a problem that can be solved by learning to use a formula or procedure. If others persist in demanding a decision, they clearly don't understand.

> **For instance. . .**
>
> In the Second World War, when Herman Goering was told that an allied fighter had been shot down over a German city way behind Axis lines, suggesting that the Allies had developed a long-range fighter, Goering said emphatically that he 'knew' such a development was impossible: 'I officially assert that American fighter planes did not reach Aachen . . . I herewith give you an official order that they weren't there.'

Like Goering, modern universities, too, deal mainly in certainties, leaving students unprepared for the real world of uncertainties, where they will have to make value judgements and decisions.

3.2 The filterers

As we all know, decisions create anxiety, so to avoid it this type of non-decision-maker filters out all information, about which decisions might have to be made. In his book *Vital Lies, Simple Truths,*[4] Daniel Goleman explains that the mind protects itself against anxiety by dimming awareness of information that might create it. This causes a blind spot: a zone of blocked attention and self-deception.

> **For instance. . .**
>
> Researchers of cognitive dissonance in the 1950s found that consumers would continue to read advertisements for a new car after they'd bought it, but would filter out all information about other brands, fearing post-purchase misgivings.

When such soothing inattention becomes a habit; it comes to shape our character. Then these habits are passed on from parent to child. Indeed, this might even have an evolutionary origin. When our ancestors were under attack it was important to avoid the urge to attend to a painful wound. So the pain and terror of the moment were numbed by the endorphin system, so they could make a cool assessment without having their judgement distorted by fear and panic that could be paralysing.

For modern man physical pain is a relatively rare event. More common is psychological pain, when our self-esteem is threatened, for example, or when we suffer loss. We meet these challenges with the same alarm system tuned by millions of years of primal threats. The antidote is the same: filtered information, dimmed awareness and denial. To avoid anxiety, some professionals, like doctors, lawyers and social workers, filter out information, which may call for them to make difficult decisions.

> **For instance. . .**
>
> Over a half of those who commit suicide visit their doctor in the month before they kill themselves. Of those who die from an overdose, 80 per cent do so with a prescription they have recently obtained.

Michael Weissberg, who directs emergency psychiatric services at a university hospitable, argues that all victims and perpetrators of abuse give multiple clues that they are in trouble, yet lies and rationalisations are often believed because of the anxiety of acknowledging the truth. Denial is easier and it protects the observer from having to make a decision about what action to take if the abuse is acknowledged. A high incidence of child abuse goes on despite some contact with authorities, like teachers, therapists, police officers and social workers, who are inclined to accept explanations at face value.

> **For instance. . .**
>
> A doctor's wife brought her child to an orthopaedist with a sprained ankle, but the X-rays revealed a fracture. Seven months later she took her to another doctor with another broken bone. Only after the third fracture was abuse suspected. The mother finally admitted throwing her daughter against a wall to 'discipline' her. The family's friends and relatives had known about the injuries, but had not intervened.[5]

Most of us respond in a similar way, when we have to make a difficult decision or a judgement that involves considering material that causes us anxiety. We see an item on the news involving cruelty to animals or children and we filter the news by changing the channel. During the Holocaust the perpetrators and bystanders alike were surprisingly inventive in devising ways in which they could limit what they would allow themselves to take onboard morally; in effect, they would anaesthetise their moral sensitivity.

What makes a good decision-maker?

1. No opt-out

It's obvious from this that the best decision-maker is one who does not allow herself to have an opt-out clause. She accepts that in one way or another she will have to make a decision:

1 either she will decide to do something;
2 or she will decide not to;
3 or she will decide not to decide.

2. Metacognition

Beyond that, good decision-makers realise that our decisions and judgements are easily influenced by our System 1 thinking and by intuitions that are very likely to be unreliable. They realise that they must monitor their decision-making by using their metacognition to recognise and counter unreliable intuitions that would otherwise lead them to make poor decisions. For this they use a strategy involving careful and thorough deliberation to arrive at their decisions. In other words they work through the three stages of the 'progressive method' of smart thinking:

As you can see below, the final stage of decision-making involves four steps. In the next three chapters we will examine these in detail.

Decision-making

1 Evaluating each solution – the likely effects, good and bad?
2 Assessing risk – what are the chances of it succeeding, how effective will it be and what are the risks of failure?
3 Making the decision
4 Reflecting on the decision

Smart Thinking - The Progressive Method

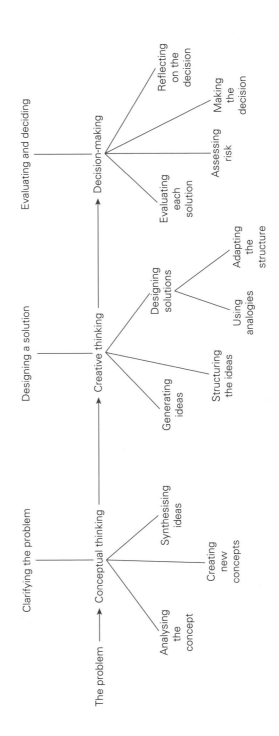

In summary, the progressive method is a process that starts with the careful clarification and analysis of the problem that we did in Stage 1 with conceptual thinking. Then we generate our ideas, structure them and design possible solutions as we did in Stage 2. Now we must evaluate each of these solutions to assess their likely effects, then assess the probability of each one succeeding and, on this basis, make a decision, using a rational, objective method to compare each option. Then, finally, we must reflect on our decision, learn from it and assess its effectiveness.

Working through these steps places good decision-makers at the centre of things, monitoring their own thinking. They have the confidence and ability to think about their thinking while they think, changing it where it needs to be changed. In this way they learn to recognise those moments when they need to be on their guard:

1   When their intuitions are likely to be unreliable.
2   When they make complex decisions.

1. Unreliable intuitions

In some situations there is no substitute for our intuitive thinking. But we have to learn to recognise these by carefully reflecting on the process we work through to come to our decision. Otherwise many of our judgements and decisions will be made by routine intuitions before we know it, leaving us vulnerable to the sort of mistakes we saw in chapter 1:

1   The narrative fallacy
2   Simplifying heuristics:
2.1   Representativeness
    2.2   Belief bias
    2.3   Anchoring effect
    2.4   Availability bias
    2.5   Affect heuristic

2. Complex decisions

There are also complex problems that cannot be solved by resorting to routine, intuitive thinking. If we do, we can easily find ourselves sweeping aside careful deliberation about, say, a serious moral dilemma, on the grounds that our intuition about it 'just feels right'. To solve these we must resort to the more deliberative, reflective System 2 thinking.

3. Counterintuitive thinking

Once we have realised that we're in a situation in which our intuitive responses cannot be relied upon, we must then set about thinking counterintuitively about the options open to us. A good decision-maker will think the unthinkable and challenge his normal intuitive response that might seem at first overwhelmingly convincing.

In chapter 1 we found that our initial intuitive responses are often influenced by the *availability bias*. When we are asked to estimate the frequency of something, we come to our decision by retrieving from our memories instances of it happening. The ease with which we can call up such examples determines how large we judge the frequency to be: if we can easily retrieve them, then we judge that it is likely to be large.

For instance. . .

If you were a local politician on a committee deciding on the spending priorities for next year, you might have to decide the amount that should be spent on a policy intended to reduce the number of teenage pregnancies. How important you decide this is will depend upon your estimate of the frequency of this occurring. If you rely on your intuition, this might depend upon how easily you can recall examples of it occurring in your own experience.

Not surprisingly we are not very good at making these sorts of estimate. A recent Mori survey of 14 countries found that people thought 15 per cent of teenagers aged 15–19 gave birth each year, whereas the official figures showed that it was only 1.2 per cent. In the US the figure was estimated at 24 per cent, when in fact it was only 3 per cent.[6]

As with all the simplifying heuristics listed above, in the *availability bias* we substitute one question for another: instead of estimating the frequency of something we answer a simpler question by reporting our impression of how easy it was to retrieve an example from memory. Good decision-makers, however, challenge their initial estimates and consider the possibility that, although they seem overwhelmingly convincing, they may not be accurate.

Simplifying heuristics: substitute a simpler question for a more difficult one.

Obviously, to counter these failings we need to think counterintuitively, using a method that harnesses our System 2 thinking to ensure we evaluate each option rationally, calculate risk accurately and come to the best decision.

4. Assessing risk and probabilities

As this demonstrates, our intuitive preferences consistently violate the rules of rational choice. Nowhere is this more obvious than in our assessment of risk and probability. Although not all of our intuitions are untrustworthy, their reliability is based on something that is unknowable.

Definition
An intuition is something we know without knowing how we know.

Our confidence in them is subjective, which is not a good indicator of accuracy. It is often based on irrelevant things, so, without knowing it, we may be answering the wrong question.

For instance. . .

An investor may decide to invest in Ford shares, because he likes the look of the cars. But this may have little to do with how well the company is run, the competition it faces or even the reliability of the cars themselves.

With the *narrative fallacy* our confidence is based on how convincing and compelling are the stories that we create from the facts we have collected. In none of these cases is the confidence generated any substitute for a rational evaluation of probability.

For instance. . .

Terry Odean, a finance professor at the University of California at Berkeley, studied the trading records of 10,000 individual investors spanning a seven-year period. He analysed every transaction, nearly 163,000 trades. Investors sold one stock and then reinvested in another, confident in the story they had created that told them one stock was bound to rise while the other would fall.

He compared the results of the two stocks over the following year. The results were unequivocally bad. On average the shares sold did better than those bought by a significant margin: 3.2 per cent per year. And over and above that there were the substantial costs involved in making the two trades.[7]

The *narrative fallacy* and all the simplifying heuristics demonstrate just how much System 1 thinking is based on subjective confidence. It is a feeling, not a judgement. Whether we are experts or novices we tend to be more confident about our decisions and the stories that support them than is justified. Consequently, we stop our search before we have gathered all the available evidence.

Try this. . .

In each of the following pairs, which historical event happened first? Also indicate your level of confidence in your decision on a scale of 0 to 10, with 10 meaning perfect confidence and 0 indicating a guess.

a) Signing of the Magna Carta   b) Birth of Mohammed
a) Death of Napoleon   b) Louisiana Purchase
a) Lincoln's assassination   b) Birth of Queen Victoria

Tests conducted among graduates, undergraduates, doctors, even CIA analysts, showed that their confidence rating was much higher than the accuracy of their answers warranted: those who were 100 per cent confident achieved only 80 per cent accuracy; those who were 90 per cent confident 70 per cent accuracy; and those who were 80 per cent confident 60 per cent accuracy.[8]

To be a good decision-maker we have to learn to be wary of such overconfidence. Unless we gather all the available evidence and conduct a rational, objective analysis of the risks, we will be relying on subjective responses that leave us vulnerable to simplifying heuristics.

What makes a good decision-maker?

1 No opt-out
2 Metacognition – they know how to monitor their thinking
3 Counterintuitive thinking – they know how to challenge their intuitions
4 They know how to assess risk and probabilities

What makes a good decision?

Over the next three chapters we will learn how to make a good decision. But, first, what exactly is a good decision?

1. Based on all the available information

In view of what we've just said, it's not surprising to stress the importance of basing a decision on all the evidence available. Even when we make the most significant decisions of our lives, so confident are we in our intuitive impressions that we can fail to search for outside views that might challenge them.

> **For instance. . .**
>
> A chef who decides to set up his own restaurant in the middle of a busy city might be inclined to emphasise his own talents and abilities as the key factors in the likely success of the project. So, he is likely to be reluctant to search beyond his personal impressions for statistics about the success of similar projects. The city may be overpopulated with restaurants all competing in the same limited market and struggling to survive. As a result, the success rate may be very poor, despite the undoubted talents of their owners.

In these cases it is all too easy to emphasise what *we* can do to the exclusion of other factors. Our projections, therefore, are likely to be little more than best-case scenarios.

2. Realistic

To make these projections more realistic we need to subject our project to 'reference class forecasting', that is, consult the statistics for similar cases, similar businesses in similar markets. Instead of relying just on our personal impressions, we need to make a rational assessment of the potential gains and losses, and the probability of failure. There appear to be a number of reasons why many project designers underestimate the odds they face as they take on risky projects. As we have seen:

1 We tend to focus too heavily on our own talents and what we can do, while ignoring the skills and plans of our competitors;
2 Similarly, we ignore the statistics for the market that we plan to enter: how crowded it is and the failure rate of similar projects.

According to one study, whenever the founders of innovative start-ups have been asked to put a figure on the extent to which the success of their company depends upon what they do, the figure has never been less than 80 per cent. In reality it depends as much on the skills and achievements of their competitors, and on changes in the market.

3 We focus on what we know, not what we don't know.
4 And by emphasising our skills and what we can do, we develop an illusion of control: we feel confident about explaining the past and predicting the future, which encourages us to take risks that we should avoid. As Nassim Taleb insists, we have an inadequate grasp of uncertainty in the environment; we neglect the influence of luck.

3. Meets all our objectives

You could say that a good decision will meet our preferences as completely as possible, although what we prefer is often not what we value and it is this that represents a deeper understanding of our ultimate objectives. You might have a strong preference to smoke a cigarette, but you know this would go against what you value most: to give up smoking completely.

Moreover, our assessment of what we prefer is not always reliable. Daniel Kahneman draws the distinction between the 'experiencing self' and the 'remembering self'.[9] The experiencing self records what we actually experience, while the remembering self creates, out of a few critical moments, a vivid, memorable story, which we keep for future reference. Despite the distorted account of the experience, it is this that tends to determine our preferences.

> **For instance. . .**
>
> Our holiday may have been disappointing, but our remembering self creates a positive story out of the anticipation and excitement of travelling to the resort, the most memorable events while we were there and then the return home.

Clearly, a decision that fails to meet our objectives, because it is based on inaccurate predictions drawn from a distorted account of our preferences, is a poor decision. It is also an obvious challenge to the rational agent model, which assumes that each individual has consistent preferences, knows them clearly and can make rational choices that maximise them.

4. Meets our objectives efficiently

But that's not all: a good decision should not only meet our objectives, but do so at the minimum cost, energy and unwanted side effects. We have to test our preferred option by asking ourselves whether there are other more efficient means of achieving our objectives. Have we dismissed these for good reason? In our hasten to get on with something and implement our plans we often overlook these.

We also have to take into account all the side effects: the indirect advantages and disadvantages; the unintended consequences that we would otherwise not have seen. A good decision is one that has involved standing back from our preferred choice to take account of these.

> **For instance. . .**
>
> As a result of reconsidering the different options, an organisation that is planning to expand its product range might realise that it already has the talent and skills lying unused in its present workforce, if it decides to adopt one option rather than another.

5. Acceptance

Nevertheless, after taking into account all these factors, a decision can clearly appear to be the best, yet still fail, if it overlooks the human factor. Those who have to implement it might be reluctant to work this way or consumers might not be keen on the product. So, to everyone's surprise what appeared to be the weaker option produces better results.

For instance. . .

After the Second World War it was thought that cake mixes would be very popular with the modern busy housewife. So companies produced mixes to which women only needed to add water. But the sales were disappointing. Then the psychologist Ernest Dichter found that women wanted to feel more involved in the process and that mixes, which required them to add eggs and sometimes milk, would sell better. They would feel that they are actually 'making' the cake, rather than just adding water. So, ironically, the most successful solution was, in fact, the least convenient.

What makes a good decision?

1 Based on all the available information
2 Realistic
3 Meets all our objectives
4 Meets our objectives efficiently
5 Acceptance

Psychometric problems – the decision analysis test

To test that you have the skills to make good decisions some employers use the decision analysis test (DAT). Unfortunately, these don't assess the full range of abilities you will use when you make decisions in the real world, which are represented by the three stages of smart thinking. The first two stages have now brought us to the point where we can now make a choice between different solutions.

Try this. . .

Parents on the touchline

In previous chapters we have worked on the problem of parents on the touchline shouting at officials, coaches and particularly at their children. We have generated ideas, structured them and then designed possible solutions. Now use these as we work through the next three chapters, so that you can make an informed decision as to what might be the best solution to the problem.

In contrast, the decision analysis tests concentrate exclusively on how well you make judgements. You are given information in a written, graphic or tabular form. Then you are expected to analyse key concepts in the information and find patterns in it, from which you make your own judgement and decide on the best answer from a list of possible answers.

So, although they don't test the full range of abilities you will need when you make decisions in your professional life, they do assess your ability to make judgements in situations of uncertainty, when the information you have is complex and incomplete or ambiguous, rather than simply apply rules that you have learned. In addition, some tests, like the UKCAT (UK Clinical Aptitude Test), ask you to complete an exercise in metacognition by indicating the level of confidence that you have in your decisions.

DATs are designed to assess the following abilities:

- To find concepts in complex information.
- To analyse concepts and information.
- To synthesise information, combining it to make new connections and inferences.
- To find patterns in the information.
- To use these patterns to find the right answer.
- To make your own value judgements.

The test is presented in the form of a deciphering problem, an exercise in code-breaking, with information contained in text, tables and other forms. This is divided between 'Operators' or 'General rules' and 'Specific information' or 'Basic codes'. You are then set a number of questions, each one having four or five possible answers from which to choose.

For instance. . .

While cleaning a fourteenth-century tapestry at the British Museum a previously undetected code is found woven into the fabric. This consists of a series of letters and numbers grouped together in sequences as coded messages. Your job is to decipher the codes. On the basis of the information that you are given make a judgement as to what you think it means.[10]

Operators/General rules

A = multiple
B = opposite
C = down
D = group
E = danger
F = noble
G = into
H = special

Specific information/Basic codes

1 = I
2 = you
3 = man
4 = horse
5 = sword
6 = tree
7 = brave
8 = move
9 = take
10 = fight
11 = creature

12 = castle
13 = goblet
14 = search

What is the best interpretation of the coded message: C12, 1, 9, F(B3)

A. Down from the castle, the noblewoman takes me as her equal.
B. The countess was my downfall.
C. I am taking the duchess into the castle.
D. I took the countess down from her castle.
E. The duchess and I found our downfall at the castle.

Answer

As we have found in previous problems, the most effective strategy is to write down all the information you have and set it out clearly. In this case write out a literal translation, grouping all the elements with commas and brackets as they are shown in the original. Then look at the possible answers and eliminate those that omit elements or combine them incorrectly.

Literal translation: down (castle), I, take, noble (opposite (man))

Starting with C12 or 'down (castle)', (A) and (D) have these elements, but (B) omits 'castle' and (C) swaps 'down' for 'into', so both of these can be eliminated. We can retain (E), although it has separated 'down' from 'castle', and 'down' has been translated into 'downfall', which is a more complex concept.

The next element is 'I', which the three remaining answers have, but when we come to 'take' (E) does not include this, so it can be eliminated. The final element, 'noble (opposite (man))' could be translated as 'noblewoman', as in (A), or as 'countess', as in (D). However, (A) also includes the concept 'as her equal', which is not included in the code, so the correct answer cannot be (A), which leaves us with (D).

Try this. . .

What is the best interpretation of the coded message: F(7,3), E8, 5, B(G6)

A. The brave duke pulled the dangerous sword out of the tree.
B. The brave duke risked pushing the sword into the tree.
C. The duke bravely moved away from the treacherous tree with sword in hand.
D. The knight pulled the sword out of the tree.
E. The knight risked pulling the sword out of the tree.

Summary

1 We all tend to avoid decisions by shielding ourselves from the anxiety of having to make them.

2 To avoid the overwhelming influence of our System 1 intuitions we have to resort to System 2 thinking by using our metacognition and counterintuitive thinking.

3 Good decision-makers go beyond intuitions and personal impressions and assess risks and probability rationally.

4 The decision analysis test assesses our ability to make our own judgements in situations of uncertainty.

What's next?

No matter who we are, how much experience we have had or the success that we have achieved, we all struggle to make good decisions. You can see this graphically illustrated in the demise of RBS in 2007. The disastrous deal to buy ABN Amro, which wrecked RBS, was not an impetuous decision made in haste and regretted at leisure. The board met 18 times to discuss it and still decided unanimously to go through with it.

As we have seen, it is difficult to overcome the beguiling appeal of our intuitions and personal impressions. Their influence can be overpowering. They cloud our judgement by obscuring any other possibility. This is the challenge we face. In the next three chapters you will learn the steps you need to take and skills you need to develop to resist the appeal of this and make good decisions based on careful, rational evaluation.

How to evaluate our solutions

In this chapter you will learn. . .

- How to assess each solution on all the practical issues it raises.
- How to predict the likely responses to each solution.
- The importance of co-operation and trust to the success of each solution.
- How maximising our own self-interest often results in a situation we least want.
- How our reference points distort our judgement about the potential benefits of different solutions.

Unfortunately, our evolution has left us without the skills to be good decision-makers. For the most part our ancestors survived by learning a system of rules and patterns of behaviour, with which they complied without much thought. Beyond the uncomplicated decision whether to comply with these reaction patterns and survive or disregard them and in all probability be killed, they had little need for the rational and reflective decision-making skills that complex decisions demand.

For virtually all of the 4–5 million years of our existence we have been programmed in this way for survival, not rational thought. Like our ancestors, for the most part we make decisions in accordance with accepted patterns of behaviour guided only by our intuitions. To overcome these limitations we have worked through the first two stages of the three-stage method of smart thinking and learned how to think conceptually and creatively. Now we have to complete the final stage: decision-making.

Decision-making

1 Evaluating each solution – the likely effects, good and bad?
2 Assessing risk – what are the chances of it succeeding, how effective will it be and what are the risks of failure?
3 Making the decision
4 Reflecting on the decision

In this chapter we will learn how to evaluate each of our solutions. To do this we conduct a series of mental simulations on one solution after another to see what is likely to be the effects of adopting them. As you do this you will find it helpful to do three things:

1 Assess the **practical consequences** of each solution;
2 Try to predict the likely **responses and decisions of others?**, who will be affected by it, so you can adjust the solution to make it more effective;

3 Evaluate the influence of your **reference point** on your evaluation of the problem – our preferences vary with our situation, so we have to take this into account as we evaluate each solution.

1. Practical consequences – costs and benefits

Our aim is to get a picture that is as complete and objective as possible, while escaping the intuitive biases that might otherwise blinker us from seeing something, which afterwards we realise we should have seen. To avoid this and evaluate each solution exhaustively we must consider the negative aspects of each one, like the cost, the time needed, the problems that will be created and the likely consequences, as well as the positives, like the time and money that might be saved, the improvements in the morale of employees and the greater opportunity for more creative contributions.

Take into account. . .

Costs and benefits
Direct and indirect effects

This has to include not just the direct, but also the indirect, effects, which we easily overlook if we fail to work through the mental simulations of what might happen.

For instance. . .

An organisation might realise that by adopting one solution it can make better use of skills in its workforce that at present lie unused. Similarly, a company might be considering whether to move into a new market. The indirect effects of this on suppliers or customers might make one option more viable than another.

To work through these factors in a structured and routine way, ask yourself the following practical questions:

Practical questions

1 WHAT exactly will have to be done to implement the solution?
2 HOW will it be done? Timescale? Will it be done in stages? Will it require special expertise or finance?
3 WHO will be responsible for the work? Who will be in charge? How many will it take?
4 TIME – when is it likely to be implemented? Will it have to wait until the resources can be gathered together or things have been arranged?
5 PROBLEMS – what problems are likely to arise? How can they be avoided or overcome?
   5.1 Effectiveness – is it more effective than the other solutions?
   5.2 Complexity – is it unnecessarily complicated?

5.3 Economy – is it too expensive to implement?

5.4 Convenience – will it be simple to implement or cause problems for a lot of people

5.5 Compatibility – will it be compatible with systems that already operate?

5.6 Safety – are there safety concerns with it? Would it present dangers to those who implement it and then to those who will have to operate it?

5.7 Legality – does it infringe existing laws that will have to be reformed? Will special licences have to be obtained and certain legal requirements met?

5.8 Morality – does it raise serious moral issues?

5.9 Public opinion – will it turn public opinion against the organisation? Will it lose customers?

5.10 Public information – will it be necessary to hold public meetings or write articles or get well-known people to explain through the media what is entailed? What will have to be done and how it will affect people?

6 CONSEQUENCES – what are the likely consequences of the solution?

6.1 On those directly affected? Individuals and communities?

6.2 What will be the direct and indirect effects on not just those in the vicinity, but those more distant in geography and time e.g. the future generation?

2. Predicting the responses and decisions of others

However, there is another more complex set of problems that we have to consider. For our solution to be effective we need a clear idea of how people will react to our decision.

Take into account. . .

What others may think and do in response.

We have to be able to predict events and the decisions others will make, so that we can assess the likelihood that things will develop as we believe they will. For that we need an accurate idea of what motivates their behaviour: what do they want; what are they likely to do to get it; what decisions are they likely to come to in response to our decision?

The importance of this lies in the fact that it deals with the unpredictability of situations. Once we have answered these questions, we can make better decisions without relying on misleading intuitions.

1. Classic decision-making theory

At the heart of classic decision-making theory are two interconnected theories, which are familiar to anyone who lives in modern western society. Indeed, they lie at the core of much of our thinking, our choices and how we understand the way society, the economy and governments work:

1   Rational agent theory
2   Expected utility theory

1.1 Rational agent theory

The economics that most of must learn as part of everyday life, and particularly at schools and universities, is grounded in the belief that all of us are

1   rational,
2   self-interested,
3   and, therefore, seek to maximise our own self-interests.

As economists teach it, rational agents have a complete knowledge of the market, compare all the choices available and then choose that which maximises their own self-interest.

1.2 Expected utility theory

As for what we want, this is settled by the expected utility theory or, more generally, expected value theory – in this case 'value' is calculated in terms of the satisfaction of preferences. We make our decisions by determining how likely something is to occur, estimating the likely value or utility of the outcome and then multiplying the two.

> **Most likely to satisfy our preferences = Value x Likelihood**

The optimum choice is the one that has the largest product: the one that is most likely to satisfy our preferences.

This theory plays a central role not just in the rational agent theory, but in modern economics and social science in general. It answers the question that we ask when we make decisions: what choice should I make when I'm not sure of the outcome of my actions? The answer comes in the form of a principle: choose the act which has the highest expected utility.

1.3 Problems

However, it also points to a number of problems that affect the quality of our decisions and the factors we must take into account as we make our choice.

1. Preference maximisation

Unfortunately, expected utility theory answers the question, 'What choice should I make when I'm not sure of the outcome of my actions?', by simplifying the range of possible outcomes. It is only concerned with utility and a restricted definition of it at that. Utility is a concept for quantifying the desirability of the outcome of a particular decision. It does not necessarily mean the more commonplace and broader definition as 'usefulness'.

> **For instance. . .**
>
> It might be more useful for you to buy a 4-wheel-drive vehicle, but buying a sports car might be more desirable.

Moreover, the interpretation of utility as desirability often fails to meet our deepest needs and values. As desirability it means that which maximises our preferences. But, as we saw in the previous chapter, what we prefer is often not what we value and it is this that represents a deeper understanding of our ultimate objectives. What's more, all preferences count the same. So the process we go through to decide what to do is just to add them up, when we all know that some desires are much more valuable than others.

> **For instance. . .**
>
> You might desire to buy the sports car, but you also have the desire to save up to buy your own home or go back to college to get a qualification. You might desire to spend your money at the local bar each night, but you also have the desire to feed your family.

2. The rational optimiser

To add to this problem, both of these theories assume that the ideal decision-maker will always attempt to arrive at the optimal decision that maximises his self-interest by assembling all the facts, computing them with perfect accuracy and making his decision, which will accurately fulfil his perfectly defined goals. However, this is not only far from what we do in practice, but far from what we could possibly do.

> **For instance. . .**
>
> It means that as we do our shopping in the supermarket each week we must assess every product on every shelf by comparing it with every other product to see if we could maximise our utility by buying it. Failure to do so would mean we have not made a rational choice.

3. Self-interest

Similarly, theories grounded on the assumption that we behave in ways that efficiently serve to maximise our self-interest, struggle to explain altruism and other 'non-self-regarding behaviour'. While they capture the effects of an individual's competitiveness as she strives to maximise her own self-interest, the effects of our co-operative behaviour remain elusive. We donate blood for no reward, we give to charity, we return wallets to unknown individuals and many work for modest pay at socially useful jobs.

> **For instance. . .**
>
> In an experiment at University College London participants had to pay to avoid getting electric shocks or avoid giving them to strangers. On average they were prepared to sacrifice twice as much to save a stranger from getting a shock as they were prepared to sacrifice to avoid it themselves. Indeed, the Princeton psychologist Dacher Keltner found evidence that compassion is 'an innate human response embedded into the folds of our brains'.[1]

2. Consider co-operation as well as competition

But how does all this affect the way we evaluate our solutions? Well, as you make your evaluation of each solution and try to decide what strategy is most likely to bring the results you want, consider whether co-operation, and not just competition, might bring about the best outcome. After all, we learn to do this from an early age. We form associations, we strike deals, we compromise with others for their benefit as well as ours and we join trade unions and clubs that promote our common interests and ideals.

Take into account. . .

Co-operation as well as competition.

In all of these cases we expect the product of co-operation to be greater than we could achieve alone. To judge each of your solutions on the basis of the competitiveness model alone would be to ignore the benefits of co-operation. Indeed, these benefits were known to our earliest ancestors and clearly made evolutionary sense.

For instance. . .

Michigan biologists have concluded that humans would have wiped themselves out, if they had been selfish above all else. Our earliest state was quite different from the ruthless competitiveness we have come to accept as part of modern economic theory. This is not, as we are often led to believe, an inevitable expression of our nature. Primitive hunter-gatherer tribes have been found to punish selfish behaviour that violates an equitable order.[2]

In fact it has only been over the last two to three centuries that we have been guided by this theory of society as just a loose collection of isolated individuals, all of whom should be free to maximise their interests in competition with others. According to this theory, it follows that by definition as each individual maximises his happiness, so too does society as the sum of these individuals.

Yet, definitions apart, the evidence suggests otherwise. By seeking to maximise their own self-interests, often not only do individuals not serve the interests of society as a whole, but fail to achieve what they intended.

For instance. . .

In all the events leading up to the financial crisis of 2007/8 those involved all acted rationally to maximise their own self-interest. The banks offered cheap and easy credit to mortgage applicants. Then they packaged these mortgages up and sold them on as investments, thereby freeing themselves of any risk and responsibility if people could not repay the loans.

Estate agents, too, acted rationally to maximise their own self-interest. For them it was clearly in their self-interest to sell properties and take their commission whether or not buyers could afford it. That was not their problem; it was the banks'. And millions of people maximised their self-interest by taking out large mortgages beyond their means to buy expensive houses, calculating that as long as prices continued to rise they would get their money back with profit.

All of this was done with people rationally maximising their own self-interest, yet it resulted in a situation that nobody wanted: lost jobs, collapsed banks, repossessions, homelessness, lost savings and huge costs to the average person in the form of higher taxes, pay freezes, declining real incomes, loss of social benefits and, for many, survival that ultimately depended on charity and food banks.

3. Interdependence and game theory

One of the many lessons to learn from this is that we live in an interdependent world. Societies are not just a loose collection of isolated individuals, in which our individual actions and their consequences can be hermetically sealed. When we make our decision on the best solution to adopt, we have to trace the indirect as well as the direct consequences of our actions and anticipate what others may think and do in response.

> Societies are interdependent, not just loose collections of isolated individuals.

Treat it like a game of chess. Each person must take into account what the other player thinks. We must put ourselves in the other person's position and try to calculate the best outcome, knowing that what he thinks and does is a key element in that calculation. We must take into account not only what we think and what the other person thinks, but what we think the other person thinks we think.

Take into account. . .

> Not only what you think and what the other person thinks, but what you think the other person thinks you think.

Although the circularity of this might seem to have no end, don't despair! This is game theory and John Nash found a solution in his concept of 'Equilibrium': a point that is reached when each person chooses his best strategy in response to what others choose to do, so that each person's strategy is best for him when the others are pursuing their best strategies.

Principle

Interdependence: the outcome for one person depends on what all the other people choose to do and vice versa.

Try this. . .

Case study: Zipcar

When Robin Chase founded the car-sharing startup Zipcar with Antje Danielson, she wanted to provide urban dwellers with a convenient, reliable, fast access to cars, which would not only bring environment benefits, but would reduce the costs of using cars for many. But to make this work she had to find this 'equilibrium' point, where she would be pursuing her best strategy, while others were pursuing theirs.

She needed to lease cars, negotiate secure parking places, buy insurance and set up a credit card system for payment. This meant negotiating with a number of organisations, including the owners of parking lots, owners of land upon which parking lots sat, car manufacturers, car rental companies and insurance companies.

To make matters more difficult, some of these saw Zipcar as a threat to their business, so she needed to think carefully about their likely responses before she negotiated with them, so she could anticipate these, the problems they foresaw and their willingness to trust her and co-operate with her largely untested business model. Many car-sharing organisations in the past had failed because of the high cost of overheads, like cars, insurance and parking spots, so she had to get this right.

For example, she realised that when she met car manufacturers she would have to allay their fears that Zipcar would be a competitor and disrupt their business. So to convince them that this was not the case she emphasised that Zipcar would, in effect, be merely aggregating people who only wanted a fraction of a car and wouldn't have bought a car on their own. For those who might go on to buy a car, she insisted that Zipcar should be viewed as a 'try before you buy' offer. Their members would always find a clean car that never breaks down, which they would then keep in mind when they came to buy one of their own.[3]

(The complete case study, along with others, can be found on the companion website: www.he.palgrave.com/smart-thinking .)

The Prisoners' Dilemma

A simplified example of this is the well-known 'Prisoners' Dilemma' problem. This demonstrates not only the importance of taking into account the interdependence of our relations with others and of calculating the impact of what we think and decide to do on what others think and decide to do, but also the importance of co-operation to a strategy designed to maximise our interests.

Try this. . .

Two prisoners are being interrogated separately about a crime they both committed jointly. The police know they can get convictions for both men on a lesser charge, but they are determined to get a conviction on the more serious charge. So, they give each prisoner a choice: he can either inform on his partner ('defect') or else remain silent ('co-operate' with his partner). But the men know that if both of them remain silent and co-operate with each other, the police will have nothing on them, except on the lesser crime for which they will each be sentenced to one year in prison.

So the police offer each man an inducement: if one of them confesses (defects) and implicates the other, he will be given immunity from prosecution and be let free, while his partner will get 20 years in prison. However, if both confess and implicate each other, then they will both go to jail for five years. What would you do in this situation?

		B	
		Confess	Not confess
A	Confess	5 yrs/5 yrs	Go free/20 yrs
	Not confess	20 yrs/Go free	1 yr/1 yr

(A's payoffs are listed first in each cell.)

Answer

You probably realise that your best strategy is to co-operate with each other. But your decision depends on what you think your friend will do. You might believe there is no way you can trust him not to defect, confess his part in the crime, implicate you and walk away free, while you're sentenced to 20 years. You also realise that he is probably thinking exactly what you're thinking, that you too will not be able to resist confessing in the expectation that you will go free.

So, you conclude you have no choice, but defect and confess your part in the crime. If your friend is foolish enough not to confess, then you will be walking out of the police station free. If, however, he confesses too, then at least you will have avoided going to jail for 20 years. So, like the banks, the estate agents and the home-buyers in the financial crisis in 2007/8, both of you, using impeccable logic, reason yourselves into the worst outcome: in this case, a longer jail sentence than you needed to have served.

Take into account. . .

You may maximise your self-interest with impeccable logic, but end up in a situation you least wanted.

In summary, using the table above, this is how it looks from A's perspective:

1 If B confesses, A should confess too, otherwise he will go to jail for 20 years.
2 If B does not confess, either A will go free if he confesses, or go to jail for one year if he too decides not to confess.
3 Therefore, whatever B does A should confess.

But, of course, the same is the case for B, so they both confess and get five years each (10 years total). The best solution is to refuse to confess (to co-operate), this way they will both get a sentence of one year in jail (two years total). By following their own rational self-interest, each of them has ended up being worse off than they needed to have been.

Trust

As you can see, each prisoner bases his decision on what he thinks his partner will do, and that's the same for us all. The more we get to know other people the more accurately we can predict who will co-operate and who will defect. It's not irrational to co-operate if the chances are good that we have chosen our partners wisely. But this means our behaviour is partly based upon trust and, if we live in societies that tolerate cheating and we learn to expect it in most exchanges, we are much more likely to cheat too. If you believe there is no chance that others will co-operate, you realise it makes no sense for you to co-operate.

> **For instance. . .**
>
> If you are convinced that the USA, China and India will not co-operate in reducing their emissions of greenhouse gases, then you are unlikely to agree yourself. A country like Britain contributes 2 per cent of all greenhouse gases. If the British government were to prevent all emissions, within two years the growth in China's emissions would more than make up for that.

Other examples are not difficult to find. The 40-year-long arms race between the two superpowers during the Cold War squandered huge quantities of economic resources until the climate of mutual mistrust was broken by leaders going out on a limb and agreeing to actual cuts and inspections. The same could be said of the Arab–Israeli conflict, where mistrust breeds more mistrust in an endless cycle of violence and death.

Take into account. . .

> Who you can trust? Can I co-operate with them? Is it in both our interests to co-operate? How can I generate their trust in me?

Who can I trust?

So what strategy should we adopt to get the best out of any situation, when we don't know whether we face co-operators or defectors? In his book, *The Evolution of Co-operation*,[4] Robert Axelrod explains how he set about finding out by inviting people to submit computer programs which would take on the role of one of the prisoners. Each program was paired with another and then made a series of 200 decisions. This 'iterated' form of the Prisoners' Dilemma replicates much more accurately the sort of extended relationships we develop between each other.

And, significantly, in the same way we do, each program would learn about each other: they would be able to decide whether to co-operate or defect on the basis of what had taken place in previous decisions. If you are not going to see the person in front of you again, defection makes the obvious rational choice. But, if you know you will be meeting them regularly in the future, you will want to create a good reputation, one that people can trust. Likewise with the computer programs: in the iterated Prisoners' Dilemma they too built reputations.

Take into account. . .

If you're going to see the other person regularly, you will want to create a good reputation as someone who can be trusted.

In the first tournament there were 16 programs, followed by a second some months later with 62, allowing entrants to learn from the previous tournament, so they could develop even more effective programs. But in both cases the same program won: the simplest, the 'tit-for-tat' program. This co-operated on the first move, but after that it would do exactly what the other player did on the previous move. As Axelrod pointed out, this program had important characteristics:

1   It was '**nice**': in the sense that it would never be the first to defect. Indeed, nice rules were much more successful on average than those that started by defecting.
2   But it was also '**tough**': it would retaliate by punishing defectors immediately the next time around.
3   And yet it was also '**forgiving**': in the sense that it would reward co-operation on the next move. It was always ready to re-establish fruitful co-operation.
4   And finally, it was '**clear**': it was so simple that other players had no problem in working out what they were dealing with.

It seems to suggest that the old saying, 'Cheats never prosper', really is true and the common belief that nice guys never win is quite wrong; that is as long as they are also tough, forgiving and clear. Opponents quickly came to realise that tit-for-tat couldn't be pushed around, so it was far better to co-operate with it.

Co-operation inexorably becomes the dominant strategy.

Moreover, as Axelrod pointed out, once pockets of co-operators become established as people realise they will have future encounters, they will outperform the defectors, who no one will be willing to trust. Their success will mean their numbers will rapidly increase and their strategy of co-operation will dominate. Even if defectors try to exploit the situation, tit-for-tat's toughness will punish them, so they cannot spread. Co-operation will quickly become the established way of doing things.

As this demonstrates, people do not simply behave in a purely competitive manner. More likely, they co-operate with others, taking advantage of the many benefits that society offers them.

3. Reference points

As you can see, our behaviour is a lot more complex than traditional theories have allowed and we must understand this if we are to make good decisions. Classical economics avoids the problems we have seen here by focusing on two situations (monopoly and perfect competition) where mutual expectations play no part. As a result, we have consistently oversimplified the notion of the individual as rational and self-interested with clear preferences that are consistent from one situation to another.

Indeed, Tversky and Kahneman found that our preferences are far from being consistent. In prospect theory,[5] the treatise that won them the Nobel Prize for economics, they found three key mechanisms to System 1 thinking that help explain our decision-making behaviour:

1. Our evaluation of a situation or problem is always relative to a reference point.

In other words, our preferences vary with our situation, our reference point. This is often the status quo, but it can also be a goal in the future. Not achieving this goal we regard as a loss, while exceeding it as a gain.

For instance. . .

You hear that you have been successful in getting a job in the top law firm in your city. This is an excellent opportunity, one that you never thought you would get. But just before you accept it, you hear that an application you sent off that was quite a long shot has been successful. This is a once-in-a-lifetime opportunity for a young lawyer to work at the UN Human Rights Council. You accept this eagerly.

But then, just two weeks before you are set to leave, the project is called off, so the job is no longer there. You still have the other one, but it now seems a disappointment. Your reference point has changed.

Take into account. . .

Check your reference point. Is this distorting your judgement, preventing you from seeing all the benefits of a solution?

2. Principle of diminishing sensitivity

The impact of events on us is always related to some benchmark, they are never standalone events. If we have £1,100 and we lose £100, the loss is felt less than if we only had £200 and lost the same amount. As a result, investors tend to be more affected by changes in their wealth than by the wealth itself.

3. Loss aversion

Most people are loss aversive: losses affect them more than gains. Indeed, Kahneman found that the loss aversion ratio is 1.5 to 2.5 times the impact of gains. And there may be good evolutionary reasons for this: 'Organisms that treat threats as more urgent than opportunities have a better chance to survive and reproduce.'[6]

Try this. . .

Problem 1: which do you choose?
   Get £900 for sure OR 90 per cent chance to get £1,000

Problem 2: which do you choose?
   Lose £900 for sure OR 90 per cent chance to lose £1,000

Most people are 'risk averse' in Problem 1: the subjective value of gaining £900 is more than 90 per cent of the value of the gain of £1,000. But in Problem 2 most people choose the gamble. The explanation for this is the mirror image of the explanation of the risk-aversion choice in Problem 1: the negative value of losing £900 is much more than 90 per cent of the negative value of losing £1,000. As Kahneman makes clear 'The sure loss is very aversive, and this drives you to take the risk.'[7]

   This explains why, despite being risk averse, we find ourselves taking some extremely risky decisions when we are facing potential losses.

For instance. . .

If we buy an investment that quickly increases in value we frequently sell it to take the profits. But if we buy an investment that promptly falls in value, we frequently hang onto it indefinitely hoping it will regain its original value.

When they are faced with possible losses, people take the riskier option and cling onto their investments when they are losing value. This explains why companies frequently change their CEOs, whose investments result in losses. It is not because the new CEO has a better record or could turn the business around, but because of the *Sink-hole fallacy*: the outgoing CEO is encumbered by previous decisions and is reluctant to cut her losses. By contrast the new CEO can ignore past investments and cut her losses. In the same way, sunk costs keep people for too long in poor jobs and unhappy relationships.

Take into account. . .

Check that your decision is not influenced disproportionately by your aversion to losses in contrast to the possible gains.

What we must take into account

As you evaluate each possible solution work your way through the following 10 things that we have discussed. Your aim is to reach an objective decision free of the intuitions and misleading oversimplifications that can dominate our thinking.

What we must take into account

1 Practical questions.
2 Costs and benefits.
3 Direct and indirect effects.
4 What others may think and do in response.
5 Co-operation as well as competition.
6 Not only what you think and what the other person thinks, but what you think the other person thinks you think.
7 You may maximise your self-interest with impeccable logic, but end up in a situation you least wanted.
8 If you're going to see other people regularly, you will want to create a good reputation as someone who can be trusted.
9 Check your reference point. Is this distorting your judgement and not allowing you to see the benefits of one solution over another?
10 Check that your decision is not influenced disproportionately by your aversion to losses in contrast to the possible gains.

Summary

1 To escape our intuitive biases we must assess each solution in a series of mental simulations.

2 The outcome of our decision depends on what others may think and do in response.

3 Co-operation may be a more effective way of achieving our objectives than competition alone.

4 Knowing who to trust and developing their trust in us will determine the success of the solution we choose.

5 Our preferences are not consistent from one situation to another: they are determined by the reference point.

What's next?

Each time we make a decision we try to assess what might happen in very complex circumstances; much more complex than traditional theories lead us to believe. So we have to learn to map out the territory and navigate our way through it. This isn't easy, but if we follow what we have learned in this chapter and check each item that we have listed, our decisions are likely to be more reliable and predict accurately what in fact will happen. Now we need to understand uncertainty and how to measure risk, which we will tackle in the next chapter.

Assessing risk: Decision-making under uncertainty

In this chapter you will learn. . .

- How to make decisions under uncertainty.
- How to calculate risk using the expected value theory.
- About the importance of luck and Black Swans.
- How to use Bayes's Theorem and a simpler method to calculate risk.
- The three most confusing ways of communicating risk.

Perhaps the one thing above all else that distinguishes the modern world from the past is not the advances of science, the discovery of the new world, technological advances or even space travel, but understanding risk: realising that man is not the helpless prey of forces beyond his control at the mercy of the gods or nature. Once this point was passed it was possible to think the future would not be like the past.

For much of our history the illusion of certainty was an important evolutionary response. Accepting values and rules without question was not only important for our integration into our cultural group, but secured our survival by programming us to react without thought to predators. We have sought belief systems in religion, astrology and superstitions for the same purpose: to create the illusion of certainty.

A new standard of reason

But by the mid-seventeenth century a new standard of reason had emerged, which accepted that, apart from propositions that were necessarily true, yet uninformative, we could not aspire to certainty, just reasonable judgements based on partial evidence of the real world. In other words, propositions were

- either true necessarily and analytically, but said nothing beyond their own terms

  or

- contingent and uncertain, but said something about the real world.

The new scientific method was grounded in an inductive theory that set out how experimenters could bridge the evidential gap: how they could move from partial evidence to universal laws and explanations by making their own carefully considered judgements. On this basis they could understand and control the world better.

Understanding uncertainty

Today, understanding how to make decisions under conditions of incomplete information is one of the most urgent challenges we face. Yet in our schools and universities we are still taught against a background of an illusory world of certainties, not a world that is difficult to understand, where events are difficult to predict and where accidents and errors are a constant, daily reality.

Despite the comforting assurances that we are taught, we can almost never have all the information we need to make a decision with certainty, so most of our decisions will involve an undeniable amount of risk.

For instance. . .

We accept beyond question that if someone's fingerprints are found on a murder weapon, then he is certainly the murderer. Originally, this confidence was based on the work of Sir Francis Galton, who, in the 1890s, calculated that the chance that two fingerprints would match randomly was one in 64 billion.

But he didn't look at the whole fingerprint, just at the 'points of similarity', where the ridges either end or split. His estimate was based on every point: typically 35 to 50. Today, however, the practice is to declare a match when only eight to 16 are found, yet we still regard our conclusions as certain.

The classic method of calculating risk is the 'expected value theory'. As we saw in the last chapter, this uses the simple idea that the expected value of a risk is the value of its possible outcome discounted by the probability of it being realised.

EV = P (Prize) x R (Risk)

The obvious use of this is when you are thinking about investing money, buying insurance or taking a gamble. The risk is only thought to be worth taking if the expected value equals or is greater than the expense of the risk.

Try this. . .

You have just bought a second-hand washing machine with a year's warranty on it. You realise that it could cost you a lot if it breaks down outside the warranty, so you wonder whether it would be worth extending this. The price of the new warranty would be £60, compared with the average cost of repair at £260. The chances of it breaking down are 1 in 10. Is it worth it?

Answer

Multiply the prize (the cost of the average repair – £260) by the risk (1 in 10).

$$260 \times \frac{1}{10} = 26$$

Then compare this with the price of the warranty (£60) to see if it would be worth it. As you can see, compared with the expected value (£26), the cost of the warranty would not be worth it.

Under and over-weighting

Unfortunately this doesn't tell the whole story. Even though it lies at the heart of the rational choice model in economics and other social sciences, the expected value theory, by which values are weighted by their probability, is not reflected in our System 1 thinking, which places different weights on the importance of the characteristics of a situation. There are a number of reasons for this.

1. Loss aversive

As we saw in the last chapter, we are loss aversive, so when we face potential losses we are inclined to take desperate gambles that we would not have considered in other circumstances. The thought of accepting a loss is too painful and the hope of avoiding it is just too enticing to make a sensible decision and cut our losses.

> **For instance. . .**
>
> In a war the losing side will often fight on beyond the point at which the other side is certain to win. Defeat is simply too difficult to accept, even though it is just a matter of time.

2. Vivid events

Similarly, we over-weight the probability of something occurring if a recent event, like an aircraft crash, has attracted our attention. This is the *availability bias* that we examined in chapter 1. The ease with which we can reconstruct the event in our minds to create a vivid image of it increases our sense of the inevitability of a similar event occurring. So we over-weight the probability.

> **For instance. . .**
>
> We hear all the time that air travel is the safest form of travel. In 2013 there were only 90 commercial aircraft accidents. Only nine involved fatalities – a total of 173 people – out of 32 million airline departures. That means less than one flight in 300,000 had an accident and only one in 3 million was fatal. Yet we hear of an aircraft crash and almost immediately we over-weight the danger, vowing only to go by train or car in future. It has been estimated that the death toll on American roads in the year after 9/11 increased by 1,595.

This is also another example of the *narrative fallacy*. We favour the narrated, the compelling story, with its causal cement binding it together to seem almost inevitable.

We understand it in hindsight, so we believe it was predictable at the time. The ease with which we can create a coherent, persuasive story convinces us that it was always going to happen. Yet subjective confidence is a feeling not a judgement; it is no substitute for rational evaluation.

3. Luck and Black Swans

In our attempt to make sense of the world the stories we find most compelling are those created out of personal choices and intentions knit together in what seems like an irrefutable, causal explanation that excludes any possibility of uncertainty or luck. We are comforted by stories that convince us we live in a world we control, full of reassuring certainties and predictable events. We fail to reckon with the influence of luck and what Nassim Taleb describes as Black Swans.

> **Definition**
> Black Swans: that small number of unexpected events which explain much of what's important going on in the world.

Despite what we are often told, we don't live in simple atomistic societies that are just the sum of their parts, a loose collection of isolated individuals. We live in societies that generate nonlinear effects, what Taleb describes as 'scalability'. While some individuals, like prostitutes, dentists and doctors, are rewarded according to their individual contributions, others, like best-selling novelists, sportspeople, recording artists and internet entrepreneurs, generate income far beyond the same level of work. This is 'scalability'. These are the effects of nonlinear forces in society from which, importantly, Black Swans are born.

> **For instance. . .**
> Financial investors in the city can generate profits and losses at an almost inconceivable rate. This can, and regularly does, result in financial crashes that are unpredictable: 1978, 1985, 1987, 1994, 1997 and 2007, all were Black Swans.

In such a complex world unpredictable and devastating events occur regularly: the rise of the internet, the personal computer, the fall of the Soviet Union and 9/11. Yet economists and financial risk management analysts rely on computer models that fail to take account of them. Indeed, Daniel Kahneman argues that:

> *Our comforting conviction that the world makes sense rests on a secure foundation: our almost unlimited ability to ignore our ignorance[1] . . . people who spend their time, and earn their living, studying a particular topic produce poorer predictions than dart-throwing monkeys who would have distributed their choices evenly over the options.[2]*

How to make decisions under uncertainty

As we have seen in previous stages, the most stubborn problems we have to deal with concern our System 1 thinking and our intuitions that guide our interpretation of uncertainty. But this is compounded by the confusing way in which uncertainty is presented, often deliberately. To tackle both of these problems we have to understand three things:

1 The problems created by the way uncertainty is presented
2 How to calculate the degrees of uncertainty – the risk
3 How to present these risks clearly

1. The problems created by the way uncertainty is presented

In most situations we are aware that there may be uncertainties, but we're not sure how great these are. This is not necessarily our fault, but the way in which the uncertainty is presented, accidentally and deliberately clouding our minds. When issues like climate change and smoking present a threat to commercial interests, the response is often to play down the level of risk or simply to confuse people.

> **For instance. . .**
>
> An internal document of a cigarette company privately concedes that its main tactic to counter the publicity about the dangers of passive smoking is to create doubt by confusing the issues: 'Doubt is our product since it is the best means of competing with the "body of facts" that exist in the mind of the general public.'[3]

And it is not just the ordinary person who is confused by this. Trained professionals of all kinds struggle to understand information and assess risk. Judges, lawyers and jurors struggle to understand the evidence of probabilities laid before them, leading to confusion and unsafe convictions that later have to be overturned.

The problem is that their professional training has left them ill-equipped to make these sorts of calculations. Doctors often know the error rates of a clinical test and the base rate of a disease, but not how to infer from this the chances that a patient with a positive test has the disease. Consequently, many patients undergo unnecessary procedures, including surgery. In Germany each year around 100,000 women have part of their breasts surgically removed after a positive test, when in fact most positive mammograms are false.[4]

> **For instance. . .**
>
> A prominent figure in medical research and teaching in Germany with over three decades of experience was given this problem. The probability that a woman has breast cancer is 0.8 per cent. If a woman has breast cancer, the probability is 90 per cent that she will have a positive mammogram. If she does not have breast cancer the probability is 7 per cent that she will still have a positive mammogram. Imagine a woman who has a positive mammogram. What is the probability that she actually has breast cancer?[5]

He studied it for about 10 minutes and then guessed that it was around 90 per cent, although he wasn't sure. The problem was also presented to 48 doctors with an average of 14 years' experience, ranging from recent graduates to heads of departments.

The results:

The estimates ranged from 1 per cent to 90 per cent; a third thought it was 90 per cent certain; a third estimated the chances to be 50 to 80 per cent; and a third estimated it to be lower than 10 per cent – half of these estimated it at 1 per cent. The median estimate was 70 per cent. Only 2 per cent gave the correct estimate of around 9 per cent, but for the wrong reasons.

David Eddy, former consultant to the Clinton administration on health care, gave essentially the same question to a number of American doctors: 95 per cent estimated the probability to be about 75 per cent, nearly 9 times more than the actual figure.

Although most doctors grossly overestimated the risk of breast cancer given a positive mammogram, this was not a question of ability, but of training – the lack of the right skills.

1. The framing effect

One reason why we so frequently get these sorts of calculations wrong is the way in which the information is framed – the words that are used to present it. We are influenced more by this than by the objective data. Indeed, the impact is even stronger when it triggers off our intuitive responses, like our tendency to be loss aversive.

For instance. . .

In the last chapter we found that we tend to prefer a sure thing over a gamble when the outcome is good (risk averse), but we tend to reject the sure thing and accept the gamble when both outcomes are negative (risk seeking). It is easy for governments and organisations to exploit this just by framing their promotional material in the right way. Presented with the same objective outcomes, our preferences can be reversed just by changing the formulation.

2. Stereotypes and the conjunction fallacy

Not only do we have to be cautious about the way a problem is framed, but also about the stereotype that it might project in our minds. The likelihood of something occurring is judged not by its probability, but by the ease with which we can classify things according to their similarity with a stereotype. This is an example of *representativeness*, one of the five simplifying heuristics we listed in chapter 1.

For instance. . .

In the case of Linda, in chapter 1 (page 17), Tversky and Kahneman listed eight characteristics, including 'f) Linda is a bank teller' and 'h) Linda is a bank teller and is active in the feminist movement'. They asked undergraduates at several major universities to list them from the most probable to the least probable and found that 83 to 92 per cent placed *h* higher than *f*. Yet the conjunction rule says that the probability of two events occurring together is less than the probability of either one of them occurring separately.

In problems like these, probability is set against similarity judgements. And, almost inevitably, similarity with a stereotype wins out. The more detail we give to a possible event, the lower is its probability. Yet our System 1 thinking works in the opposite direction: more detail makes the event more plausibility as it begins to match more closely one of our stereotypes.

The conflict is between our System 2 thinking and its attempts to calculate probabilities, and our System 1 thinking and its eagerness to see a form appear that is representative of a stereotype. The most representative outcome combines all the personality details into a coherent, persuasive story, the plausibility of which we then substitute for probability.

Try this. . .

Let's say you are at a party, where you have a brief conversation with somebody called John. As you are leaving, you pick up a coat, but later realise you have picked up his by mistake. You need to get in touch with him so you can exchange coats, but, although you know the company he works for, you don't know in what department.

1. The base rate

In the absence of specific information, other than his first name and his appearance, you will go by the 'base rate': the number of things of a particular kind – in this case the number of employees in each department.

You realise that the number of people employed in production is greater than in any other department, so the chances are that he is more likely to be found there, than elsewhere.

2. Personal characteristics

Your next step is likely to involve recalling your impressions of the type of person he seemed to be, his personality, what he talked about, how he behaved and his appearance.

3. Stereotypes

Then you will probably retrieve or construct a stereotype of an employee you might typically find in each of these departments and search for the closest match with John's personality.

You now have three things:

1 The base rate.
2 Your impressions of John's personality, about which you will have some doubts, because you only talked to him for about 15 minutes.
3 The similarity of this to a stereotype.

Most people concentrate on 3, ignoring 1 and 2. We substitute a judgement of representativeness for the problem we should be tackling.

> **Principle**
>
> **The rule is when you have doubts about the quality of the evidence, let your judgement of probability stay close to the base rate.**

2. How to calculate the degrees of uncertainty – the risk

Now we reach a complex stage, particularly for those of us who don't feel confident about doing mathematical calculations. However, don't despair; there is a simpler way of dealing with the problem. But first we must look at the complex method. This is Bayes's Theorem developed by the eighteenth-century theologian and mathematician Thomas Bayes. It is a method for calculating the probability of a hypothesis being true or an event coming about, given certain data.

> **Principle**
>
> **The probability of some event coming about is the sum of probabilities of the different ways it _can_ come about. In essence what we are after is the number of times something happened, divided by the number of times it _could_ have happened.**

> **For instance. . .**
>
> If you have just received a positive result from a test for cancer, you want to know the chances that you _could_ actually have cancer. So you calculate the proportion of people who get a positive test and have cancer and then divide this by the proportion that receive positive results, both accurate and inaccurate.

That is the simple problem we are trying to solve. Keep this clearly in mind as we tackle the technical algebraic formulation, which is the way it is normally presented – bear with me, it will get easier. What we are dealing with is two things: the data D (such as a positive test) and a binary hypothesis H – a hypothesis that could be true or untrue (H and not-H, such as the disease and not the disease). The calculation that we make to discover the chances that this data (this positive test) could be accurate is the following:

$$p(H\text{-}D) = p(H)p(D\text{-}H) \div p(H)p(D\text{-}H) + p(\text{not-}H)p(D\text{-not-}H)$$

p(H-D) is the posterior probability: _the answer we're looking for_
p(H) is the prior probability: _the probability of having the disease (this is the base rate of the disease)_

p(D-H) is the probability of D given H: *the probability of getting a positive test, if you have the disease*

p(not-H) is the probability of not-H: *the probability of not having the disease*

p(D-not-H) is the probability of D given not-H: *the probability of a person without the disease getting a positive test result*

For instance. . .

You are a doctor in a major hospital systematically screening patients for a new and dangerous blood disease. The incidence of the disease among the population is currently 1 per cent, but there are fears it could spread without prompt medical action. The test that you perform is 90 per cent reliable: that is 90 per cent of people suffering from the disease give a positive reaction to the test. 80 per cent of people without the disease give a negative reaction.

What is the probability that a patient who gives a positive reaction actually has the disease? What, in the light of your answer to the above question, do you tell your patient?

Using this data in the formula above we get the following, from which we can then reach the answer we want:

$$p(H-D) = 0.01 \times 0.9 \div (0.01 \times 0.9) + (0.99 \times 0.2)$$

$$= 0.009 \div 0.009 + 0.198$$

$$= 0.009 \div 0.207$$

$$= 0.0435$$

$$= 4.35\%$$

You probably didn't find it too difficult to substitute the data in the formula and work out the equation. But there is a simpler way of working on this sort of problem. This should make it clearer what we're doing and why.

In a problem like this we are dealing with two things: the base rate (the chances of having the disease or not having the disease in the population as a whole) and the reliability of the test:

Base rate

1 Chances of having the disease – 1 per cent.
2 Chances of not having the disease – 99 per cent.

Reliability

3 Test is accurate – 90 per cent of those who have the disease test positive; 80 per cent without the disease test negative.
4 Test is inaccurate – 10 per cent with the disease give a negative reaction; 20 per cent without the disease give a positive reaction.

This gives us four possible combinations that can be presented simply in the following way:

A	B
C	D

A = 1 x 3 – the chances of having the disease and testing positive
B = 4 x 2 – the chances of not having the disease and testing positive
C = 3 x 2 – the chances of not having the disease and testing negative
D = 4 x 1 – the chances of having the disease and testing negative

In the case above involving the screening for a blood disease this translates in the following way:

$$A = 1 \times 0.9 = 0.9$$
$$B = 99 \times 0.2 = 19.8$$
$$C = 99 \times 0.8 = 79.2$$
$$D = 1 \times 0.1 = 0.1$$

0.9	19.8
79.2	0.1

Using these categories there is a formula that simplifies the one above for calculating the probability that a patient who gives a positive reaction actually has the disease:

$$\frac{A}{A + B}$$

Once we substitute the figures above, we are left with a very simple equation to solve:

$$\frac{0.9}{0.9 + 19.8} = \frac{0.9}{20.7} = 4.35\%$$

In this form it is not only clearer *what* you have to do, but *why* you have to do it: the logic behind it is clearer. Using this method, work out the solution to the following problem taken from *Thinking, Fast and Slow*.[6] It presents exactly the same sort of information as the problem above. Like most standard Bayesian problems, we have two items of information: the base rate and the reliability of the evidence, in this case the reliability of the witness's testimony.

Try this. . .

A cab was involved in a hit-and-run accident at night. Two cab companies, the Green and the Blue, operate in the city. You are given the following data:

- 85 per cent of the cabs in the city are Green and 15 per cent are Blue.
- A witness identified the cab as Blue. The court tested the reliability of the witness under the circumstances that existed on the night of the accident and concluded that the witness correctly identified each one of the two colours 80 per cent of the time and failed 20 per cent of the time.

What is the probability that the cab involved in the accident was Blue rather than Green?

Answer

Base rate – the incidence of Blue and Green

1 Chances of being Blue = 15 per cent.
2 Chances of being Green = 85 per cent.

Reliability

3 Accurate – 80 per cent of the observations.
4 Inaccurate – 20 per cent of the observations.

$$A = 3 \times 1 = 80\% \times 15\% = 0.12$$
$$B = 4 \times 2 = 20\% \times 85\% = 0.17$$

$$\frac{A}{A + B} = \frac{0.12}{0.12 + 0.17} = \frac{0.12}{0.29} = 41 \text{ percent}$$

We found the answer by applying the principle that we made clear above. We divided

1. all the times that it was correctly identified as blue

by

2. all the times when it *could* have been blue, which in turn is made up of

=

all the times it was correctly identified as blue

+

all the times when blue cabs were incorrectly identified as green cabs.

3. How to present these risks clearly

Problems that are presented in the usual algebraic form as probabilities and percentages are so confusing that we do one of two things as we search for ways of sidestepping the difficult calculation:

1. Ignore the base rate

When Kahneman presented the cab problem to students the most common answer was 80 per cent, in other words they did what many of us do: simply ignore the base rate and go with the witness statement.

2. System 1 thinking

Alternatively, we resort to System 1 thinking and rely on our intuitive responses, searching out ways of creating a causal story, perhaps by uncovering grounds for applying a stereotype of careless blue cab drivers recklessly endangering people's lives.

We struggle with information in this form, because this is not the sort of input the mind has learned to process over millions of years.

For instance. . .

If you arrange to meet up with your friends at a restaurant and, when they arrive, you notice that three of them are driving red cars and four black cars, you don't say to yourself 57 per cent are driving black cars and 43 per cent are driving red cars. Even less likely do you say that there is 0.57 probability of black cars and 0.43 probability of red cars. You express it in frequencies: four out of seven are driving black cars and three out of seven red cars.

It was only in the seventeenth century that the mathematical theory of probability was developed and only in the nineteenth century that percentages became common after the metric system was institutionalised in Paris after the French Revolution. Even then it was only in the second half of the twentieth century that we began using percentages and probabilities as part of our everyday language to express degrees of uncertainty. According to Gerd Gigerenzer, for much of our evolution our minds learned to process risks in terms of 'natural frequencies', which demand less computation.

Representation

In creative thinking we found that the key to solving many problems lies in their representation: represent the problem differently and the solution seems so obvious that you wonder why you didn't see it in the first place. The same is true here. In both the blood screening and cab problems we converted the data into four numbers from which we could easily calculate the answer.

For instance. . .

A doctor observes 100 people, 10 of whom have a new disease. Of these, 8 display a symptom, while 4 of the 90 without the disease also show the symptom. The doctor, therefore, has four numbers to work with, four frequencies:

1 Disease and symptom – 8
2 Disease and no symptom – 2
3 No disease and symptom – 4
4 No disease and no symptom – 86

If she then observes a new patient with the symptom, she can easily see that the chances that this person has the disease is

$$\frac{8}{8+4} = \frac{2}{3}$$

This corresponds to the way we collected and processed information prior to the invention of probability theory.

For instance. . .

In a murder trial an expert witness might tell the jury that the DNA found at the murder scene matched the suspect's DNA and there was only a 0.00001 probability or 0.001 per cent chance of being anyone else's. Although it is difficult to get a clear sense of the significance of this, it does sound pretty convincing.

But now present it as a frequency and things become a lot clearer. It means that out of every 100,000 people, one will show a match. So how many people are there who could have committed the murder? If the city, in which this occurred, has a 10 million adult population, there are 100 inhabitants, whose DNA would match the sample on the victim.

When the information is presented in this form as a frequency, there is much less confusion and, as a result, much less variation in responses. Earlier in this chapter (page 255) we described a problem that was presented to an experienced doctor in Germany concerning a woman who had received a positive mammogram and wanted to know the probability that she actually had breast cancer. The doctor, along with many others, struggled to produce an answer. In fact estimates ranged widely from 1 to 90 per cent. But now try to calculate it when the problem is expressed as a frequency.

Try this. . .

Eight out of every 1,000 women have breast cancer. Out of these 8 women with breast cancer, 7 will have a positive mammogram. Of the remaining 992 women who don't have breast cancer, some 70 will still have a positive mammogram.[7]

Answer

As you can see, it is now much easier to work out the answer. Only 7 of the 77 women with a positive mammogram (7 + 70) actually have breast cancer: in other words, one in 11, or 9 per cent.

Forms of communication that lead to problems

Given the confusion that surrounds the way this sort of information is presented, it's easy to understand how we frequently draw the wrong conclusions. To avoid these mistakes it helps to be aware of the three types of communication that most often produce them:

1 Single-event probabilities
2 Relative risks
3 Conditional probabilities

1. Single-event probabilities

The simplest way of avoiding each of these is to specify the reference class, which you do when you use frequencies.[8]

> **Definition**
> The reference class is that class of events or objects to which a probability or frequency refers. When a probability is given without one, you have no clear idea what the probability is referring to.

Statements that include single-event probabilities, by definition, specify no reference class: they refer to just single events.

> **For instance. . .**
>
> Many weather reports, today, make statements like, 'There is a 30 per cent chance of rain tomorrow.' But what exactly do we take this to mean? Although you might be able to think of more interpretations, it could mean one of three things:
>
> 1 it will rain for 30 per cent of the time;
> 2 in 30 per cent of the area; or
> 3 on 30 per cent of the days that are like tomorrow.[9]

A statement expressing probability in this way can never be proved wrong: unless it shows what difference it makes to the world it cannot be tested. It is therefore meaningless. This type of confusion can be avoided quite simply by using frequencies instead, because they make clear the reference class: 'It will rain on 10 days in August.' This can be tested; it can be falsified, so it is not meaningless.

2. Relative risks

Equally ambiguous are statements that present information in the form of relative risks. In 1995 the results of a study were reported in a press release which stated, 'People with high cholesterol can rapidly reduce . . . their risk of death by 22 per cent by taking a widely prescribed drug called pravastatin sodium.'[10] Like many similar reports, the benefits were reported in the form of a 'relative risk reduction'. But what does 22 per cent mean in this context? It appears that most people believe it means that out of 1,000 people with high cholesterol, 220 of those will be prevented from dying.

> **When they are presented in the form of a relative risk reduction, the benefits always appear more impressive.**

In fact it means something quite different. Presented in the form of an absolute risk reduction you can see the difference. Out of 1,000 people who took the drug over five years 32 died, whereas out of those who did not take it 41 died. The absolute risk is the number of those who die without treatment minus those who die with treatment. The study showed that the drug reduced the number of people who die from 41 to 32 in 1,000. So the absolute risk reduction is 9 in 1,000 = 0.9 per cent.

As you can see, presenting the evidence as a relative risk reduction can be very misleading. The benefits look more impressive. In a different context, it can also increase people's anxiety.

For instance. . .

Since the oral contraceptive pill was made available in the 1960s there have been a number of scares. In Britain a few years ago information was released in the following form: 'combined oral contraceptives containing desogestrel and gestodene are associated with around a two-fold increase in the risk of thromboembolism' (a blockage of a blood vessel by a clot).

Phrased in this way, as a relative risk, this information caused understandable alarm among women, many of whom stopped taking the pill, resulting in an increase in unwanted pregnancies and abortions.

Relative risk – When the information is presented as a relative risk it says only how much more likely thromboembolism is, if one takes the pill, than if one does not: the chance doubles. It does not show how often thromboembolism actually occurs.
Absolute risk – In this form the information shows that thromboembolism increases from about 1 to 2 in 14,000 women.[11] In other words, the risk is a lot less alarming.

3. Conditional probabilities

The confusion of this third type of communication is felt beyond statements of probability. In general most of us struggle with conditional reasoning, in which a proposition takes the form, 'If A, then B'. The most common mistake it to confuse 'If A, then B' with 'If B, then A', when this would be an example of illicit conversion. In many cases it is legitimate to do this, but not in others. For example, I can argue that 'If Stanley is a dog, then he is an animal', but I cannot argue that 'If Stanley is an animal, then he is a dog.'

Definition
Conversion is the process of interchanging the subject and the complement of a sentence.

The same problem arises in the form of conditional probabilities. The chances that a test will detect a disease are frequently presented as a conditional probability:

If a woman has breast cancer, the probability that she will test positive on a screening mammogram is 90 per cent.

But many doctors then go onto to commit the fallacy of illicit conversion by confusing this statement with

If a women tests positive on a screening mammogram, the probability that she has breast cancer is 90 per cent.

Gigerenzer points out that, despite the obvious problems, this is the standard way in which risk is communicated in the press and the way drug companies advertise and report the benefits of treatment. As we have seen, the solution is simple: present the information in the form of frequencies instead.

Summary

1 Understanding how to make decisions under conditions of incomplete information is one of the most urgent problems we face.

2 In such a complex world unpredictable and devastating events occur regularly.

3 Calculating risk using the expected value theory fails to take account of the weight we place on the importance of different characteristics in any situation.

4 In most Bayesian problems we have two items of information to deal with: the base rate and the reliability of the evidence.

5 To simplify the calculation of risk and avoid the most common errors convert the information into frequencies.

What's next?

Nassim Taleb explains that 'Black Swan logic makes *what you don't know* far more relevant than what you do know.'[12] Unfortunately, we don't learn about Black Swans, those unexpected events that have extreme impact, which explain much of what's important going on in the world. Instead, we favour that which can be narrated, about which a causal story can be written. We search for causes that exclude the possibility of Black Swans and uncertainty. We comfort ourselves that we live in a world of certainties and known predictabilities.

Only recently have we begun to accept the possibility of uncertainty and how to measure and take account of it. This has given us the tools to plan our actions on the basis of acceptable risks. In the knowledge of this we can now move to the last two steps of decision-making and compare all our solutions, evaluate each one against the others, choose the best one and then reflect on our decision to see what we can learn from it.

How to make a good decision

In this chapter you will learn. . .

- How to do a comparative evaluation of all the solutions.
- How to create an algorithm that frees us from unreliable intuitions.
- How to use grid analysis to lay out our preferences in an objective, rational way.
- How to use paired comparisons to see the relative importance of different options.
- The importance of reflecting on our decisions.

As we have worked our way through each of the three stages of smart thinking we have had one clear aim: to elevate our thinking above the appeal of our intuitions and first impressions. Nowhere is the conflict between smart thinking and our intuitions clearer than when we finally choose which solution to adopt. We have evaluated each solution, assessed the risk of each one, now we have to compare and evaluate them against each other and decide which one to choose.

But how do you do this without resorting to intuitive, impressionistic judgements? The problem is that you are comparing things that are not of the same kind, so on what do you base your judgement? You want to buy a house and you have a number to choose from: one has good-sized rooms, but no view; another has a good view, but is remote; another has good-sized rooms, a wonderful view, but needs a lot of work doing on it; while another has small rooms, a good view, but sits on a busy road.

The problem: you are comparing things that are not of the same kind.

Creating an algorithm

One answer is just to trust to your gut reaction, your intuition. If you are a professional you will describe this as your professional judgement. Your training and experience has given you a certain ability that those who are not similarly trained learn to respect.

Yet this is less reliable than you might think; even less than a simple algorithm. Over the past 50 years there have been roughly 200 studies that have compared the accuracy of the predictions of clinicians and other professionals with statistical algorithms and in every case the accuracy of the professionals' predictions have been matched or exceeded by a simple algorithm. Studies have ranged from the selection of stocks by investment managers to the choice of medical treatment by doctors and in each case 'an algorithm that is constructed on the back of an envelope is . . . certainly good enough to outdo expert judgment.'[1]

For instance. . .

Obstetricians knew that, if an infant was not breathing within minutes of its birth, there was a danger of brain damage. To determine the danger doctors and midwives used their professional judgement. But different professionals focused on different things with the danger that critical signs would be missed.

One day in 1953 an anaesthesiologist, Virginia Apgar, was asked how she would improve the situation, so she jotted down five variables: heart rate, respiration, reflex, muscle tone and colour and three scores: 0, 1 and 2 depending on the robustness of each variable. With this a consistent standard could now be used. Since then it has been adopted by countries around the world and is credited with saving hundreds of thousands of lives. Indeed, the 'Apgar score' has even been made into an acronym for learning purposes: **A**ppearance (skin colour), **P**ulse (heart rate), **G**rimace (reflex), **A**ctivity (muscle tone) and **R**espiration.[2]

What this shows is that a simple, mechanical method combining a few variables, applied consistently, can outperform the subtleties of professional judgement that we have all learned to respect.

1. Characteristics

Now we can adopt a similar method to choose between our different solutions. By constructing our own algorithm, as we did when we generated our ideas using trigger questions in chapter 9, we can create a simple and effective method for comparing things that are not of the same kind. However, here we need to go one stage further by building in our own principle of evaluation, like the Apgar score.

For instance. . .

If you were a manager of a restaurant and you were about to interview candidates for the vacant post of assistant manager, you could, of course, just rely on first impressions. But we all know how unreliable these can be. So, the first step is to list certain characteristics or, in this case, personality traits that you think the assistant manager should have:

- A sense of responsibility
- Professional image
- Optimistic outlook
- Good at motivating people
- An eye for detail
- Sociability – interested in people

If you were deciding which house to buy or which job offer to accept, you would adopt the same strategy. You would compile a list of those things that you are looking for. It doesn't have to be a long list – six is probably enough. But they should be as independent from one another as possible, so you can assess each one reliably without one influencing another.

2. Weighting

Now consider whether any of your characteristics are more significant than the others. If some are, then you will have to weight them. Say, there is one characteristic that is more significant, how much more? Is it twice or three times as important?

For instance. . .

You might be lucky enough to have three job offers. Which one do you choose? The first thing you do is to list those characteristics you most want in a job:

1 Good salary
2 Opportunity to develop your skills through in-house training
3 Opportunity to travel
4 Freedom to use your own judgement
5 Creative challenges
6 Fast track career plan within the organisation

But above all, you may want the opportunity to travel in your work. So you will have to decide how important this is: is it twice or three times as important as the others?

Of course, you may not need to do this: they may all be as equally important. It will depend upon how accurate and discriminating you can be about your preferences.

3. Questions

Then you need a series of factual questions on each characteristic that you can ask to gather the information you need. It is important to get the phrasing right, so that it gathers precisely what you need. If you are interviewing applicants for the post of assistant manager in the restaurant, each one will have to answer exactly the same questions.

For instance. . .

When you come to ask questions about the candidate's sociability, her interest in people, you might ask questions about her social life, the frequency of interaction with friends, her interest and participation in sports and any other interests that may involve meeting people and socialising. Someone whose interests involve spending a lot of time on their own might find social interaction a strain.

Asking questions like this on each of the characteristics that you have identified counteracts the influence of our first impressions, which can then distort our responses to the person and heavily influence our judgement. It is also important to gather information on each characteristic and give it a score before moving on to the next. As you look at each house you would take one characteristic, say, the size of the rooms, and gather all the information on that before moving on to the next characteristic.

4. Score each characteristic

The next step is to score each characteristic, say, on a scale of one to five. To do this, of course, you should have a clear idea of what constitutes a weak candidate and scores just one and what constitutes a strong candidate who scores five.

5. Add up the scores for each characteristic

Finally, after you have interviewed an applicant, before moving onto the next interview, calculate those scores that have been weighted and then work out the evaluation by adding up all six scores. The total will give you an objective score for comparison.

Creating an algorithm

1 Characteristics
2 Weighting
3 Questions
4 Score each characteristic
5 Add up the scores for each characteristic

Once you have done this you will have a clear, reliable indication of which candidate to hire, which job to accept or which house to buy. Research shows that this is a much more reliable method of doing a comparative evaluation and making the right decision, than just trusting to our intuitions. That's not to say that you should ignore your intuition entirely. It adds value, but only after you have completed a disciplined collection of objective evidence that you have evaluated according to a rigorous process. The determining factor must always be the objective evidence.

All of our decisions that involve comparing and choosing between different options involve these sorts of calculations, even when we are not fully conscious of it. No matter what the decision, we have to assemble the information and make a comparative evaluation of each option with the rest.

Try this. . .

Let's say that you are the editor of a local newspaper. You get the following information pass across your desk.

A local man is setting out that morning to swim the 10 treacherous miles across the local estuary. As he is raising money for the children's ward of the local hospital, which is threatened with closure, he's inviting the paper along to cover the story with a photographer. He is being sponsored by a large supermarket that advertises with the paper.

Should you cover the event and run the story, bearing in mind that you have a number of similar stories and events all competing for coverage? Which should you concentrate your resources on? Of course, your guiding principle, the ultimate goal, is to make the paper a success by increasing its circulation, which will attract more advertising revenue. So, like the Apgar algorithm, list a set of, say, six characteristics that will guide your choice.

Answer

Although you might not have experience in this area, you should be able to create a list of characteristics, something like the following:

1 Does it improve the paper's standing in the local community?
2 Local stories sell papers
3 Keep advertisers happy with good coverage
4 Coverage of charities is always popular
5 Names of local people sell papers
6 Pictures sell stories

Now you would have to list, say, five questions to ask about each characteristic, so you could rate each one, arrive at a total and make an objective comparison. For this exercise, take the fifth characteristic – names of local people sell papers – and list five questions that you would ask about this.

Answer

Perhaps the important questions to ask about this concern the level and type of involvement of local people. A story with just one person involved might not be as valuable as one that involves a number.

1 How many people are involved in the story?
2 Are they central to the story or just peripheral?
3 Do we have an interesting story that includes them?
4 Can we get pictures of them?
5 Can we get quotations from them?

Try this. . .

Case study: wave power

Now, using the same method, tackle the following case study. You can find the full account of it on the companion website www.he.palgrave.com/smart-thinking, but the core details are as follows.

Resolute Marine Energy was set up to provide communities with cheap water using renewable energy in the form of ocean waves. Now the management had a decision to make. They could go in one of three directions. They could develop a wave-driven system that would produce electricity to power a desalination plant. While this would mean that they could apply for US government grants to cover the development and testing costs, they would have to find a partner to develop a desalination plant to plug into their wave energy converter.

The second direction would involve developing their wave-powered system to use hydraulics to power a desalination plant, rather than electricity. An all-hydraulic system had many advantages. They would be producing water, rather than electricity, and the profit margin on water production was higher than that on electricity. However, this strategy would require investment from the private sector, which had yet to be sold on wave energy. It also would require a desalination partner.

The third direction involved developing an all-in-one solution, in which they would produce not only fresh water, but electricity as well. This way the company would not need a partner: it would own both the wave energy conversion system and the desalination plant. However, it would be more technically challenging and, therefore, require more investment.

In making their decision the management would have to decide which direction would add more value to the company. At the heart of it was the question what sort of company should they be: an energy company, a water company, or something more complex.[3]

Grid analysis

Grid analysis adopts a similar strategy, which could complement the method that uses an algorithm. Once we have worked through our characteristics asking our questions, we need a simple, practical method of laying out our preferences. Grid analysis does this, making our preferences clear so we can make a rational and objective decision.

For instance. . .

Let's say you are buying a second-hand car. You have asked all your questions, done your research and gathered as much data as you can on each one. You have been to the different garages, seen the cars and taken them out for test drives. Now you want to reveal your preferences: what you think would be the best buy.

Grid analysis works by getting us to list our options as rows on a grid and the factors or characteristics we must consider as columns. We then score each option/factor combination and weight them, if necessary, to reflect their relative importance as we did with the algorithm. Finally we add up the total scores to give us a clear picture of our preferences.

How does it work?

Grid analysis involves a few very simple steps.

Grid analysis – the steps

1 Draw up a grid with your options listed as a row and the factors you want to consider as columns. For example, if you were buying a car, the options would be the different cars that you are considering and the factors would be cost, reliability, economy and so on.
2 Work your way down each column scoring each option to see how well it rates for each factor, using a scale of 0 (poor) to 5 (excellent).
3 Now work out the weighting of each factor, say, from 1 to 5, indicating the relative importance in your decision. A less important factor might be rated as 1, indicating that its relative importance will make no difference, while a factor that is vital would be rated at 5. Note that you are not rating these factors against each other, but in accordance with the importance they have in your decision, so it is perfectly possible for two factors to be given the same weighting. If you're unsure of the relative weighting of factors, you can estimate them by using paired comparison analysis (page 277).
4 Now multiply each of the scores you recorded in step 2 by the relevant weighting for each factor.
5 Finally, add up the weighted scores for each option to find the car you most prefer.

Try this. . .

Let's say you have identified the following factors as the most important in making your choice from the four cars:

Cost
Mileage
Economy
Engine size
Reliability

First draw up a grid with your options listed as a row and the factors you want to consider as columns, with an extra row for the weights that you are giving to each of the factors. Work your way down each column scoring each option, using a scale of 0 to 5.

Answer

Step 2: although the results will be different, your grid should look like the following:

Factors	Cost	Mileage	Economy	Engine size	Reliability	Total
Weights						
Car 1	2	3	4	2	4	
Car 2	4	3	3	3	2	
Car 3	5	4	3	2	4	
Car 4	2	5	4	3	4	

Step 3: now work out the weighting of each factor from 1 to 5.

Answer

Factors	Cost	Mileage	Economy	Engine size	Reliability	Total
Weights	5	3	4	2	4	
Car 1	2	3	4	2	4	
Car 2	4	3	3	3	2	
Car 3	5	4	3	2	4	
Car 4	2	5	4	3	4	

Finally, steps 4 and 5: multiply each of the scores you recorded in step 2 by the relevant weighting for each factor and then add up the weighted scores for each option to find the total that shows the car you most prefer.

Factors	Cost	Mileage	Economy	Engine size	Reliability	Total
Weights	5	3	4	2	4	
Car 1	10	9	16	4	16	55
Car 2	20	9	12	6	8	55
Car 3	25	12	12	4	16	69
Car 4	10	15	16	6	16	63

Paired comparison analysis

However, as we saw in step 3 above, there are those situations in which you are not sure of your priorities and the weighting you want to give them. Your evaluative criteria might be too subjective to produce any objective data on which to base your decision.

For instance. . .

You may have just completed your university education and you are wondering what to do next year: should you extend your education by doing a master's degree; should you travel to see countries that you have always longed to; should you go straight into employment; or should you do voluntary work for a cause close to your heart?

Paired comparison analysis gives you a means of comparing these different options with each other, so that you can see the relative importance you place on each one. Although it originated from the earliest psychometric tests used by psychologists, today it is widely used in a range of different contexts. It involves pairing each item with each of the others, giving them a value and then producing a ranking that reveals the priority you attach to each one. In this way you can reveal the relative importance of different competing things.

How does it work?

Like the others this method involves a series of very simple steps:

Paired comparisons – the steps

1 List the options you want to compare.
2 Give each one a letter.
3 Draw up a grid matching the number of options with a square for each one along the row and column headings. This is so you can compare each option with one another.
4 Mark the options as row and column headings on the grid.
5 Now block out those squares where an option is compared with itself and those that are duplicating comparisons already dealt with elsewhere. This ensures that you only make each comparison once.
6 Within each of the remaining blank cells compare the option in the row with the one in the column. For each cell, decide which of the two options is more important and enter the letter of the most important option into that cell.
7 Enter also the difference in importance between the two options, ranging from 0 (no difference: each has the same importance) to, say, 3 (major difference: one is significantly more important than the other).
8 Finally, calculate the total for each option by adding up the values for each option in the squares. It may be useful to convert these into percentages of the total score.

Try this. . .

Take the first situation we described: you have just completed your university education and you are wondering what to do next year. You have four options to choose from:

A. You could extend your education by doing a master's degree.
B. You could travel to see countries that you have always longed to.
C. You could go straight into employment.
D. You could do voluntary work for a cause close to your heart.

Now draw a grid, labelling the square in each row and column with the letters representing your four options and block out those squares in which you would be comparing each option with itself.

Answer

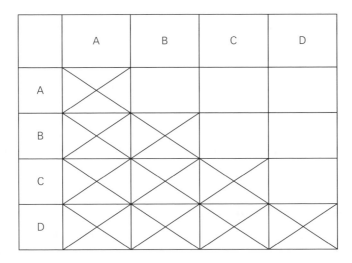

Now block out those squares in which you would be duplicating a comparison done in another square.

Answer

In the remaining squares compare each option and decide which is more important, entering the letter of that option into the square. Then enter a figure, 0–3, indicating the relative difference in importance between the two.

Answer

You should now have a grid in which all the remaining squares have both a letter and a number.

	A	B	C	D
A	✕	B 3	C 2	A 1
B	✕	✕	B 2	B 1
C	✕	✕	✕	C 2
D	✕	✕	✕	✕

Finally, calculate the total for each option by adding up the values for each one in the squares and convert these into percentages of the total score.

Answer

You now have scores that look like this:

A = 1 (9%)
B = 6 (55%)
C = 4 (36%)
D = 0 (0%)

As you can see, the paired comparison technique is an effective way of revealing the relative importance of doing different things, where our priorities may not be clear to us.

All of these methods give us a means of comparing options in an objective and rational way that liberates us from the unreliability of intuitions and first impressions. Now we can make a decision confident that we have made the right one.

Reflecting on the decision

Once you have made your decision, it's important to find time to reflect on it. Our immediate concern will be whether our decision has been effective, whether we have chosen the best solution. And, if our decision affects others, directly and indirectly, we need to know how it has affected them and whether we could have done better. To get a clear idea of these issues, work through the following questions, which raise the same issues that we discussed in chapter 15:

1 Has your decision been accepted by those who are affected? If this is within an organisation, does it make their jobs more fulfilling by allowing them to think for themselves and use a wider range of their abilities?
2 Have the costs and benefits been as you had predicted?

3 Have you noticed any unexpected direct and indirect effects? How serious have these been?

4 Have other people responded as you thought?

5 Do you need to adjust things to generate more trust and co-operation?

6 Did your reference point prevent you from seeing all the benefits of one solution, thereby distorting your judgement?

7 Was your decision influenced disproportionately by your aversion to losses in contrast to the possible gains?

However, it is not just the *product* of our thinking that's important; it is also the *process*. Indeed, in as far as this will affect other decisions in the future, this is arguably more important.

In chapter 10 we underlined the importance of reflective thinking as a means of learning from our decisions. Now it is time to do just that: to look back on the completed episode of thought, so we can better understand the way we have used our abilities at each stage and what we need to do to improve them. As we have seen, this form of self-monitoring lies at the heart of smart thinking and metacognition. Without it we fall prey to unreliable intuitions.

Summary

1 The problem is how to compare things that are not of the same kind.

2 The accuracy of a simple algorithm matched or exceeded professional judgement in over 200 studies.

3 Using grid analysis we can lay out our preferences clearly so we can make a rational and objective decision.

4 Paired comparisons are useful when we are not sure of our priorities and the weighting we want to give them.

5 Reflecting on our decision is important not just for the decision itself, but to improve our skills.

Conclusion

We began this book with 'the old South Indian Monkey Trap' from Robert Pirsig's best-selling book, *Zen and the Art of Motorcycle Maintenance*. The monkey is trapped, not by anything physical, but by an idea, one that has served him well in the past, but has now turned against him. We, too, are confronted with the same problem: our intuitions, which have served us so well in the past, trap us in routine thinking. We struggle to think creatively and conceptually about complex problems, producing decisions that result in situations we least wanted.

Smart thinking has shown us how to escape this trap. Learning to think conceptually and creatively opens up new insights and ways of seeing things nobody else has seen. With the skills and methods we have learned we can now solve problems we never thought possible and make the right decisions.

Decision-making

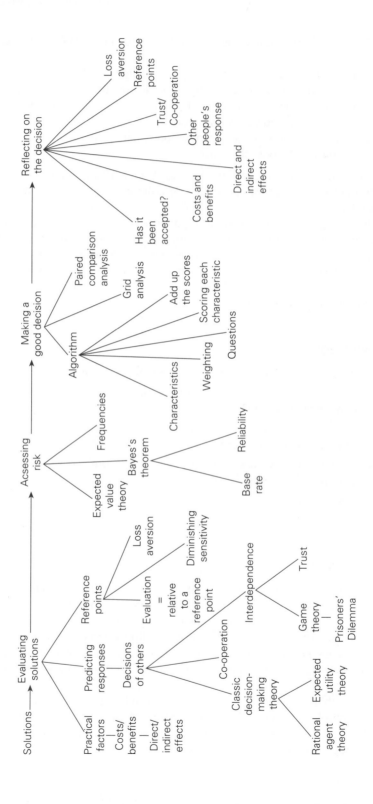

How will this improve my grades and employability?

In this chapter you will learn. . .

- About the importance of decision-making in making ideas our own.
- How this can produce a depth of conviction that results in essays and presentations that are far more persuasive.
- How this can help us find our own voice in everything we write.
- That dissertations are designed to give examiners a window into our thinking and decision-making.
- That learning to be a good decision-maker gives you skills that are essential to all organisations and professions adapting to change in the twenty-first century.

If everything were certain, there would be no decisions to make, just problems to solve. Decision-making would have nothing to do with academic work. Yet, in fact, it has everything to do with it. It is at this point that we start to think for ourselves, when we escape a form of learning that reduces us to mere recyclers of received opinion. We begin to make ideas our own by testing and integrating them within our own network of beliefs and understanding.

When we evaluate an argument, the strength of the evidence that supports it, or the clarity with which it is expressed and developed, we are making a decision as to what degree our criticisms should affect our belief that the argument is true or false. Even though it might not direct us to an action, such a decision does direct us to a belief, on which directly or indirectly an action will depend.

- Making a decision marks the point at which we start to think for ourselves.
- At this point we make ideas our own.
- Making a decision shapes our beliefs and values.

Decision-making in our academic work

All of this points to the obvious fact that coming to a judgement and making a decision lie at the heart of all academic work. Yet in universities around the world these skills are rarely taught. Students and teachers alike are inducted into education systems that encourage them to believe that such skills are irrelevant. Teachers are assumed to be the authoritative sources of certainties, about which no decision has to be made. In this there are three associated assumptions that hinder the development of our skills to think conceptually and creatively to produce new ideas, and to make decisions:

1. Single answers

We are encouraged to believe that there is a single best answer to every problem, which can be found by applying set techniques and conventional logic that needs to be learned and then applied over and over again.

2. Teachers know all the answers

Similarly, we enter universities believing that teachers are the gold standard in knowledge: they know the answers and it is their limited responsibility to pass this on to their students.

3. Students are recyclers

The converse of this is that students need only develop the skills to reproduce orthodox opinion accurately, to recycle received opinions and all the associated beliefs, values and attitudes.

And, of course, these assumptions lead us to conclude that, as we have all the facts, we are no longer making a decision, just working out a problem. In fact, of course, in the real world this is very rarely the case. Almost always we are confronted with situations that are uncertain and full of risk. For good reason, therefore, when employers consider applications from graduates they want to know how good they are at making value judgements of their own and coming to a decision.

How will decision-making skills improve my work?

The modern world is characterised by a standard of reason that accepts there can only ever be partial, incomplete evidence. To bridge this evidential gap we must make reasonable judgements. Except for formal subjects, like logic and mathematics, there is no subject or profession in which value judgements and decisions can be avoided. Evidence has to be weighed and value judgements made about its strength. Even though some generalisations are supported by a substantial body of evidence, that evidence is capable of being interpreted in different ways depending on who does the interpreting and their background, experience and values.

> Evidence has to be weighed and value judgements made about its strength. It is capable of being interpreted in different ways.

1. Seminars

The importance of this shows up immediately we start a presentation in a seminar or begin to contribute to the discussion. If we have evaded the responsibility to make our own judgements and decisions and, instead, relied upon the judgements of the authorities we have read, our arguments, justifications and explanations will often come across as unpersuasive, lacking the depth of conviction that will make them convincing.

Conviction

This highlights a common assumption about people who have convictions that makes us so suspicious in academic work about value judgements and decision-making. We often dismiss as biased anybody who has a clear conviction about something. It seems to suggest that bringing a process of reasoning to a conclusion in this way is to have a closed mind, when in fact you can always have a conviction about something and still be willing to assess it when new information appears.

It leads many people to assume that if it is just one person's opinion, or it can be shown that somebody else thinks differently, then it is biased to one side of the argument and cannot possibly be true.

For instance. . .

In an argument that has become familiar over recent years, it is claimed that, despite overwhelming evidence, you are biased in thinking that the Earth is 4.6 billion years old, because, as there are religious groups who believe it to be no more than 6,000 years old, this is just one side of the argument.

Obviously, someone can still be right about one side of the argument, even though someone else is equally convinced about the other. Indeed, she can still be right even when *everyone* else is convinced of the other side of the argument.

For instance. . .

In 1633 Galileo was forced to retract his opinion that the Earth went round the sun, because the overwhelming weight of opinion was against him, but he was still right.

Reasons for suspecting bias

In none of these cases are we entitled to call someone biased. We are only entitled to if we can show evidence that his reasons for supporting an argument are prejudiced: that he has prejudged an issue and is unwilling to suspend his judgement and play devil's advocate to test his argument. When people have a vested interest in something that goes beyond just being convinced about it, we have good grounds to suspect that bias might play a part in his or her judgement.

For instance. . .

A government might form a new commission to devise policy to improve the public's diet and tackle the problems of obesity and alcoholism. If they were then to appoint onto this commission the heads of food and drink companies, who make their profits from selling junk food and alcohol, we would have good grounds to suspect that they are likely to be biased and self-serving in their judgements.

But still these are only good grounds for 'suspecting' bias. The best thinkers are often convinced by one side of an argument, but are still able to suspend their judgement, play devil's advocate and subject the arguments that support their view to the severest criticism.

> The best thinkers have convictions, yet are still able to suspend their judgement, play devil's advocate and criticise their convictions.

2. Essays

All of this points to the overwhelming importance of decision-making for our academic work in that it places us at the heart of our own ideas. If we evade the responsibility of making our own decisions by relying instead on the judgements of authorities, we sidestep this key stage in learning, when we begin to think for ourselves. Rather than assess the effectiveness of explanations, weigh up the risks of evidence being unreliable and come to a rational decision, we sidestep this responsibility and simply borrow the judgements and decisions made by others.

- The overwhelming importance of decision-making for our academic work is that it places us at the heart of our own ideas.
- If we evade this, our arguments, justifications and explanations in seminars and in essays will tend to be unconvincing.

The effects of this show up in our essays, where the problems are more long term and difficult to solve.

Illiteracy

By recycling the ideas of those we read we evade the responsibility to think and process ideas at a deeper level. We become surface-level processors, who merely describe and reproduce other people's ideas accurately, rather than analyse concepts and ideas, assess evidence and critically evaluate arguments by subjecting them to our own ideas, values and beliefs. Inevitably, we find ourselves struggling to express ideas that are not ours in a language we do not command. As a result we show all the signs of deep-seated illiteracy.

> If we evade the responsibility to make our own decisions, we will fail to process the ideas at a deeper level and show all the signs of illiteracy.

This should come as no surprise. After all, writing is a form of thinking, the most difficult form. So, if our thinking breaks down, because we are not at the centre of our ideas, then the language, too, will break down. We will stumble from one unconvincing explanation to another as we struggle to give shape to our ideas; our fluency of expression will break down; our sentences will no longer mean what we meant them to mean. In all important respects we will become illiterate.

- We struggle to express ideas that are not ours in a language we do not command.

- Writing is a form of thinking, the most difficult form.
- If our thinking breaks down, because we are not at the centre of our ideas, then the language, too, will break down.
- We will struggle to give shape to our ideas; our fluency of expression will break down; our sentences will no longer mean what we meant them to mean.

Sadly, many bright, literate students enter universities, only to leave illiterate. They may know more and they will have read many things. But these will not be *their* ideas: they will struggle to develop them with any confidence; their arguments will be weak and their explanations unconvincing.

While at university they have not shared the needs of a genuine thinker, so they have not been involved in what they are writing at a deeper level. When they have been asked to express themselves they have not been expressing *their* ideas, but what they think their teachers think they ought to think. For the most part they have been content just to recycle the opinions of authorities, while their teachers have settled for teaching them *what* to think, rather than *how* to think.

> **Many of us do not express *our* ideas, but what we think our teachers think we ought to think.**

How can we avoid this?

We can routinely do simple things. Make our own decision, but only after we have worked through the three-stage method of smart thinking (see the flowchart on p288) and harnessed our System 2 thinking to process the ideas at a deeper level.

This means:

> 1 Analyse the concepts that are used in an argument to resolve the ambiguities.
> 2 Design alternative solutions to choose from.
> 3 Assess the evidence and then decide which of these is most likely to be true.

Finding your own voice

Once you have done this you are likely to find for the first time that you have found your own voice, which will come through clearly in everything you write. Your writing will glide across the page almost effortlessly with an elegance that is genuinely your own. It will be easier to understand and will always be more compelling, because your own thoughts and convictions are driving it.

Decision-making and finding your own convictions are central to this. As writing is a form of thinking, discovering what you think is vital to discovering your own voice.

Discovering what you think ───────────────▶ Discovering your own voice

The problem is that normally when we write our essays and dissertations we aim it at some unknown, anonymous reader, which encourages us to adopt a more universal, less personal form of communication. This becomes clumsy and cumbersome. The

Smart Thinking

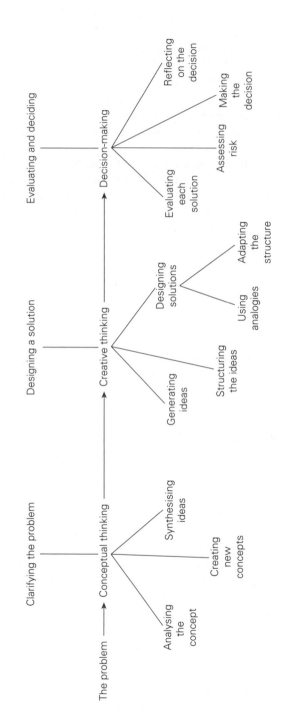

further we depart from the rhythm of the spoken word, the more difficult it is to understand what we say.

- Once you have found your own voice, your writing will be clearer and more compelling, because your own thoughts and convictions are driving it.
- Writing is a form of thinking, therefore discovering what you think is vital to discovering your own voice.

The first person

This problem is made worse by the advice we're often given that our writing must be both impersonal and passive. This means there's an embargo on all forms of the first person pronoun 'I'. We are then told that when we can't avoid it we must disguise our identity by talking about 'the author's opinion', 'in the opinion of the present writer' or similar hedging devices like 'It is thought that' and 'It has been suggested that'.

Then, ironically, when we are on the receiving end of this, we use our critical thinking skills to get beneath this unhelpful subterfuge to distinguish between fact and opinion. We want to know by whom it is 'thought' or 'suggested' and, if it is more than one, how many 'think' or 'suggest' it and what proportion: is it a majority, only a few or about 50/50?

Objectivity

You may think this flies in the face of everything we say about upholding the highest standards of academic integrity. If academic writers are expressing their own opinions they should uphold these standards of honesty and own up that this is 'my' opinion and you may not agree with it. The reason for this unconvincing subterfuge is that our aim is objectivity: to judge an argument on its consistency and how well it is supported by the evidence and not on the individual who has made the argument. We cannot accept an argument that only rests on someone's subjective conviction.

But, as we know, none of us have all the facts. So, after assessing all the evidence, finally we have to bridge the evidential gap between the facts and our convictions by making a value judgement. At that point the advice that has some integrity would say, own up to your value judgements, rather than try to disguise them in these unconvincing ways. They are a necessary and unavoidable part of what we do.

- We disguise our own value judgements, when in fact they are unavoidable.
- We have to bridge the evidential gap between the facts and our convictions by making a value judgement.
- To uphold our academic standards of honesty we should own up to them.

3. Dissertations

Although your dissertation assesses a range of skills, at the heart of it, running through every week and month that you work on it, is a series of decisions. In effect, you are being assessed on how well you can make the important decisions that will result in the successful completion of a large, independent research project involving different sources, methods and skills.

The one thing that knits all this together is your ability to make good decisions. Unlike essays, there is nowhere to hide. Dissertations are designed to give examiners a window into your thinking and decision-making. Do you make good decisions? Did you have good reasons for deciding the way you did? It must be *your* decisions and *your* value judgements that determine the shape that it takes.

> **Dissertations are designed to give examiners a window into your thinking and decision-making.**

> **1** You must justify why you decided to adopt the methods that you did to gather and validate your evidence.

As we know, a key element of smart thinking is metacognition: the ability to think about our thinking, to be aware of the *process* of thought, not just the *product*. Dissertations are equally concerned with this. You will have to explain why you decided to use the methods, techniques and instruments that you did: why did you decide to use case studies, questionnaires or interviews to gather your material?

- You must be able to show how you validated your results;
- That you understand and can justify the research methods you've chosen to gather and evaluate your evidence.

> **2** You must decide on the focus, direction and organisation of your work.

You choose the questions for which you want answers or the hypothesis you want to test. In the process, you will show that you can manage a large research project, organise your own schedule, set targets, maintain your motivation throughout and produce a well-reasoned and organised presentation of the results. In short, you will show yourself, your examiners and future employers that you have the personal resources to take on a large project and succeed.

> **3** You must decide how you are going to assess the arguments you read in your sources.

Then you will have to come to your own judgement as to how far you agree or disagree with your sources. You must decide whether your criticisms justify taking a different approach, interpreting the evidence differently, or choosing a different methodology.

> **4** You will have to assess the value of different forms of evidence, coming to a measured, well-reasoned judgement as to their reliability and relevance.

You will decide whether to use primary or secondary sources or a combination of both. Your decision will draw upon other decisions that you will have to make: how reliable they are, how representative and the strength of the conclusions you can draw from them.

> 5 You will judge how best to process the material and how you are going to draw conclusions from it.

Once you have decided how you are going to process your material and analyse your data, you will have to justify these decisions in the chapter in your dissertation on research methods.

> 6 You will have to design the eventual structure of your dissertation.

You will have to decide what chapters to include, the order in which to take them and then the structure of each chapter.

> 7 You will have to choose the content of each chapter.

You will have to decide on how you will present the analysis, the arguments and the evidence you include, and how you will pull all of these elements together to create a fluent, cohesive and persuasive piece of consistent reasoning.

It's the justification that is important

All of this may sound daunting, but, of course, it is not, once you realise that we all have to make decisions and all of them are based on value judgements, none of which can be shown to be right or wrong beyond doubt. We have to let go of the assumptions of certainty; that we are being assessed on a criterion of right and wrong. This runs through everything we have said about decision-making. All we can do is provide convincing, well-reasoned justifications for the decisions we made and evidence that we were able to learn from it when things went wrong.

This is what examiners are looking for. They accept that things may not go to plan. If your decisions turn out not to produce reliable results, it's important to be candid about it. Let examiners know about any variations from your original plan and the disadvantages of the methods you chose and how you overcame these problems. It is not the product, but the process that is important.

It is worth remembering our two key principles about creative thinking:

> 1 **We don't have to be right at each step.**
> 2 **There is no single way of getting to where you want to be.**

Employability

What we learn from our dissertation is good preparation for the decisions we will have to make in our professionals lives. Like our examiners, employers know there is no certainty in advance of making a decision. At best, there are well-reasoned decisions, clearly and rationally justified.

Unfortunately, as we have said so often, our learning as undergraduates has been grounded in the assumptions that there are right answers and certainties. Not only is this style of thinking vulnerable to the accelerating rate at which knowledge becomes obsolete, but it leaves us struggling to solve problems and make decisions in conditions of uncertainty. As a result, most of us are likely to be poor decision-makers, preferring instead to do what we have done throughout our undergraduate studies: seek out authority and follow its lead. This, in turn, condemns us and the organisations we work for to repeat the past.

> **Most of us seek out authority and follow its lead, condemning organisations to repeat the past.**

The effects of smart thinking

The only way of countering this is to become a smart thinker. These skills are vital to employers in the twenty-first century.

> **1** Avoiding System 1 thinking and unreliable intuitions

Smart thinking will help you see the dangers of allowing your decisions to be easily influenced by your System 1 thinking and its unreliable intuitions. You will realise that you must monitor your decision-making: you must use your metacognition to recognise and counter unreliable intuitions that would otherwise lead you to make poor decisions.

> **2** A strategy for decision-making

Unlike most graduates, you will have a rational strategy involving careful and thorough deliberation to arrive at your decisions. You will evaluate each of the solutions to a problem to assess their likely effects. You will then be able to assess the probability of each one succeeding and the risks of failure. On this basis you will make a comparative evaluation using an algorithm or grid analysis and make a decision. And then, finally, you will reflect on your decision, learn from it and assess its effectiveness.

> **3** Someone who can live without certainty

Although this might seem a relatively simple thing to do, we all crave for certainty in our lives; that sense of predictability that if you do one thing other things are sure to follow. And, of course, this is reinforced by our education, which teaches us to expect certainty.

To borrow Bertrand Russell's phrase, smart thinking teaches those who study it 'how to live without certainty and yet without being paralysed by hesitation'.[1] By working through the stages of smart thinking, it places good decision-makers at the centre of things, monitoring their own thinking. They have the confidence and ability to think about their thinking while they think, changing it where it needs to be changed.

> **Working through the stages of smart thinking places good decision-makers at the centre of things, monitoring their own thinking.**

Why are these skills important to employers?

If you were an employer, you would want to employ someone who understands risk and is not driven to make decisions on the basis of her intuitions alone. Employers know that someone who can work systematically in this way, rationally evaluating all the options before making a decision, is more likely to make a decision that safeguards and promotes the interests of the organisation, than someone who merely responds to her intuitions without reflection.

> **1** Risk

To understand, calculate and then represent risk accurately you need to have developed certain skills. As we have seen, those who don't have these skills miscalculate it and fail to represent it clearly, even those professionals who have to advise their patients and clients about serious challenges that might threaten their lives.

Smart thinking teaches us not only how to calculate risk accurately, but how to work through the stages to reach a well-based, rational decision. In this way we can impose order on the confusion, so that we can better understand the situation and assess the levels of uncertainty and risk. Then, after we have worked through these stages, we can present our findings and recommendations in clear, well-argued presentations that lay out the facts for a decision to be made.

- Employers realise the importance of the skills needed to calculate risk and present it clearly.
- They also want employees who can work through the stages to reach a well-based, rational decision.

> **2** Smart thinkers can create different alternatives to choose from, rather than be wedded to one option without knowing why.

Most employers are aware of the *confirmation bias*, even though they may not know it by that name. We make up our minds about something and then our System 1 thinking searches for examples and evidence that confirm our beliefs, while we resolutely ignore alternatives and block information that conflicts with them. Daniel Goleman describes the way our minds block all information that causes us anxiety and, of course, few things cause us more anxiety than being forced to think differently.

> **We make up our minds, ignore alternatives and block information that conflicts with our beliefs.**

So, it should come as no surprise that employers value those who can generate new ideas, who can design different solutions and evaluate each one without closing their minds to alternatives. Using our conceptual and creative thinking skills we can create structures out of the information and ideas we have, different representations of the problem, so that we can see the possible solutions and the decisions we might make.

Creating such representations in the conceptual and creative stages is an indispensable part of problem-solving and decision-making. Learning to speculate, to conduct mental experiments to see what would happen if you did certain things, guarantees an open mind, which is important to all professions and organisations.

- Employers value those who can design different solutions without closing their minds to alternatives.
- Creating different representations is an indispensable part of problem-solving and good decision-making.

> **3** Smart thinkers know how to evaluate alternatives rationally

All employers need people who can rationally evaluate each option, compare them, and then lay out clearly the problem and the options open to the organisation. By learning how to be a smart thinker, you will have the skills to present clear, rational justifications for the solutions you are recommending, based on a rational assessment of the risk of each option and the measures that need to be taken to manage the levels of risk.

Psychometric tests

In chapter 14 we saw that employers assess our abilities to make decisions using the decision analysis test (DAT). The emphasis in this is to see how well we can process complex and incomplete or ambiguous information and come to our own judgement in conditions of uncertainty. This underlines the point we discussed at the beginning of this chapter: that making a decision is not a simple process of applying conventional logic, but one that involves coming to our own carefully considered judgements.

However, this only assesses a limited range of the abilities that we use in making a decision. Some employers are likely to test a wider range of abilities using tests that assess our ability to evaluate solutions, tackle Prisoners' Dilemma problems, calculate risk, and conduct comparative evaluations of competing solutions.

Summary

1 Decision-making places us at the heart of ideas, from where we can begin to think for ourselves.

2 By making the ideas our own, our explanations and arguments are not only more convincing, but by finding our own convictions we find our own voice.

3 In our dissertations we are being assessed on how well we can make a series of important decisions.

4 Employers need people who can evaluate different solutions, assess risk and make decisions in conditions of uncertainty.

Conclusion

Over the last four chapters we have learned how tempting it is to escape the demands of decision-making by seeking shelter in our System 1 thinking with all its intuitions. To make the problem worse, we have been used to education systems that have taught us to rely on authorities with all their instant certainty. But we now know that in our academic work and in the real world we have to confront uncertainty if we are to make the ideas our own and show employers that we have the skills to make difficult decisions, rather than just search out authorities to follow their lead.

Conclusion

B. F. Skinner once said that 'Education is what survives when what has been learned has been forgotten.'[1] There are probably very few teachers who don't see some truth in this. Good thinkers are not defined by what they know, but what they can do with it. The paramount responsibility of all universities should be to produce people who can think for themselves, generate their own ideas and reveal new insights that push back the frontiers of our understanding and change our societies for the better.

Yet we are taught as if education is limited just to passing on a body of knowledge. Still, the problem is not entirely our teachers': they are as much a victim in this as we are. We are all socialised into cultures and education systems that translate education as the mere acquisition of knowledge. From an early age we are tested on how much we know and no matter what time of the day the chances are if you turn on your TV you will stumble across a game show awarding prizes to contestants who can recall the most information.

Instead of promoting our creative and conceptual skills to generate new ideas and design solutions to the most difficult problems, we praise those who show prowess in the lower cognitive skills to memorise and recall information. As a result, those inventive, entrepreneurial successes of our own time, like Steve Jobs, Bill Gates and Mark Zuckerberg, are known for having dropped out of our education systems and for having found their own way.

It is no surprise, therefore, that teachers so easily settle into a role as authorities with the limited responsibility of teaching students *what* to think, rather than *how* to think, even though in the process they ignore the enormous untapped potential that leaves their classrooms every year. And, by the same token, as students we just as easily accept that to be educated all that is necessary is to listen attentively, patiently record the facts, consign them to memory and then reproduce them faultlessly in exams.

Employers

However, around the world employers are beginning to realise the inadequacy of this. Many are now sidestepping university degrees as a qualification for a post and, instead, directly testing applicants themselves to see if they have the skills they need. They have concluded that an education based on the low level cognitive skills of comprehension and recall are irrelevant to their needs. Some are excluding any knowledge of school-leaving exam results and degrees, relying instead on the results of tests.

For instance. . .

In August 2015 Ernst & Young, a major accountancy firm, announced that they would choose which applicants to interview based entirely on their performance in online tests. They will keep all details of schools and universities, along with degree classifications, from recruiters. This follows the announcement by PricewaterhouseCoopers, rated the top graduate employer by the *Sunday Times* for the past 12 years, that they would ignore A level grades. Ernst & Young explained that 'It found no evidence to conclude that previous success in higher education correlated with future success in subsequent professional qualifications undertaken.'[2]

Relying on psychometric tests instead of degree results not only gives employers a more accurate indication of the thinking skills they are after, but access to a wider pool of talent, while giving every candidate the chance to demonstrate their strengths and potential.

So, as teachers what can we do?

Like the monkey in 'the old South Indian Monkey Trap', we are trapped by an idea. We need to think conceptually by lifting the bonnet of the concept of 'education' to reveal the pattern of ideas beneath that is controlling our thinking, and then learn to think differently. As Keynes put it, 'The difficulty lies not in the new ideas, but in escaping from the old ones.'[3]

Once we have done that we need to teach our students the principles of smart thinking, particularly the importance of metacognition and counterintuitive thinking that will help them use their System 2 thinking. If we can transform their learning experience by teaching them that there is more than one way to get where you want to go and you don't have to be right all the time, they will begin to realise that they have important and valuable ideas of their own: a genuine contribution to make to their own learning.

No longer intimidated by the fear of failure, they will be less likely to seek refuge in just memorising and recalling information and begin, instead, to think creatively by generating ideas and designing their own solutions. In the process they will learn to cope with uncertainty, manage risk confidently and make their own decisions.

As students what can we do?

Similarly, as students we need to challenge our conventional ideas about education and accept that ours is not the simple, imitative role as a mere recycler of received authoritative opinion. We need to learn to become smart thinkers, who can suspend their judgement, ask naïve questions and generate ideas and insights that others fail to see. The key to this is to accept that you have an important, valuable contribution to make to your own education; that your role is not just one of blind respect for authority. Be inspired by the expectation that you will succeed, rather than fearing you will fail.

With the skills and methods you have learned in this book you can begin to produce your own insights: those blinding flashes of inspiration when we realise for ourselves the truth of something. It's not until you have thought deeply about an idea yourself – analysed it, generated your own ideas about it and tested it against your own experience – that you make it genuinely your own. Years later when you look back, what you will remember about your intellectual progress, the peaks that look down on the clouds of knowledge, are the insights you generated yourself that still shine brightly.

Notes

Introduction

1 Paul Tillich, *The Shaking of the Foundations*, (1949) (Harmondsworth: Penguin, 1964), pp. 118–21.
2 Arthur Koestler, *Darkness at Noon*, (1940) (London: Vintage, 2005), p. 81.
3 Bertrand Russell, *History of Western Philosophy* (London: Allen & Unwin, 1967), p. 14.

Chapter 1

1 J.M. Keynes, *The General Theory of Employment, Interest and Money*, (1936) (London: Snowball Publishing, 2012), Preface, p. viii.
2 This problem comes from the philosopher Ludwig Wittgenstein.
3 P.B. Medawar, *Induction and Intuition in Scientific Thought* (London: Methuen, 1969), p. 26.
4 Medawar, *Induction and Intuition*, p. 53.
5 Nassim N. Taleb, *The Black Swan* (London: Penguin, 2008), 11–12.
6 Evans, J. St. B., Barston J., & Pollard P., 'On the Conflict between Logic and Belief in Syllogistic Reasoning', *Memory and Cognition*, II, pp. 295–306.

Chapter 2

1 Immanuel Kant, 'Answering the Question: What Is Enlightenment?', *Berlinische Monatsschrift*, December 1784, pp. 481–94.
2 Huxley, Aldous, 'Green Tunnels' in *Mortal Coils*, (1922) (Harmondsworth: Penguin, 1955), p. 114.
3 Sylvia Nasar, *A Beautiful Mind* (London: Faber and Faber, 2001), p. 69.
4 O.R. Frisch, *What Little I Remember* (Cambridge: Cambridge University Press, 1979), p. 92.
5 Daniel Kahneman, *Thinking, Fast and Slow* (London: Penguin, 2008), p. 44–5.
6 *New York Times*, 1 April 1934.
7 Ernest Dimnet, *The Art of Thinking* (London: Cape, 1929), p. 187.
8 Peter Ackroyd, *Newton* (London: Chatto & Windus, 2006), p. 26.

Chapter 3

1 This example is from the *Guardian Unlimited* crossword page which you can find at www.guardian.co.uk/crossword.
2 P.B. Medawar, *Induction and Intuition in Scientific Thought* (London: Methuen, 1969), p. 48.

Chapter 4

1 Bertrand Russell, *The Problems of Philosophy*, (1912) (Oxford: Oxford University Press, 1986), p. 28.
2 For this I have adapted an example found in Arthur J. Cropley, *Creativity in education and learning* (London: Kogan Page, 2001), p. 111.
3 Gary Wolf, 'Steve Jobs: The Next Insanely Great Thing', *Wired* magazine, 1994–2003.

4 Both of the examples in this chapter of this sort of psychometric problem have been modelled on similar examples in C.R. Wylie Jr.'s book, *101 Puzzles in Thought and Logic* (London: Dover Publications, 1957).

5 J. Silveira, 'Incubation: The Effect of Interruption Timing and Length on Problem Solving and Quality of Problem Processing', 1971, in J.R. Anderson, *Cognitive Psychology and Its implications* (Basingstoke: W.H. Freeman, 1985).

6 Dorothea Brande, *Becoming a Writer*, (1934) (London: Macmillan, 1984), p. 151.

7 Brande, *Becoming a Writer*, p. 160.

8 Brande, *Becoming a Writer*, p. 149.

9 Brande, *Becoming a Writer*, p. 151.

10 P.D. Smith, 'The genius of space and time' *The Guardian*, 17 September 2005.

Chapter 5

1 Palle Yourgrau, *A World without Time* (London: Penguin, 2007), p. 2.

2 Yourgrau, *A World without Time*, p. 7.

3 Ludwig Wittgenstein, *Philosophical Investigations*, (1953) (Oxford: Blackwell, 1992), p. 32.

Chapter 6

1 P.B. Medawar, *Induction and Intuition in Scientific Thought* (London: Methuen, 1969), p. 26.

2 Medawar, *Induction and Intuition*, p. 53.

3 Gary Wolf, 'Steve Jobs: The Next Insanely Great Thing', *Wired* magazine, 1994–2003.

4 Arthur J. Cropley, *Creativity in education and learning* (London: Kogan Page, 2001), pp. 38–9.

5 Thomas S. Kuhn, *The Structure of Scientific Revolutions* (Chicago: University of Chicago Press, 1971), pp. 89–90.

6 Albert Einstein, *Ideas and Opinions* (London: Souvenir Press, 1973), p. 340.

7 During, Alan, *Asking How Much Is Enough*, citing a personal communication from Michael Worley of the National Opinion Research Center, University of Chicago, September 1990; quoted in Peter Singer, *How Are We to Live?* (London: Mandarin, 1994), p. 50.

8 These two problems come from J. Metcalfe & D. Wiebe, 'Intuition in Insight and Non-insight Problem Solving', *Memory & Cognition*, 15 (1987), pp. 238–46.

9 These two problems come from William H. Batchelder & Gregory E. Alexander, 'Insight Problem Solving: A Critical Examination of the Possibility of Formal Theory', *Journal of Problem Solving*, vol. 5, no. 1 (Fall 2012), pp. 56–100.

Stage 2

1 Ernest Dimnet, *The Art of Thinking* (London: Cape, 1929), p. 48.

2 William Blake, *Auguries of Innocence*.

3 Harvey Mackay, *Swim with the Sharks Without Being Eaten Alive* (New York: Ivy Books, 1988), p. 162.

Chapter 8

1 Charles Handy, *Beyond Certainty: The Changing Worlds of Organisations* (London: Hutchinson, 1995), p. 104.

2 Sylvia Nasar, *A Beautiful Mind* (London: Faber and Faber, 2001), p. 129.

3 *The Observer*, 10 September, 1995.

4 Lecture, University of Lille, 7 December 1854.

5 *New York Times*, 1 April 1934.

6 Ernest Dimnet, *The Art of Thinking* (London: Cape, 1929), p. 187.

7 Peter Ackroyd, *Newton* (London: Chatto & Windus, 2006), p. 26.

8 Simon Singh, *Fermat's Last Theorem* (London: Harper, 2007), p. 228.
9 J.S. Mill, *Autobiography,* (1873) (New York: Signet, 1964), p. 100.
10 Nasar, *A Beautiful Mind*, p. 160.
11 Arthur J. Cropley, *Creativity in education and learning* (London: Kogan Page, 2001), p. 11.

Chapter 9

1 Arthur J. Cropley, *Creativity in education and learning* (London: Kogan Page, 2001), pp. 45–6.
2 Thomas S. Kuhn, *The Structure of Scientific Revolutions* (Chicago: University of Chicago Press, 1971), pp. 4–5.
3 Kuhn, *The Structure of Scientific Revolutions*, p. 96.
4 Rudolf Flesch, *The Art of Clear Thinking* (New York: Harper & Row, 1951), p. 121.
5 Boris Starling, *Visibility* (London: Harper, 2007), p. 14.

Chapter 10

1 Herbert A. Simon, *The Sciences of the Artificial* (Cambridge, Mass: MIT Press, 1996), p.132.
2 Simon, *The Sciences of the Artificial*, p. 108.
3 Edward de Bono, *The Use of Lateral Thinking* (Harmondsworth: Penguin, 1974), p. 29.
4 Lecture, University of Lille, 7 December 1854.
5 A fuller account of this example can be found in Richard D. Altick, *Preface to Critical Reading*, Fifth edition (New York: Holt, Rinehart and Winston, 1969), pp. 283–5.
6 LSATTestQuestions.com

Chapter 11

1 D. Hofstadter, 'Analogy as the Core of Cognition', in D. Gentner, K. Holyoak & B. Kokinov (eds), *The Analogical Mind: Perspectives from Cognitive Science* (Cambridge, Mass: MIT Press, 2009), pp. 499–538.
2 Adrian Desmond and James Moore, *Darwin* (London: Michael Joseph, 1991), p. 420.
3 Karl Duncker, 'On Problem Solving', *Psychological Monographs*, 58 (1945), Whole No. 270.
4 M.L. Gick & K.J. Holyoak, 'Analogical Problem Solving', *Cognitive Psychology*, 12 (1980), pp. 306–55; K.J. Holyoak & K. Koh, 'Surface and Structural Similarity in Analogical Transfer', *Memory & Cognition*, 15 (1987), pp. 332–40; quoted in Cummins, *Good Thinking*, p. 175.
5 Denise D. Cummins, *Good Thinking* (Cambridge: Cambridge University Press, 2012), p. 105.
6 I owe this example to Cummins, *Good Thinking*, pp. 168–9.
7 http://www.globalresearch.ca/the-financial-sector-a-house-burning-down/12735
8 'To Pluck a Rooted Sorrow', *Newsweek*, April 27, 2009.
9 Michael Scriven, *Reasoning* (New York: McGraw-Hill, 1976), p. 213.
10 J.S. Mill, *Utilitarianism,* (1861) (London: Fontana, 1970), p. 288.

Chapter 12

1 'Texas judge won't hang 'em high', *Guardian Weekly*, 19 October 2012.
2 Sir Arthur Conan Doyle, 'The Problem of Thor Bridge' in *The Case-book of Sherlock Holmes* (1927) (London: Penguin, 1951), p. 153.
3 Silva Nasar, *A Beautiful Mind*, p. 12.
4 Simon Parker, 'Rebuild government around people's values', *Guardian Weekly*, 20 April 2011.
5 This problem comes from William H. Batchelder & Gregory E. Alexander, 'Insight Problem Solving: A Critical Examination of the Possibility of Formal Theory', *Journal of Problem Solving*, vol. 5, no. 1 (Fall 2012), pp. 56–100.
6 Howard Thomas, *Brighter Blackout Book* (London: George Allen & Unwin, 1939).

Chapter 13

1 A.S. Munroe, 'Is Your Design a Life Sentence?' *Machine Design* (1995), 26 January, p. 156; quoted in Arthur J. Cropley, *Creativity* (London: Kogan Page, 2001), p.157.
2 I am grateful to Marcus Groombridge LLB (Hons) Cert. PFS of Joseph Oliver Ltd for this example.
3 'Texas judge won't hang 'em high', *Guardian Weekly*, 19 October 2012.

Chapter 14

1 Christopher Caldwell, *Select All*, 1 March 2004.
2 John Cohen, *Behaviour in Uncertainty* (London: Allen & Unwin, 1964), pp. 142–3.
3 S. Finkelstein, Jo Whitehead, Andrew Campbell, *Think Again* (Boston, Mass: Harvard Bus Press, 2008), p. 41.
4 Daniel Goleman, *Vital Lies, Simple Truths* (London: Bloomsbury, 1998).
5 Michael Weissberg, *Dangerous Secrets* (New York: W.W. Norton & Co., 1983); quoted in Goleman, p. 178.
6 Ipsos MORI's new global survey, 'Perceptions are not reality: Things the world gets wrong', 29 October 2014.
7 Daniel Kahneman, *Thinking, Fast and Slow* (London: Penguin, 2012), p. 213.
8 Denise D. Cummins, *Good Thinking* (Cambridge: Cambridge University Press, 2012), p. 50.
9 Daniel Kahneman, *Thinking, Fast and Slow*, p. 381.
10 This has been adapted from the 2011 UKCAT Sample Questions.

Chapter 15

1 *The Guardian*, 28 November 2014.
2 *The Guardian*, 28 November 2014.
3 'Robin Chase, Zipcar and an Inconvenient Discovery', *Learning Edge Case Study Topics* at MIT Sloan Management website: https://mitsloan.mit.edu/LearningEdge/Pages/Case-Studies.aspx
4 Robert Axelrod, *The Evolution of Co-operation* (London: Penguin, 1990).
5 Daniel Kahneman and Amos Tversky, 'Prospect Theory: An Analysis of Decision under Risk', *Econometrica*, 47(2), March 1979, pp. 263–91.
6 Kahneman, *Thinking, Fast and Slow* (London: Penguin, 2012), p. 282.
7 Kahneman, pp. 279–80.

Chapter 16

1 Kahneman, *Thinking, Fast and Slow* (London: Penguin, 2008), p. 201.
2 Kahneman, p. 219.
3 Robert Proctor, *Cancer Wars* (New York: Basic Books, 1996), pp. 101–10.
4 Gerd Gigerenzer, *Reckoning with Risk* (London: Penguin, 2002), p. 229.
5 Gigerenzer, p. 41.
6 Kahneman, p. 167.
7 Gigerenzer, p. 42.
8 Gigerenzer, pp. 34–6.
9 Gigerenzer, p. 33.
10 Quoted in Gigerenzer, p. 34.
11 In fact these figures may themselves be uncertain. It seems the risk for women on the pill ranges from 2 in 7,000 to 2 in 100,000, Jain, B.P., McQuay, H., & Moore, A., 'Number Needed to Treat and Relative Risk Reduction', *Annals of Internal Medicine*, 128 (1998), pp. 72–3; quoted in Gigerenzer, p. 207.
12 Nassim Taleb, *The Black Swan* (London: Penguin, 2008), p. xix.

Chapter 17

1 Daniel Kahneman, *Thinking, Fast and Slow* (London: Penguin, 2012), p. 226.
2 Kahneman, pp. 226–7.
3 'Resolute Marine Energy: Power in Waves', *Learning Edge Case Study topics* at MIT Sloan Management website: https://mitsloan.mit.edu/LearningEdge/Pages/Case-Studies.aspx

Chapter 18

1 Bertrand Russell, *History of Western Philosophy* (London: Allen & Unwin, 1967), p. 14.

Conclusion

1 B.F. Skinner, 'Education in 1984', *New Scientist*, 21 May 1964.
2 Judith Burns, 'Accountancy Firm Scraps Education 'Barrier'', *BBC News*, 3 August 2015.
3 J.M. Keynes, *The General Theory of Employment, Interest and Money*, (1936) (London: Snowball Publishing, 2012), Preface, p. viii.

Bibliography

Ackroyd, Peter *Newton* (London: Chatto & Windus, 2006).

Altick, Richard D. *Preface to Critical Reading*, Fifth edition (New York: Holt, Rinehart and Winston, 1969).

Axelrod, Robert *The Evolution of Co-operation* (London: Penguin, 1990).

Batchelder, William H. & Alexander, Gregory E. 'Insight Problem Solving: A Critical Examination of the Possibility of Formal Theory', *Journal of Problem Solving*, vol. 5, no. 1 (Fall 2012), pp. 56–100.

Cummins, Denise D. *Good Thinking* (Cambridge: Cambridge University Press, 2012).

Cropley, Arthur J. *Creativity in education and learning* (London: Kogan Page, 2001).

de Bono, Edward *The Mechanism of Mind* (Harmondsworth: Penguin, 1971).

de Bono, Edward *The Use of Lateral Thinking* (Harmondsworth: Penguin, 1974).

de Bono, Edward *Lateral Thinking for Management* (London: Penguin, 1990).

Desmond, Adrian and Moore, James *Darwin* (London: Michael Joseph, 1991).

Duncker, Karl 'On Problem Solving', *Psychological Monographs*, 58 (1945), Whole No. 270.

Einstein, Albert *Ideas and Opinions* (London: Souvenir Press, 1973).

Finkelstein, S. Whitehead, Jo Campbell, Andrew *Think Again* (Boston, Mass: Harvard Bus Press, 2008).

Flesch, Rudolf *The Art of Clear Thinking* (New York: Harper & Row, 1951).

Frisch, O.R. *What Little I Remember* (Cambridge: Cambridge University Press, 1979).

Gick, L. & Holyoak, K.J. 'Analogical Problem Solving', *Cognitive Psychology*, 12 (1980), pp. 306–55.

Gigerenzer, Gerd *Reckoning with Risk* (London: Penguin, 2002).

Goleman, Daniel *Emotional Intelligence* (London: Bloomsbury, 1996).

Goleman, Daniel *Vital Lies, Simple Truths* (London: Bloomsbury, 1998).

Handy, Charles *Beyond Certainty: The Changing Worlds of Organisations* (London: Hutchinson, 1995).

Handy, Charles *The Empty Raincoat* (London: Arrow, 1995).

Handy, Charles *The Hungry Spirit* (London: Hutchinson, 1997).

Hofstadter, D. 'Analogy as the Core of Cognition', in Gentner, D. Holyoak, K. & Kokinov, B. (eds), *The Analogical Mind: Perspectives from Cognitive Science* (Cambridge, Mass: MIT Press, 2009), pp. 499–538.

Holyoak, K.J. & Koh, K. 'Surface and Structural Similarity in Analogical Transfer', *Memory & Cognition*, 15 (1987), pp. 332–40.

Kahneman, Daniel *Thinking, Fast and Slow* (London: Penguin, 2012).

Kahneman, Daniel and Tversky, Amos 'Prospect Theory: An Analysis of Decision under Risk', *Econometrica*, 47(2), March 1979, pp. 263–91.

Kuhn, Thomas S. *The Structure of Scientific Revolutions* (Chicago: University of Chicago Press, 1971).

Lehrer, Jonah *The Decisive Moment* (Edinburgh: Canongate, 2009).

Mackay, Harvey *Swim with the Sharks Without Being Eaten Alive* (New York: Ivy Books, 1988).

Medawar, P.B. *Induction and Intuition in Scientific Thought,* (London: Methuen, 1969).

Metcalfe, J. & Wiebe, D. 'Intuition in Insight and Non-insight Problem Solving', *Memory & Cognition*, 15, (1987), pp. 288–94.

Nasar, Sylvia *A Beautiful Mind* (London: Faber and Faber, 2001).

Poundstone, William *Prisoner's Dilemma* (New York: Anchor, 1992).

Ruggiero, Vincent Ryan *The Art of Thinking* (New York: Harper & Row, 1988).

Scriven, Michael *Reasoning* (New York: McGraw-Hill, 1976).

Simon, Herbert A. *The Sciences of the Artificial* (Cambridge, Mass: MIT Press, 1996).

Simon, Herbert A.& W.G. Chase, 'Skill in Chess', *American Scientist* 61 (1973), pp. 394–403.

Singh, Simon *Fermat's Last Theorem* (London: Harper, 2007).

Taleb, Nassim N. *The Black Swan* (London: Penguin, 2008).

Weissberg, Michael *Dangerous Secrets* (New York: W.W. Norton & Co., 1983).

Wilson, John *Thinking with Concepts* (Cambridge: Cambridge University Press, 1976).

Index

References to illustrations are printed in bold.